Quality Education in Rural Learning Ecologies in Zimbabwe

Quality Education in Rural Learning Ecologies in Zimbabwe

Obstacles and Opportunities

Edited by
Christopher Ndlovu

PETER LANG
Lausanne • Berlin • Bruxelles • Chennai • New York • Oxford

Library of Congress Cataloging-in-Publication Data

Names: Ndlovu, Christopher, 1969– editor.
Title: Quality education in rural learning ecologies in Zimbabwe:
obstacles and opportunities / edited by Christopher Ndlovu.
Description: New York: Peter Lang, 2023 | Includes bibliographical
references.
Identifiers: LCCN 2022028052 (print) | LCCN 2022028053 (ebook) |
ISBN 9781433198267 (hardback) | ISBN 9781433198274 (ebook) |
ISBN 9781433198281 (epub)
Subjects: LCSH: Education, Rural—Zimbabwe
Classification: LCC LC5148.Z55 Q83 2023 (print) | LCC LC5148.Z55 (ebook) |
DDC 370.9173/4096891—dc23/eng/20221005
LC record available at https://lccn.loc.gov/2022028052
LC ebook record available at https://lccn.loc.gov/2022028053
DOI 10.3726/b19865

Bibliographic information published by the **Deutsche Nationalbibliothek.**
The German National Library lists this publication in the German
National Bibliography; detailed bibliographic data is available
on the Internet at http://dnb.d-nb.de.

Cover design by Peter Lang Group AG

ISBN 9781433198267 (hardback)
ISBN 9781433198274 (ebook)
ISBN 9781433198281 (epub)
DOI 10.3726/b19865

Published by Peter Lang Publishing Inc., New York, USA
info@peterlang.com - www.peterlang.com

This publication has been peer reviewed.

Table of Contents

List of Figure

List of Tables

Preface

If those in a crisis situation take the initiative and institute effective and relevant corrective measures that can extricate them from the predicament they are facing, progress and sustainable development can be realised. The common old adage says, 'There could be nothing for them without them.' Events throughout the world have aptly demonstrated that solutions that are imposed from above or by external players and agencies, without the involvement of key and direct stakeholders on the ground, always produce ineffective results.

In this single volume, we seek to emphasise on the need for rural stakeholders in the education sector, i.e. learners, teachers, and communities in general, that it is through their active involvement in changing learning activities and conditions in their ecologies that they can indeed transform these environments and make them relevant and useful. This book will not only describe the deplorable conditions that learners and teachers experience in rural areas in Zimbabwe, but will also explain and recommend that stakeholders in rural learning ecologies proactively participate as change agents in transforming learning and teaching conditions and activities in their environments. Perceptions on the viability of externally-driven change that is not context-specific is questioned through our various contributions in this book, as we emphasise on uniqueness instead of universality in terms of the curriculum design and implementation. Our main argument is that people should teach and learn what will enable them to put food on their tables, and that which will not make them stranded and always look for external assistance.

This book will make you realise that, if homes are transformed into active learning centres; that if communities fund their own learning programmes, and utilise their heritage in learning and teaching, and craft a curriculum that is grounded in local culture and needs, then issues perceived as obstacles in rural learning ecologies would be turned into opportunities. Our view is that, standardised practices, or what are usually termed 'international best practices' make people look for external solutions for challenges that are peculiar to a specific environment. A common thread that runs through all the presentations in this book is that, stakeholders in rural learning environments should capacitate themselves through utilising locally-available resources, to *inter alia*, motivate both learners and teachers, produce goods and services that are relevant to the needs and aspirations of the local people, and make sure that communities take care of the welfare of the teachers.

There are more opportunities than obstacles in the education sector in rural ecologies. If this collection contributes to that realisation, then it will have achieved its core mission.

Acknowledgments

This book is the brainchild of Lupane State University's Educational Foundations Department whose niche is anchored on improving learning in rural learning ecologies. The editor who is a National of Institute of Humanities and Social Sciences (NIHSS) funded scholar acknowledges this institution for the role it played in the origination of this book. The book would not have been successful without the wonderful work of all the contributors who fully applied themselves in coming up with these innovative chapters. Compiling the chapters into this book although not easy, was such an eye opener to the potential that lies in working together under Ubuntu philosophy. Indeed, all the chapters attest to the fact that we need to have a paradigm shift if learning in rural ecologies is to be improved. Thank you all! Great appreciation also to the publishers, Peter Lang, and their editorial team for their role in the publication of this book.

List of Abbreviations

4IR – Fourth Industrial Revolution
ADM – African Diaspora Marketplace
AGM – Annual General Meeting
ARTUZ – Amalgamated Rural Teachers Union of Zimbabwe
BEAM – Basic Education Assistance Module
CALA – Continuous Assessment Learning Activities
CPLP – Communidale dos Paises Lingua Portuguesa
DFID – Depart for International Development
ECD – Early Childhood Education
GDP – Gross Domestic Product
HNT – Human Needs Theory
HTA – Home Town Association
ICT – Information and Communication Technology
IGATE – Improving Girls Access Transforming Education
LOM – National Ethic Minorities Consultative Committee
MDGs – Millennium Development Goals
MNOs – Mobile Network Operators
MOOCs – Massive Open Online Course
MoPSE – Ministry of Primary and Secondary Education
NGO – Non-Governmental Organisations
O. Level – Ordinary level
ODL – Open and Distance Learning
POTRAZ – Postal and Telecommunications Regulatory Authority of Zimbabwe
SDA – School Development Association
SDC – School Development Committee
SDGs – Sustainable Development Goals

SDP – School Development Plan
SIDA – Swedish International Development Agency
SPA – School Parents Assembly
STEM – Science, Technology, Engineering and Mathematics
TOC – Theory of Change
UNESCO – United Nations Educational Science and Cultural Organisation
USAID – United States Agency for International Development
USF – Universal Service Fund
VOIP – Voice Over Internet Protocol
WVZ – World Vision Zimbabwe
ZARNet – Zimbabwe Academic Research Network
ZIMSEC – Zimbabwe School Examination Council

1. *Online learning opportunities for quality rural learning ecologies*

NTANDOYENKOSI SATAMWE & NHLANHLA MKWELIE

Introduction

Dube (2021) declares that rural learning ecologies in third-world countries remain disadvantaged concerning the access to quality education compared to their counterparts in urban areas. There are several attributes of rural learning ecologies that adversely affect the access and provision of quality of education. They include a lack of qualified teachers, poor working conditions, poor internet connectivity, lack of electricity, and competing priorities between accessing education and domestic chores (Belay, 2020). These affect the rural learners' access to quality education as well as academic achievement. The problems of rural learning ecologies are further worsened by the continued under-resourcing of schools. However, adopting an online learning mode for rural learners remains vital. Extant literature reveals that Online learning has improved the access to learning resources during the COVID-19 pandemic period. Therefore, this chapter explores online learning opportunities for quality rural learning ecologies.

The concept of online learning

The concept and practice of online learning are not new in the educational field, but what is new is its implementation in rural learning ecologies. According to Hlalele (2013), a learning ecology is an environment that is consistent with how learners learn. Hlalele further highlights that most rural learning ecologies have low access to online resources due lack of internet connectivity and electricity. However, when online learning is well implemented in rural areas, it has great potential to support deep and meaningful learning among rural learners. Online education is viewed as a subset of distance learning that provides more flexible access to educational experiences than face-to-face learning (Liaw & Huang, 2003).

Dube (2021) asserts that online learning has become one of the vital modes of learning during the COVID-19 pandemic period because of social distancing measures. It is no more optional as it used to be during the pre-COVID-19 pandemic era but has become a necessity in every learning ecology. Different countries use different terms to refer to online learning such as 'web-based learning', 'e-Learning', computer-mediated learning, and virtual learning. Rossi (2009) describes online learning as access to learning experiences via electronic means such as the Internet. Online learning has its roots in distance learning. Moore (2011) notes that the distance, in online learning is not defined by the physical distance but by 'transactional distance'. Transactional distance is an interaction gap or barrier caused by the physical separation of students from their lecturers. Algahtani (2011) opines that online learning involves learning experiences in synchronous or asynchronous environments using different digital devices with internet access. Abbad et al. (2009), conceive online learning as any learning that is enabled electronically. Online learning has been defined as any web-based learning (LaRose, Gregg, & Eastin, 1998; Keller & Cernerud, 2002). Ngozi, Onoimiuko, and Ebere (2020) posit that the online learning mode provides learners with opportunities to interact with the learning content found in different formats such as videos, audios, word documents, slideshows, and PDFs. In addition, Majumdar (2006) notes that the advent of the online instructional model has changed drastically the learning environment as well as the roles of both learners and teachers. Majumdar (2006) asserts that the major hallmark of this learning transition is the shift from teacher-centred to learner-centred paradigm.

Online instructional model

Algahtani (2011) has identified three distinct ways of using online learning in education, which are the adjunct, blended, and wholly online. The adjunct online learning model is when online learning is used as an assistant in the traditional classroom model (Algahtani, 2011). The blended learning model is the combination of traditional face-to-face learning and online learning whereas the wholly online model is total online learning (Algahtani, 2011; Zeitoun, 2008). Zeitoun (2008) has gone further to sub-divide the wholly online learning model into synchronous and asynchronous learning. The online Instructional Model is shown in Figure 1.1.

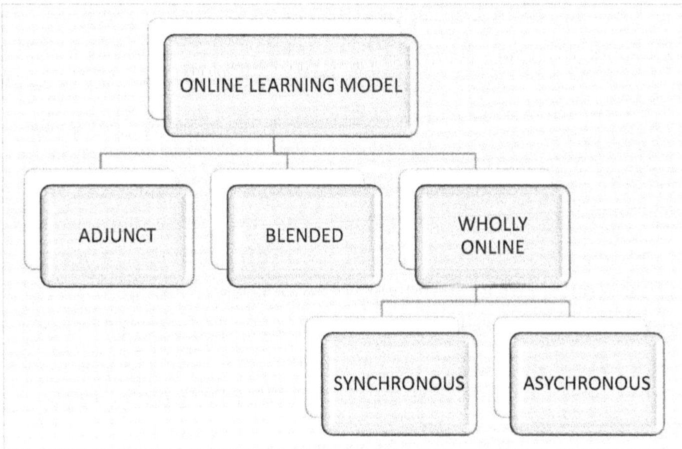

Fig 1.1: Online Instructional Model [Source: Adapted from Algahtani, 2011, p. 404]

Role of teachers and learners in the online learning

Marsh (2012) argues that the teacher's role has always been central in providing a structured and engaging teaching and learning environment to learners. Thus, the role of the teacher in the online learning environment remains indispensable. Abaidoo and Arkorful (2014) affirm that the online learning model has changed the role of a teacher from being a knowledge provider to that of a facilitator of knowledge construction during the learning. Thus, in an online learning environment, the role of the teacher is to help students to be responsible for their learning. Marsh (2012) notes that the role of a learner has been changed from being a passive learner to an active learner, from a dependent learner to an autonomous learner. This is in line with the contemporary teaching principles which advocate for self-regulated learning.

Benefits of online learning

The adoption of online learning in the education field, especially in rural learning ecologies has several benefits. The benefits include flexibility in terms of time and place. Smedley (2010) posits that the adoption of online learning by learning institutions provides the students with much flexibility in terms of time and place of delivery. Students can access the learning material at any time and from anywhere. Moreover, it provides a more individualised learning experience and personalised learning support, which is necessary for self-regulation (Abaidoo & Arkorful, 2014). Online instruction improves communication among students and between students and lecturers through collaboration. Amer (2007) asserts that online learning supports and encourages independent learning. Moreover, online learning promotes the development of 21st-century skills such as critical thinking, problem-solving, innovation, communication, and collaborative learning. Marsh (2012) says that online learning helps the learner to share learning resources and it promotes learner collaborative learning principles. Marsh further states that online learning increases student engagement in learning. Marsh (2012) argues that online learning can provide diverse ways of learning, thereby allowing different learning styles, as well as greater access to learning. Furthermore, online learning facilitates the construction of a potentially richer learning environment that enhances meaningful learning.

The situation of online learning in rural areas

COVID-19 has brought a threat to traditional face-to-face teaching mode but it has provided the opportunity to implement online learning mode in the new normal after the COVID-19 era. Rose (2020) argues that the advent of COVID-19 facilitated an exponential growth of online education in most parts of the world. The lack of ready access to Information and Communication Technology(ICT) is a major challenge to ICT integration in rural learning ecologies. Matthew (2021) notes that there is a remarkable 'digital divide' between urban and rural learners in terms of access to online education. This is because of inadequate hardware, and software, poor internet connectivity, and limited electricity in rural schools. Notably, there is a remarkable difference in how frequently students and teachers use technology within the classroom (Wang, Wang, Lin, & Tang, 2003).

Dube (2020) observes that in developing countries such as Zimbabwe, online learning tends to favor urban learners over rural learners. In line with this, Ramesh and Reddy (2020) echo that the urban learner has more access to online learning resources compared to the rural learner. Most learners in rural schools were left behind in their studies during the lockdown COVID-19 era because they had limited access to online learning materials. This was mostly because of limited or no electricity in most rural schools, no proper internet infrastructure, and a lack of ICT gadgets, which are key in online learning (Dube, 2020). As a result, rural learners find themselves excluded from meaningful online learning opportunities. This situation is contrary to the expectations of the values of Education for Sustainable Development(ESD), specifically Sustainable Goal 4, which seeks to ensure inclusive and equitable quality education for all. Therefore, there is a need to close the widening gap between urban and rural learners by increasing access to online learning.

Learning platforms for rural quality education

In light of the highlighted challenges, rural schools need great support through the provision of means to access user-friendly learning platforms (UNICEF, 2021). Non Governmental Organisations (NGOs) such as the World Vision Zimbabwe (WVZ) in partnership with other corporate partners empower rural school learners to access a wide range of learning resources, that include digital textbooks and e-learning platforms such as ProFuturo and Eco-School (World Vision Zimbabwe, 2021). The Eco-School was produced by WVZ with a corporate partner, Learning for Humanity from Canada. The organisation is assisting learners from 127 schools in Gwanda district in Matabeleland South province, Hwange and Lupane districts in Matabeleland province to access e-learning platforms (World Vision Zimbabwe, 2019).

The Ministry of Primary and Secondary Education (MoPSE) together with UNICEF Zimbabwe launched an e-learning platform on the 11th of March 2021(Maiden, 2021 reporting for UNICEF). The learning platform is called 'The Learning Passport'. According to Maiden (2021), the platform addresses the challenges faced by millions of children and youths worldwide to access continued quality education in times of crisis and when access is limited to traditional learning. The Zimbabwe Learning Passport contains a digital library of teaching and learning resources from the national curriculum as well as open education resources from a wide range of partners, mapped to complement the local curriculum. It creates a unique opportunity for young people to continue their studies regardless of their location, and level of education. (Maiden, 2021).

Non-Governmental Organisation's roles in rural quality education

The plight of rural schools on shortage of technological gadgets, connectivity, and the need for remote methods of teaching appealed to Non-Governmental Organisations (NGOs). NGOs such as World Vision Organisation and UNESCO set up programs for empowering teachers and learners in underserved areas. World Vision Organisation (WVO) distributed tablets and computers to learners in rural schools in some provinces in Zimbabwe (World Vision, 2020). A report from World Vision (2020), indicated that World Vison organization has also rolled out a program entitled 'Improving Girls

Access Transforming Education (IGATE)'. The program aimed at improving the education and life of a girl child. UNESCO developed a Rapid Teacher Training program on Open, Distance, and online learning programs to promote quality education in rural schools (https://en.unesco.org)

World Vision together with a Canadian-based organisation, Learning for Humanity, assisted in the construction of an e-learning centre in the Hwange district in Matabeleland North Province. The project is set to benefit about 900 learners from early childhood development (ECD) to the tertiary level. The centre provides e-learning solutions to teachers and learners. The major aim of this project is to promote education through e-learning in underserved areas. In the same province in the Lupane district in some schools, WVO distributed tablets to be used by learners in the form of PROFUTURO ICT kits. This project aimed at empowering schools with digital tools to use for online learning since the education system is fast becoming digital.

According to a report from wvi.org/stories (2021), the IGATE programme was rolled out to ensure that children are learning during the COVID-19 era despite lockdown challenges. It initiated the holiday Virtual Learning program where children receive literacy and numeracy activities via the Whatsapp mobile platform. World Vision provides access to data bundles for community volunteers and a daily literacy and numeracy challenge that can keep learners across many grades actively learning. However, this activity does not require a teacher to lead. This programme started with Four districts, Chivi, Insiza, Mberengwa, and Mangwe. It will cascade to other rural districts across the country.

In light of the need to shift traditional education to e-learning, most rural schools could not offer online learning (Dube, 2020). Teachers were neither equipped nor trained to offer this type of learning. Therefore, the United Nations Educational, Science and Cultural Organisation (UNESCO) working together with Zimbabwe's Ministry of Primary and Secondary Education developed a professional development programme for teachers to support the continuation of teaching and learning during and beyond the COVID-19 pandemic era. The empowerment is through Rapid Teacher Training on Open, distance, and online learning.

The major goal of the program is to equip teachers with skills to deliver distance education and use Information and Communication Technology (ICT) in education (UNESCO, 2020). Teachers are introduced to basic digital skills, remote learning methods, and the pedagogical use of ICTs. They are also equipped with the skills and resources to deliver and alternate the appropriate forms of remote learning using low and high-tech digital tools.

The training program was introduced in early 2021, and is ongoing. It exposes teachers to practical steps to designing an online lesson and teaching content using low-tech tools such as WhatsApp and high-tech tools such as management systems such as Google Classroom and Moodle as well as other learning management systems with offline functionality. By the end of May 2021, 1400 teachers from all provinces of Zimbabwe had been trained. The bulk was from the rural areas. The ongoing program aims to reach the most remote and marginalised areas to promote quality education through the provision of relevant 21st-century learning tools for teachers and learners in rural areas.

The role of the rural community in supporting online learning

In most rural areas in Zimbabwe, communities are working very hard to develop schools to meet 21st century standards by providing learners with relevant gadgets and developing infrastructure so that schools within the community can access Wifi (Belay, 2020). In areas where there is Tel-One network coverage, communities approach the Postal and Telecommunications Regulatory Authority of Zimbabwe (POTRAZ) to provide affordable WiFi services to schools. POTRAZ has projects set to facilitate e-learning that ran before the Covid-19 pandemic and continued during Covid -19 pandemic era. According to Muhamba (2021), the projects were run in conjunction with the Universal Service Fund(USF). The projects are:

(i) Connect a School Connect a Community
(ii) 1300 Zimbabwe Academic Research Network(ZARNet) Connectivity Project.

Connect a school connect a community

Muhamba (2021) reports that the Connect a school connect a community project was launched in 2014 and gave 60 rural schools 80 laptops for students and 10 tutor personal computers. It included solar power supplies, projectors, and servers. For instance, in Matabeleland North province, Lupane district, in schools with no electricity, some communities made contributions to the installation of solar systems. The distribution of laptops and computers to rural schools is shown in Table 1.1.

Table 1.1: Distribution of computers donated to schools in the connect a school community project

Province	Number of Primary schools	Number of Secondary School	Total schools that benefited
Mashonaland Central	4	4	8
Mashonaland East	4	4	8
Mashonaland West	4	4	8
Manicaland	4	4	8
Midlands	4	4	8
Masvingo	4	4	8
Matabeleland South	3	3	6
Matabeleland North	3	3	6
Total	30	30	60

This project was concluded in 2016 and as shown in the table the project covered very few rural schools due to connectivity challenges.

ZARNet Connectivity Project

The project aimed at providing 1300 schools with internet connectivity as well as the provision of functional websites with e-learning materials, VOIP (Voice Over Internet Protocol) telephones, email services, and e-learning video conferencing facilities (Muhamba, 2021). He further reports that the ZARNet project was done in collaboration with MoPSE and USF with 800 schools have benefited.

Table 1.2: Distribution of computers donated to schools in the ZARNet Connectivity project phase one

Province	Number of Computers	Number of printers	Number of copiers	Servers	Total number of schools that benefited
Harare	65				6
Bulawayo	185				25
Matabeleland South	263				33
Matabeleland North	270				26
Manicaland	800		1		50

Table 1.2: Continued

Province	Number of Computers	Number of printers	Number of copiers	Servers	Total number of schools that benefited
Mashonaland West	480	2			27
Mashonaland East	453				38
Midlands	550	5	1		76
Mashonaland Central	645	5	1	1	70
Masvingo	621	5		1	54
Total	4332	17	3	2	405

Mahamba (2021) reported that the phase started in 2020 and is currently ongoing. So far in 2020, 570 computers were distributed to 57 schools.

Table 1.3: Distribution of computers donated to schools in the ZARNet Connectivity project phase two

Province	Number of Computers	Printers	Total number of schools that benefited (Primary & Secondary)
Mashonaland Central	50	0	5
Mashonaland East	90	0	9
Mashonaland West	50	0	5
Matabeleland South	140	0	14
Matabeleland North	30		3
Manicaland	110	1	11
Midlands	40	0	4
Masvingo	60	0	6
Total	570	1	57

According to the report, the connectivity contract awarded to Tel-One will supply internet to 100 schools across the country. Further, POTRAZ is set to provide internet connectivity to 180 schools as well as 20 laptops to each of the schools to improve e-learning access. Covid-19 containment measures saw the banning of face-to-face learning during lockdowns. The resultant use of remote methods of teaching and learning proved to be a challenge to most unconnected rural areas. This has resulted in POTRAZ promising to set up 34 base stations, starting with the following provinces.

According to Muhamba (2021), this program will see Mobile Network Operators (MNOs) able to offer 3G coverage in the above-mentioned areas. This program will go a long way in alleviating connectivity challenges since individuals will be able to access the internet in the comfort of their homes. Thus, teachers in the marginalised areas will be able to use remote methods of teaching and learners will learn online with no problems.

Table 1.4: POTRAZ Proposed provincial base stations

Province	Location
Matabeleland South	Chikwarakwara
Midlands	Nyamara
Mashonaland Central	Nyatsatso
Mashonaland West	Mola

However, although efforts are made to improve connectivity, schools, teachers, and learners find it too expensive to fund their respective e-learning programs. Data bundles offered by MNOs are unaffordable. Magwaya (2021), says that the government urges the MNOs to provide affordable internet services to schools to enhance access to e-learning. In this light, all the three MNOs in Zimbabwe introduced a cheaper data bundle that is accessed through schools. Only schools are allowed to buy for teachers and learners.

Conclusion

In third-world countries, education inequality is still widely observed between learners in rural and urban areas. The rural-urban infrastructure disparities put the rural learner at a disadvantageous position in access to quality education. Therefore, there is a need to bridge the education disparities between privileged (urban) and marginalised (rural) learners via the online learning mode so that there is equal access to quality education.

References

Abaidoo, N., & Arkorful, V. (2014). The role of e-learning, the advantages, and disadvantages of its adoption in higher education. *International Journal of Education and Research, 2*(12), 397–410.

Abbad, M. M., Morris, D., & de Nahlik, C. (2009). Looking under the Bonnet: Factors affecting student adoption of E-Learning systems in Jordan. *The International Review of Research in Open and Distance Learning.10(2), https://doi.org/10.1973/irrodl.v10i2.596.*

Algahtani, A. F. (2011). *Evaluating the Effectiveness of the E-learning Experience in Some Universities in Saudi Arabia from Male Students' Perceptions*, Durham theses, Durham University.

Amer, T. (2007). *E-learning and Education,* Cairo: Dar Alshehab publication.

Belay, D. G. (2020). COVID-19, *distance learning and educational inequality in rural Ethiopia. Pedagogical Research, 5*(4), em0082. https://doi.org/10.29333/pr/9133

Dube, B. (2020). Rural online learning in the context of COVID-19 in South Africa: Evoking an inclusive education approach. *Multidisciplinary Journal of Educational Research, 10*(2), 135–157. DOI: 1 0.4471/remie.2020.5607

Hlalele, D. J. (2013). Sustainable rural learning ecologies: A prolegomenon traversing transcendence of discursive notions of sustainability, social justice, development, and food sovereignty. *The Journal for Transdisciplinary Research in Southern Africa, 9*(3), 561–580.

Improving Girls Access through Transforming Education (IGATE, 2015). https://wvi.org/stories (Retrieved on 18/09/21)

Keller, C., & Cernerud, L. (2002). Students' perception of e-learning in university education. *Learning, Media and Technology, 27*(1), 55–67.

LaRose, R., Gregg, J., & Eastin, M. (1998). Audio graphic telecourses for the Web: An experiment. *Journal of Computer-Mediated Communications, 4*(2), 34–45.

Maiden, J. (2021). Zimbabwe launches an innovative learning platform for children and teachers. https://www.unicef,org>Zimbabwe>press-releases

Majumdar, S. (2006). *Emerging Trends in ICT for Education & Training.* New Jersey: Sage Publishers.

Mangwaya, M. (2021). Provide affordable internet in schools: Govt. (Newsday May 17, 2021) https://newsday.co.zw/2021/05

Marsh, D. (2012). *Blended Learning Creating Learning Opportunities for Language Learners.* New York: Cambridge University Press.

Matthew, A. T. (2021). Adoption of E-Learning as a Panacea to the effects of Covid-19 on the teaching and learning of science in Nigerian Secondary Schools. International *Journal of Research and Innovation in Social Science (IJRISS), 5*(4), 115–119. *DOI:* https://dx.doi.org/10.47772/IJRISS.2021.5406

Moore, J. L. (2011). e-Learning, online learning, and distance learning environments: Are they the same? *Internet Higher Educational Journal,* 2011, *14*(2), 129–135.

Muhamba, V. (2021). POTRAZ measures to facilitate e-learning for rural & underserved communities https://techzim.co.zw/2021/03 (Retrieved 24/09/21)

NGOs target teachers to improve online learning in Zimbabwe. (2021). https://zerit.co.zw (Retrieved on 08/09/21)

Ngozi O, Onoimiuko A. C., Ebere, E. A. (2020). Online resources for e-learning in educational institutions: a case of COVID-19 era. *International Journal of Research and Review, 7*(10), 95–102.

Nyahasha, T. (2021). Econet introduces a cheaper e-learning bundle, schools buy it for students & teachers. https://www.techzim.co.zw

Ramesh, L. S., & Reddy, D. S. (2020). *Pros and Cons of E-Learning by Children in Rural Areas During Lockdown Situation And Ways To Empower It.* Proceedings of Cloud-based International Conference "Computational Systems for Health and Sustainability(CSFHS)", 5th June 2020.

Rose, S. (2020). *Medical student education in the time of COVID-19,* JAMA Doi: 10.1001/jama.2020.5227.

Rossi, P. G. (2009). Learning environment with artificial intelligence elements. *Journal of E-learning and Knowledge Society, 5*(1), 67–75.

Smedley, J. K. (2010). Modelling the impact of knowledge management using technology. *Insight Research Journal, 2*(3), 233–250.

UNESCO's rapid teacher training on open, distance, and online learning reaches 1400 teachers in Zimbabwe. https://en.unesco.org/:17 July, 2021

UNICEF. (2021). Zimbabwe launches an innovative learning platform for children and teachers.

Wang, Y. S., Wang, Y. M., Lin, H. H., & Tang, T. I. (2003). Determinants of user acceptance of Internet banking: An empirical study. *International Journal of Service Industry Management, 3*(14), 501–519.

World Vision Zimbabwe. (2019). Annual Report

World Vision Zimbabwe. (2020). Improving Girl's Access through Transforming Education (IGATE)

World Vision Zimbabwe (2021). Growing from Challenges to Opportunities to Promote Digital Transformation in Zimbabwe.

Zeitoun, H. (2008). *E-learning: Concept, Issues, Application, Evaluation,* Riyadh: Dar Alsolateah Publication.

2. Diaspora contribution to rural education

Tinashe Pikirai, Pikirai Teckla & Christopher Ndlovu

Introduction

The contributions of migrants and diaspora to sustainable development in their countries of origin and destination have been acknowledged by the 2030 Agenda for Sustainable Development, the New York Declaration for Refugees and Migrants and the Summits of the Global Forum on Migration and Development. According to Holm (2012) the world is increasingly becoming a village as migrants are now mostly found everywhere in the world and Zimbabwean migrants are not exceptional. Orozzo (2016) noted that Africa, which is largely involved in this phenomenon, is characterized by high emigration to developed countries. This process results in brain drain from countries such as Zimbabwe whilst it nourishes the stock of the developed countries with the highly skilled Zimbabwean Diaspora (IOM 2006).

The impact of brain drain from developing countries is a controversial issue on which two paradigms are opposed. Patterson (2006) argues that the first paradigm, which is the oldest and most widespread, posits that brain drain is detrimental to the economic development of the sending countries concerned. The argument of this paradigm is that emigration of an individual with a higher than average level of education and income results in a decrease in the average of people with average education in the sending country. The second paradigm is more recent and challenges the first by putting forward two brain drain effects that could be beneficial to sending countries (Patterson, 2006). The first is an incentive effect, which takes place as a result of emigration itself, and leads families to invest in the education of their children in the perspective of future emigration (Levit, 2001). As all high-skilled individuals do not emigrate, the stock of human capital could increase with this incentive effect. The second effect relates to the links that the diaspora maintains with the original home country. Saxenian (2006) asserts that it is a well known thing that Africans when they migrate to other countries they always think about home and would preferably invest home than in the foreign country. They do this through their financial transfers or their possible return, especially by their participation in scientific, political and business networks. Such networks potentially generate trade and capital flows, technology transfers, and can also contribute to the dissemination of social and institutional norms conducive to development. This article explores the contribution that diasporas can make to the home countries with much emphasis on the second and recent paradigm which looks at the positive contribution by the disporas to their mother country.

Background

Rural international migration occurs in countries of high and low levels of structural and rural transformation. Sending money across borders to rural homes is one central feature among migrants originating from rural communities. Faini (2007) argues that as a proportion of GDP, the diaspora remittances to rural areas contribute 4% to their countries' local economies. The flow of money to rural localities not only highlights the significance of remittances for households across many countries with varying levels of rural transformation but also represents a development opportunity to expand their rural transformations. Kerr (2008) argues that sending remittances is just one of many forms of engagement in the rural economy and society. Migrants contribute directly and indirectly to economic and social well-being through various channels of engagement with their home countries, including consumption of homeland goods, philanthropy and capital investments, among other activities (Rodriguez & Rodrik, 2000). Migrants' transnational economic engagement has had positive impacts in rural areas within countries across the structural and rural transformation classification continuum, suggesting that migrants' transnational engagement is a flexible tool for rural development worldwide.

Diasporas have been making contributions for a long time. This is in spite of working without policies to mobilize them. However, diaspora contributions are directly related to institutional frameworks, socio-economic settings, political environments as well as issues of perceptions, images, trust and social identification, in both the home and host country. Orozzo (2013) pointed out that while there is a growing policy interest in tapping, mobilizing and channelling diaspora contributions, these policies should be clearly defined, and the approaches should be effective in facilitating the engagement of diasporas for development.

There have been a number of regional and international efforts to bring back the Diaspora to support the nation building process. Patterson (2006) asserted that the efforts draw on the social and patriotic linkages as a starting point and attempt to put in place incentives to encourage the Diaspora to remain part of the national and institutional capacity building efforts. One can submit that international efforts to bring back diaspora helps to have development as these diaspora will bring a lot that can be used in developing their home nations. It is also encouraging for governments to note that Africans in the Diaspora have a high contribution to the national economic growth process through remittances and knowledge.

Concept of diaspora

There is no single accepted definition of the term 'diaspora', neither is there a legal recognition of the term which consequently has given rise to many different meanings and interpretations. For the purpose of this article several definitions are going to be outlined so as to give a global picture of its meaning. Generally the term diaspora comes from an ancient Greek word meaning 'to scatter about' (Ortega & Peri, 2009). Thus that's exactly what the people of a diaspora do, they scatter from their homeland to places across the globe, spreading their culture as they go. According to Patterson (2006) the Bible on the other hand refers to the Diaspora of Jews exiled from Israel by the Babylonians. Another broad definition of 'diasporas' is proposed by Goldring (2003) as referring to members of ethnic and national communities, who have left, but maintain links with, their homelands. The term conveys the idea of transnational populations, living in one place, while still maintaining relations with their homelands, being both 'here' and 'there'. In this chapter we will not capitalize the first letter of the word diaspora so as to avoid the confusion with the historic Jewish or Greek Diaspora, and purposely use the plural to reflect the diversity of populations that can be acknowledged as diasporas (Orozzo, 2013).

The idea of a diaspora is viewed by different countries in different ways. Dendir (2017) argues that some countries view diaspora as people settled in a host country on a permanent basis, labour migrants based abroad for a period of time, dual citizens, ethnic diasporas, citizens of the host country or second-generation groups. Another useful definition of 'diasporas' is provided by the UK House of Commons (Sixth Report of Session 2003–4, Volume 1) which views international migrants as people who, although dispersed from their homelands, remain in some way part of their community of origin. The emphasis is on the fact that the individuals are dispersed, possibly across several countries, but they maintain an interest and an affiliation to their home country, either 'real' or 'imagined'.

The term diasporas also refers to expatriate groups which, in contrast to migrants, applies to expatriate populations abroad and generations born abroad to foreign parents who are or may be citizens of their countries of residence. Nguyen et al. (2017) noted that the overall development potential of the people referred as diasporas can reach significant levels, involving such areas as business creation, trade links, investments, remittances, skills circulation, exchange of experiences and even impacts on social and cultural roles of men and women in the home society.

For the purpose of this article, a broad definition of diaspora can be viewed as members of ethnic and national communities, who have left, but maintain links with, their homelands. All definitions highlighted above captures the following points:

- individuals are dispersed, possibly across several countries
- but they maintain an interest or connection to their homeland and an affiliation to their home country, either 'real' or 'imagined'
- Dispersion, whether voluntary or involuntary, across sociocultural boundaries and at least one political border
- A collective memory and myth about the homeland
- A commitment to keeping the homeland alive through symbolic and direct action
- The presence of the issue of return, though not necessarily a commitment to do so

Contributions by the diaspora to rural development

Most African move around looking for income be it in towns or mines. Such that they may end up finding themselves in foreign land (Chinn & Ito, 2006). However as much as they move they always think of back home. According to Dzingirai (2017) there are even traditional idioms that suggest that the power of an African is always embedded in their rural background where in Shona they say 'Mudzimu weshiri uri medendere'. Literally this means the birds' ancestors are in its nest. The ancestors are generally regarded as the torch bearers of the African man. Thus diasporas always think of this as they work in foreign land. This gives them an attachment to their rural area. Goldring (2003) noted that the diasporas contributes a lot positively to rural ecologies

Kerr (2008) argues that diasporas have been making contributions for a long time, without waiting for policy to mobilize them and sometimes even in spite of these. However, diaspora contributions are directly related to institutional frameworks, socio-economic settings, political environments as well as issues of perceptions, images, trust and social identification, in both the home and host country. Holm (2012) asserted that while there is a growing policy interest in tapping, mobilizing and channelling diaspora contributions, the role of policies should be clearly defined, and the approaches that can effectively facilitate the engagement of diasporas for development understood to ensure that diasporas are not deprived of the ownership of their contributions

Diasporas movement to other countries results in a process called brain circulation paradigm. Saxenian (2005) argues that brain circulation paradigm is a process whereby skilled and well-connected members of the diaspora circulate human, financial and organizational capital back to the sending (developing) country, resulting in a dynamic flow of resources and know-how. Many diaspora maintain connections to homelands and demonstrate a willingness to support most activities that they would have left home. For example many Zimbabweans in South Africa have a close link with their home country such that they always strive to come back home during the festive period. Dzingirai (2017) says that many diaspora members maintain familial connections to their countries of origin. The rise in telecommunications and transportation technologies has been pivotal for the formation and sustenance of transnational connections and the efficient circulation of financial and social remittances across borders (Levitt, 2001). The contributions of the African diaspora, through individual or coordinated efforts, extend beyond supporting families. Diaspora members also volunteer, help establish professional networks, forge links with resources in more developed countries, and help to facilitate knowledge-sharing initiatives (Migration Policy Institute, 2004).

Remittance

In an increasingly globalized world community, rural international migration is often characterized by engagement or links that migrants establish with their home countries, through transnational economic and social activities (World Bank, 2011). These activities predominantly include money transfers (family remittances). Remittance refers to money that a migrant sends back to the sending country formally or informally. According to Chin and Ito (2006) remittances are private flows of funds that are transferred by people in one country to their families and friends in another country. They represent an important self-protection measure or safety net in times of natural or man-made crises and can improve poor people's resilience to shocks, particularly for rural populations exposed to climate stresses or agricultural prices volatility. Lucas & Stark (1985) argue that remittances remain a reliable source of funds even during downturns in the migrant's country of origin. Remittances have lifted millions of families out of poverty, contributing to the improvement of food security, education, health, well-being and housing for individual families (IMF, 2016).

Zimbabwean rural areas have been improved through the use of remittances (Dzingirai 2012). Most remittances are usually sent to urban areas due the increased access of financial institutions in urban areas. However the reality of the matter is that these monies always end up finding itself in the rural areas. Levitt (2001) asserts that money transfers (family remittances) contribute to rural youth development through several channels. Money transfers combined with entrepreneurship translate into employment opportunities through increased investment in rural agriculture. Capital investment is crucial for investment in non-agricultural service industries that grow alongside increased agricultural productivity in rural area (Sachikonye, 1998).

Remittances provide benefits at several levels. One of the key beneficiary of remittance is education. Meyer (2001) pointed out that in Zimbabwe a lot of money is sent from countries all over. This has led to the development of money sending registered companies such as Mukuru. However there are also a lot of unregistered companies or individuals who are into receiving money from the diaspora. Dzingirai (2012) argues whether registered or not, these institutions brings remittances to the nation. Many Diaspora prefer to invest in their own countries in assisting their relatives to educate them. They establish synergies with schools where their relatives learn. Some send remittances direct to the schools in form of tuition and school fees. Goldring (2003) noted that some small businesses will promote education for examples business in stationery, uniforms and of late ICT gadgets promotes education. Hooper & Sumption (2016) indicated that diasporas usually do activities with the assumption and hope that they might one day return and would need to have a source of local income. Such establishments invest in the education sector indirectly.

Remittances have been found to reduce income poverty in developing countries worldwide, to varying degrees (Orozco, 2013). Most rural households live from hand to mouth especially considering the effects of climate change which has resulted in many rural communities failing to have surplus hence requiring supplements which comes in hand as remittance from outside countries. Improving in food supply in turn creates a very conducive environment for education (Alcaraz, 2016). Well nourished children may not have much problem in the school hence may perform well yet lack of food results in truancy, absenteeism as well as a lot of indiscipline, which in turn impacts negatively on education. According to Ortega and Peri (2009) there is a symbiotic relationship between education and diaspora such that if diaspora sneezes financially, the local education will definitely catch a cold because of their symbiotic relationship.

The symbiotic relationship also goes on to household level. At the household level, recipients of remittances in Africa are in most instances are found to be having higher levels of education compared to non recipients (Barro, 2013). In addition recipients of remittances are more likely to have some form of savings account and a higher level of savings than those who are not receiving money from abroad. According to Holm (2012) researches made in Africa showed that about 10–20 % of the US$ 40 billion remittance flow to Africa is saved or invested in education. Ayidin (2016) noted that there is evidence showing that a 10 % increase in official international remittances as a share of gross domestic product (GDP) leads to a 2.9 % decline in the poverty in the country were remittance is being sent. Remittances also support families during national conflicts, when regular salaries and wages are often interrupted.

Remittances have long been a potent force for enabling conditions by which households enjoy higher quality of life, increased potential for upward mobility, improved material well-being and greater freedom more generally (Orozco, 2013). Bennell (2007) noted that remittances in most African countries results in high levels of rural transformation, which suggests that international remittances are an important aspect of development of rural areas. Remittance monies are fungible, thus households are able to use remittances for a variety of purposes like for education purposes for consumption, as precautionary savings or for productive investment (Orozco, 2016). In most Zimbabwean rural areas, youths assume adult responsibilities within households at younger ages, this burden can be reduced by remittances. These youths can easily manage their roles using the remittances from their seniors (Bennell, 2007).

Remittances are also known to prevent youth from having to drop out of school, from suffering from malnutrition or from losing their housing. Holm (2012) argues that remittances can be particularly effective in preventing rural youth from dropping out of school during household shocks or larger economic downturns. Enabling youth to stay in school has been shown to be associated with mental well-being among impoverished youth (Rock et al., 2016). Studies from Latin America found that remittances are important in helping households decide to keep youth in school and promote health through stable housing (Alcaraz, Chiquiar, & Salcedo, 2012; Adams & Cuecuecha, 2010). With good and quality education, rural youths are likely to get a chance to pursue quality employment opportunities. Thus it should be noted that remittances can serve as a crucial support that reap benefits well into adulthood. Remittances can facilitate rural households' investment in education. Education can positively change individuals' earning capacity over a lifetime (Nguyen, Grote, & Nguyen, 2017).

Dzingirai (2012) argues that a combination of social and financial remittances can help countries of origin improve gender equality and the empowerment of women and girls. This happens through the fact that by sending remittances to home country, this will promote more equitable social norms and also increasing the financial inclusion of women and bridging gender gaps through higher participation of women in labour markets. Levit (2001) pointed out for those women who stay home, their position as heads of households, combined with financial education gives them the tools to enhance the quality of life of their relatives. Orozco (2016) noted that when women control the inflow of remittances, either at the sending or at the receiving end, the money is more likely to be spent productively on items such as food, education, health and nutrition services.

Contribution to education

According to Baro (2013) the diaspora contributes a lot in the development of education in most countries. African Diasporans have various networks in the education sectors which results in the establishment of some form of links with their home country institutions such as universities and research centres. Diasporas sometimes are involved in collecting and distributing materials (books, computers, medical supplies, etc.) and mobilizing resources to their countries to assist in these efforts.

Most African migrants inject much needed financial and material resources where they are required most the household, particularly the rural family level, the urban poor, and provision of access to basic services. World Bank (2011) asserts that these are usually driven from the diaspora members of the society whose aim will be to improve their home countries especially their area of origin. In Zimbabwe the diaspora has helped in building from scratch areas of learning through sponsoring the building of schools. Lucas & Stark (1985) say that buildings has helped in reducing walking distances of most rural children as there has been an increase in schools especially primary schools. The diaspora has also helped in repairing dilapidated schools in most rural areas. Such initiatives are according to International Organisation for Migration (2016) are usually done mostly by diaspora who would have experienced hardships during their times at school hence they would not want other children not to experience the same situation. Of note is also fact that most of these diaspora donors may not specifically have their children.

The other contribution by diaspora in education is that of payment of fees and tuition to the disadvantaged students in their home area. Aydin (2016) argues that most of the people in the diaspora plough back in the communities that raised them through assisting in the payment of fees, buying of stationery as well as equipping the schools with equipment such as sporting equipment like balls as well as uniforms. This has helped in upgrading most of the rural schools. It has led to some schools ending up having state of the art equipment through being sponsorship from the diaspora. Sachiokonye (1998) noted that some diaspora people also are engaged in development activities in schools where they donate income generating equipment such a grinding mills, fencing school gardens and drilling boreholes. A lot of rural schools in Zimbabwe have been assisted by diaspora through installing solar panels, installing water tanks, equipment such computers (Dzingirai, 2012).

One area that diaspora have done very well is that improving treading materials in schools. International Fund for Agricultural Development (IFAD) (2008) noted that reading materials in rural schools in Zimbabwe are mostly as a result of donation from diaspora in one way or the other. One can submit that the improvement in schools are therefore mostly attributed to do diaspora contributions. These diaspora may give direct resources from their own coffers or they can mobilise resources from friends and other members in the diaspora. According to Ortega & Peri (2009) while these are good acts for personal and family socio-economic well-being, and even community development, mobilizing expertise and financial resources of the diaspora toward shared national goals has been increasing with increase in global migration.

The experiences by diaspora is very important in the development of their home areas. The experience of the diaspora at community level may be critical to community development and intra regional peace building. Successful individuals in the diaspora can become role models and provide the visionary guidance to the youth on further embracing peaceful means to nation building.

Summary

Worldwide the diaspora send a lot of things to their home country. They may send goods and money which is three times as much money to the total official development aid. In an increasingly globalized world community, rural international migration is often characterized by engagement or links that the diaspora establishes with their home countries, home towns and relatives in their country of origin through transnational economic and social activities. They support hospitals and schools in fragile situations, and transfer skills and resources through return migration. In an increasingly globalized world community, rural international migration is often characterized by engagements or links that migrants establish with their home countries, home towns and relatives in their country of origin through transnational economic and social activities. Transnational engagement activities include money transfers (family remittances), philanthropy, entrepreneurship, capital investment, homeland goods consumption and knowledge transfer. Sending remittances is just one of many forms of engagement in the rural economy and society. Migrants contribute directly and indirectly to economic and social well-being through various channels of engagement with their home countries, including consumption of homeland goods, philanthropy and capital investments, among other activities.

References

Adams, R., & Cuecuecha, A. (2010). *Remittances, household expenditure and investment in Guatemala. World Development, 38*(11), 1626–1641.

African Diaspora Marketplace. (2018). *Prior programming.*

Alcaraz, C., Chiquiar, D., & Salcedo, A. (2012). *Remittances, schooling, and child labor in Mexico. Journal of Development Economics, 97*(1), 156–165.

Aydın, Y. (2016). *The Germany-Turkey migration corridor refitting policies for a transnational age. s.l.: Migration Policy Institute,* TransAtlantic Council on Migration.

Barro, R. J. (2013). *Education and economic growth. Annals of Economics and Finance, 14*, 301–328.

Bennell, P. (2007). *Promoting livelihood opportunities for rural youth. IFAD Governing Council Round Table: Generating remunerative livelihood opportunities for rural youth.* Rome: IFAD.

Brinkerhoff, J. (2011). *David and Goliath: Diaspora organizations as partners in the development industry. Public Administration and Development, 31*(1), 37–49. Special Issue: Public-Private Partnerships: Familiar Ground, Fresh Perspectives.

Center for International Private Enterprise. (2015). *Helping diaspora investors make a difference in their home countries.* https://www.cipe.org/blog/2015/10/01/helping-diaspora-investors-make-a difference-in-their-home-countries

Chinn, M. D., & Ito, H. (2006). What matters for financial development? Capital controls, institutions, and interactions. *Journal of Development Economics, 81*, 163–192.

Dzingizirai, C. (2012). The Impact of USD – Rand Exchange Rate Remittance to Zim 2008–2015

Goldring, L. (2003). *Re-thinking remittances: Social and political dimensions of individual and collective remittances.* CERLAC Working Paper Series.

Holm, J. D. (2012, October 9). The brain drain within Africa. *The Chronicle of Higher Education.* Retrieved from http://chronicle.com/blogs/worldwise/the-brain-drain-withinafrica/30554

Hooper, K., & Sumption, M. (2016). *Reaching a "fair deal" on talent emigration, circulation, and human capital in countries of origin. Migration Policy Institute.*

IFAD. (2009). *Sending money home to Africa.* Rome: IFAD.

IOM. (2006). *Engaging diaspora as partners for home and destination countries: Challenges for policymakers.* IOM Migration Research Series, No. 26. Geneva: IOM.

IOM. (2013). *Diasporas and development: Bridging societies and states.* International Dialogue On Migration No. 22. Geneva: IOM.

Kerr, W. R., (2008) Ethnic scientific communities and international technology diffusion. *Review of Economics and Statistics, 90*, 518–537.

Levitt, P. (2001). *The transnational villagers.* Berkeley: University of California Press.

Migration Policy Institute (MPI). (2004, July). B*eyond Remittances: The Role of Diaspora in Poverty Reduction in their Countries of Origin.*

Lucas, R., & Stark. (1985). Motivation to rent. Evidence from Botswana Journal of Political Economy

Nguyen, D., Grote, U., & Nguyen, T. (2017). *Migration and rural household expenditures: A case study from Vietnam. Economic Analysis and Policy, 56*, 163–175.

Orozco, M., & Rouse, R. (2007). *Hometown associations and opportunities for development.* Migration Policy Institute.

Orozco, M. (2013). *Migrant remittances and development in the global economy.* Boulder, CO: Lynne Rienner.

Orozco, M. (2016). *Improving data on international migration: Towards agenda 2030 and the global compact on migration.* Washington, D.C.: Inter-American Dialogue.

Ortega, F., & Peri, G., (2009). *The causes and effects of international migrations:* Evidence from OECD countries 1980–2005. NBER Working paper No. 14833, National Bureau of Economic Research.

Patterson, R. (2006). *African brain circulation: Beyond the brain gain debate.* Boston: Brill Academic Publishers.

Rock, A., Barrington, C., Abdoulayi, S., Tsoka, M., Mvula, P., & Handa, S. (2016). Social networks, social participation, and health among youth living in extreme poverty in rural Malawi. *Social Science & Medicine, 170*, 55–62.

Sachikonye, L. M. (1998). Rethinking about labour markets and migration in Southern Africa, Harare Sapes

Saxenian, A. (2005). From brain drain to brain circulation. Transnational communities and regional upgrading in India and China. *Studies in Comparative International Development, 40*(2), 35–61.

Terrazas, A. (2010). *Diaspora investment in developing and emerging country capital markets: Patterns and prospects.* Washington, D.C.: Migration Policy Institute.
World Bank. (2011). *Migration and remittances.* Washington: World Bank.

3. *Improving the teaching and learning of agriculture through the use of viable school gardens in rural schools*

SIPHIWO NCUBE & CHRISTOPHER NDLOVU

Introduction

Research has established that there are multiple benefits that can be derived from running viable agricultural gardens in schools. In the 21st century, the agricultural gardens at schools garden are viewed as a places where multiple benefits are derived for the learner, the teacher, the school, and the community in general (Chitiyo & Duram, 2017). This view of an agricultural garden allows the learners to continue benefitting from the school garden even after leaving the school. This is because the agricultural garden can also be part of the community. In this scenario, the life long skills obtained during learning at school are used to improve the livelihoods of learners after school as well as that of the surrounding community. Some of the benefits provided by the viable gardens are the improved and effective teaching and learning pedagogies of agriculture and other science subjects (Sherman, 2007).

Agricultural gardens also provide a place for physical activity in which the learners can learn about concepts that may otherwise seem abstract (Sherman, 2007). The garden is also considered a therapeutic environment where learners can break away from the stressful environment of the classroom and get new motivation through exploring their immediate environment.

Despite the achievements and the visible impacts of agricultural gardens in schools in some parts of Zimbabwe as well as in some parts of Africa in generally where agricultural gardens provide both training of future food producers and also provide nutrition to hungry learners, the endeavour is still weak in the district of Lupane in Matabeleland North. What the chapter finds curious and worth looking into is that whereas there is indeed acceptance by teachers, learners and parents that gardening is beneficial, the phenomenon of agricultural gardens in schools is still weak in most of the schools in Lupane district.

Significance of the chapter

This chapter will among other things, bring to the attention of readers, the poor state of rural agricultural school gardens to relevant stakeholders including teachers, Ministry of Education officials and the community as well as show clearly to policy makers the need to refocus and allocate resources to the exercise given its relevance and importance to education, nutrition and to sustainable livelihoods. Enable the Ministry of Primary and Secondary Education to find ways of better integrating agriculture school gardens in the teaching and learning of agriculture and other science subjects as well as find ways of integrating the larger community in running viable and sustainable gardens. It is also meant to generate interest from other researchers so that they could investigate further into modern agricultural methods that can be used to establish and run viable and sustainable agricultural gardens in schools.

Theoretical framework

This chapter is informed by the generative theory of rurality as propounded by Balfour, Mitchell, and Moletsane (2008). This is a transformative social theory which sees the rural inhabitants as active actors in their own environment. It is premised on the belief that rural communities should take active roles as agents in solving the challenges they experience. It focuses on rural peoples' ability to sustain themselves, depending on resources available (Balfour, 2012). Rural people are conceived as having a great potential to influence the direction their education would take (Moletsane, 2012). A generative theory of rurality considers three variables which sum up its content (Balfour et al., 2008). The first variable is termed Forces. This refers to space and place which is occupied by people and helps in shaping their behaviour, thinking, identities and subjectivity. This theory calls for an an education system that takes into consideration the conditions in rural settings; rural peoples' beliefs and culture, social, economic and political situations which may extend to the state of rural households (Balfour et al., 2008). This variable informs teachers and learners in this case from Lupane district, on how they can manipulate their environment to develop viable and sustainable agricultural gardens in schools that will improve the livelihoods of communities in Lupane. The second variable is described as Agencies. Agencies are identified as a series of behaviours and dispositions: 'compliance and disruption, activism and entropy, and involves an exercise of will towards both ends' (Balfour et al., 2008: 101). This is how community members act upon the influence of forces, hence positive actions lead to societal transformation. This has to inform the school, parents, education officers and learners on how to respond to the forces for community transformation in Lupane district where agricultural gardens school gardens are not performing well (Balfour et al., 2008). The third element of a generative theory of rurality is Resources. This variable refer to material and emotional resources as well as to conceptual and physical resources (Balfour, 2012). Unavailability of resources in rural schools leads to poor agricultural gardens in schools that do not add value to teaching and learning processes. In the context of this chapter; teachers, learners and community members are informed on how the agencies affect the forces for the production of resources in Lupane district. This will lead to identification of the problem of shortage of resources, and ultimately stimulate the community to intervene to address the problem.

Overall, the generative theory of rurality gives teachers, learners and community members a critical view on how the community can be transformed through its initiatives and acting upon the challenges it is facing (Balfour et al., 2008). Teachers are enlightened of the interconnectedness of the factors affecting academic performance and sustainable agricultural gardens in rural settings in general, and in Lupane district in particular. The understanding of this theoretical grounding is hoped to empower all the stake holders to confront challenges of poor agricultural gardens in schools in Lupane district hence improving their academic performance and positively transforming their community.

History of agricultural gardens in schools

The teaching and learning via the use of agricultural gardens in schools is not a new approach. It started way back in the 1800s. The idea came up and has been perpetuated as a way of promoting recent trends toward going green, using sustainable agriculture, eating locally-grown food and improving the nutrition of youths (Doerfler, 2009).

In Zimbabwe, the concept of agricultural gardens in schools was born from the introduction of agriculture as a subject in schools in the 1950s (Sherman, 2007). The period saw the introduction of agricultural gardens in schools which aimed, according to the planning of the Ministry of Education at the time, at providing material for science subjects. However, even then, there were challenges in the implementation of the curricular mostly due to location of school plots and general failure to produce viable crops (Doerfler, 2009). Over the passage of time, the concept of the agricultural gardens in schools gained popularity as a result of the continued need to improve nutrition among rural children in the period after independence in Zimbabwe, that is, from 1980 onwards (Sherman, 2007). The popularity of the idea of agricultural gardens was also spurred by the issue of the worsening economic situation in the mid-1980s into the 1990s.

Currently, and in line with the Ministry of Primary and Secondary Education curriculum requirements and the updated curriculum of 2015 which emphasises hands on learning especially on practical subjects like agriculture, agricultural gardens in schools are a necessity for all schools in Zimbabwe. Agricultural school gardens play an integral role in this updated curriculum (Doerfler, 2009). They help to transform the teaching and learning process as they help to avail to the learners a practical and hands-on experience. Schools are expected to operate viable and sustainable gardens that can enhance the education experience for the learner and the teacher (Sherman, 2007). However, most of the schools in the rural areas have failed to run sustainable agricultural gardens hence the object of this chapter is to try and find ways in which rural schools could be motivated to embark on this venture seriously in Lupane district.

Challenges faced by schools in rural areas

In Zimbabwe, although the concept of agricultural gardens in schools is not a new one, it is plagued by a wide variety of challenges. These include lack of funding, lack of expertise among teachers as well as lack of manpower in general (Sherman, 2007). Zimbabwe's secondary schools vocational subjects are largely funded by the levies that are paid by the parents and the government. These sources of funding hardly meet the needs of most of vocational subjects hence in most instances, these subjects are neglected. The problem becomes much complex in rural areas where the economic status of the parents is very depressed. Most of the parents in the rural areas cannot afford to pay vocational levies (Chitiyo & Duram, 2017).

Owing to this predicament, agricultural gardens in schools in Lupane district are dilapidated and cannot be used for effective teaching and learning of agriculture. The shortage of funding is also compounded by poor financial accounting for received funds which further frustrates the few funders (FAO, 2013). While the importance of keeping financial records and of transparency in accounting is stressed in Zimbabwe, it is noted that schools are not keeping full records of produce that they sell, distribute, and cook. This makes it difficult not only in keeping track of resources invested, but also in having a clear picture of productivity of agricultural gardens in schools (Mashozhera & Pesanayi, 2016).

Sherman (2007) pointed out that understaffing and underfunding in the Ministries of Primary and Secondary Education and that of Agriculture, has resulted in, among other things: insufficient in-service training provision, insufficient agricultural extension services, insufficient subject inspectors and unfilled posts. This has compromised the quality of gardens as it has had an effect on the know-how when it comes to the implementation of agricultural gardens in schools. The problem is compounded by the fact that, generally, rural schools are shunned by qualified staff who prefer urban schools (Sherman, 2007).

Chitiyo and Duram (2017) contend that in rural schools, as alluded to earlier and in concurrence with Mashozhera and Pesanayi (2016), there is a challenge in the deployment of qualified teachers and at most, there is the missing concept and practice of learning from life as an educational approach as some teachers fail to see this linkage. At the same time, there is a general narrow perception of the role of the community in relation to agricultural gardens in schools, inputs and infrastructure, lack of adequate irrigation infrastructure, insufficient assessment of school soil conditions (FAO, 2010). Another challenge is that of capacity-building. There is generally lack of capacity in the teaching staff and in the school administration to handle and fully appreciate the role of agricultural gardens in schools in teaching and learning (FAO, 2013). To that end, there is lack of data and limited sharing of information, lessons learnt and best practices, absence of relevant training and training materials (Sherman, 2007).

Way forward for Lupane agricultural gardens in schools

FAO (2010) pointed out that any form of gardening is multi-sectoral and agricultural school gardening in particular tends to be multi-disciplinary. It relates closely to school food; it is usually partly extra-curricular; it may require equipment and infrastructural support, especially water supply; gardens may need attention out of the school term (FAO, 2010). By and large, there is need for expertise and training in garden management, financial accountability, issues of curriculum integration; monitoring and evaluation; and support and encouragement for hard working school staff. All these suggest the need for careful planning and long-term support, rather than quick fix solutions

(FAO, 2013). As alluded to earlier on, the generative theory of rurality is to be used in bringing all the concerned parties to dialogue and map a way that can lead to the transformation of agricultural gardens in schools in Lupane district. The education officers, the Lupane business community, non-governmental organisations that are operating in Lupane, teachers, learners and all other interested stake holders should come to a dialogue table and identify the potentials of the district and map out strategies that will help them to develop better agricultural gardens in schools in the district. The stake holders, guided by the generative theory of rurality, should consider some of the approaches suggested below in order to influence change in agricultural gardens in schools in Lupane district.

Starting small

The schools are urged to start on a small scale, minimising costs and steadily growing over years. With organic approaches, inputs are low, except where irrigation infrastructure is needed. Such schemes start small, taking little for granted in terms of capacity and interest (Chitiyo & Duram, 2017). Schools need to get inspiration and guidance from other schools that have managed to produce viable and sustainable gardens and choose their own pace and measure their own progress. The agriculture teacher with help of other teachers can draft a school proposal initiative that can be circulated and shared to local business people and non-governmental organisations. This should be based on the available resources and capabilities of the business community (Chitiyo & Duram, 2017). After the dialoguing stage carried out under the generative theory of rurality, it should be easy to get buy-ins from the local business community and non-governmental organisations. Chitiyo and Duram (2017) note that some schools have managed to move from relying on small external support to running their own agricultural gardens in schools without external assistance. Once such agricultural school gardens have been organised they may become critical contributors to self-reliance and also become centres of mutual support and exchange of experience and information in the community.

Agricultural school gardens as business ventures

For successful running of agricultural gardens in schools, there is need to run then as business ventures aiming at increasing productivity and gaining profit (FAO, 2010). For this to be successful, the agriculture teachers should undergo training in business and financial management skills. Applying the generative theory of rurality, the local business community can facilitate such trainings without schools incurring training expenses (Balfour et al., 2012). Under this approach to agricultural gardens, learners can be able to produce surplus in crops and poultry products that could be sold to the local community and external markets. From humble beginnings, these gardens have the potential to gather enough financing for the self-sustenance of the garden. As the school gardens develop and grow into bigger entities, the school should appoint one agriculture teacher to be full time manager of the agricultural garden (FAO, 2013). The proceeds from the agricultural garden can be used to purchase more teaching and learning materials that will improve the effectivenes of learning in the school.

Agricultural gardens in schools as community centres

A thought is rarely given to learners' potential roles in the management of the garden in planning, decision-making, organization, monitoring and evaluation. FAO (2013) alludes to the fact that malnutrition was one of the greatest challenges to the development of a healthy population in Sri Lanka after the civil war in that country. To that end, schools became pivotal in dealing with the problem and thus agricultural clubs were formed in schools and the department of agriculture in the country provided basic training to schools so as to ensure the program would be effective. Schools became centres from which agricultural growth began, and grew outwards through the establishment of gardens and nurseries which sold seedlings to the community (Chitiyo & Duram, 2017). Learners began practicing at home what they were doing at school and the knowledge of gardening grew outwards for increased benefit to the community.

Agricultural gardens in schools are a very good platform for the interaction of the school and community (FAO, 2010). Agricultural gardens in schools have given hope to learners who have acquired long life skills from the activities they do in the garden, thus the learners are learning valuable lessons that can be used to positively transform the communities. The school can also offer community members chance to share their agricultural knowledge to the learners as they will be invited as resource persons to make learning varied and exciting. Ndlovu, James, and Govender (2021) see this as an opportunity for the community elders to share their indigenous knowledges to the learners and also bring other ways of doing agriculture which can be cost favourable. If such an arrangement is made, the agricultural gardens in schools in Lupane district will flourish as the community will see them as part of their own community and support the initiative. In this way, it is envisaged that resources will be made available at all times and learners will find learning from their community elders beneficiary as they will also learn some of their traditional practices associated with agriculture .

Agricultural gardens in schools as nutrition centres

Scholarship has since established that for agricultural school gardens to achieve their full impact on the nutrition front, there should be nutrition education (Doefler, 2009). Evidently, the agricultural school gardens become some of the most convenient vehicles of achieving that initiative as they provide both the audience in form of learners and the community for that education but also the food to go with it. FAO (2013) recognises the role of food based systems in the creation of a platform for addressing sustainable development. These are the factors that are central to the development of a child, such as education, nutrition and financial independence. Furthermore, FAO (2010) contends that it is paramount to education that schools give top priority to learners' school gardening and gardening activities thus pointing to the central role of education in building resilient communities that are able to sustain their own nutritional needs.

Viable gardens provide learners with the opportunity to become familiar with and eat produce that they have grown themselves, an experience that anecdotally increases the appeal of eating vegetables (FAO, 2013). To that end, teachers are playing an important role in the incorporation of healthier foods in family diets through increased access to greens. It is notable that eating vegetables in an agricultural garden in a school program is a peer group activity, with the potential benefit of drawing on peer social influence to promote the view of consuming fresh produce as a normative practice (Doerfler, 2009). Nutrition curricular used in conjunction with some agricultural gardens programs teach topics such as food groups, nutritional and energy needs, how to read nutrition labelling, appropriate portion size, and the benefits of eating unprocessed foods (FAO, 2010).

Arguably, agricultural gardens in schools are part of the programme of achieving sustainable livelihoods and thus reducing on the costs of household insecurity in the country which can take a serious toll on the population (FAO, 2013). There are huge health and medical costs associated with poor nutrition but a sufficient supply of micronutrients can curtail that by giving longevity to the populace (FAO, 2010). Agricultural gardens, if fully and effectively implemented, can become very central in ensuring that people live long. The importance of the agricultural school gardens cannot be overemphasized in rural areas where there is abject poverty given that malnutrition does perpetuate poverty as malnourished women tend to give birth to malnourished children whose potential will be compromised in future thus perpetuating poverty (Doerfler, 2009).

Brouwer and Neelon (2013) contend that habitual life consumption of fruits and vegetables is promoted when learners are exposed to these foods at early stages of life. Also, Brouwer and Neelon (2013) posit that behavioural change has been noted amongst learners who have done gardening as a way of promoting healthy eating and physical activity. Agricultural gardens by and large, are a very good platform for the community to discuss health related matters as well as food security matters.

Research has also established lack of linkages among the following; nutrition and agriculture, agriculture and the environment, school meals and nutrition, the school garden and nutrition, and learning in relation to all of these (FAO, 2013). As alluded to earlier, these factors include the most important factor of nutrition whereby the agricultural garden at school can cater for the nutritional needs of the children by augmenting where there may be need for supplements. Agricultural gardens in schools introduce children to the process of food production. They also help learners to better understand the nature of sustainable food systems as they begin to connect with other adult growers and market gardeners. Doerfler (2009) said words to the effect that, the growing of food allows for the special intersection of communal goodness that is found in the interaction of people and plants in which food becomes a source of transformation. FAO (2013) also added that as an agricultural practice, school gardening provides learners with health, nutrition, natural resource management skills and equips them with business skills as well. Also, learners who grow up practicing agriculture through in school gardens have a better understanding of nutritional needs that help them plan their food consumption patterns.

Agricultural gardens in schools as teaching and learning centres

Equally important is the role played by agricultural gardens in the teaching and learning process. Agricultural gardens in schools have become hands-on learning for learners in an age where greater emphasis is being placed on the need to make education practical and equip learners with skills that enable them to create employment and be productive food producers of the future (FAO, 2010). Ozer (2007) was of the view that the goal of the agricultural gardens was always 'normative' and 'pragmatic'. Among the major purposes of agricultural gardens in schools has always been the need to teach through practice and shape the moral outlook of the learners (Sherman, 2007).

Whereas the origins of the agricultural gardens in schools indicate that it was predominantly for aesthetic purposes, the current view is that it should be used for effective teaching and learning.

The teachers in Lupane district should make good use of agricultural gardens to improve the academic performance of the learners not only in agriculture as a school subject, but also in all their learning areas. Doerfler (2009) suggests that gardens have been successfully used for science education due to their usability in environmental education beyond the classroom. But that is not the end as through education innovation teachers have been able to use gardens in other subjects as well, including maths, language, arts, nutrition, environmental science, and general science curricula (Sherman, 2007). There are a lot of measurements done in gardening and the precision required has made the agricultural school garden a good place for the development of mathematical skills for learners. Mashozhera and Pesanayi (2016) also argue for the development of vibrant agricultural gardens in schools saying that they give learners an all-important opportunity to interact with nature as a source of well-being and learning.

Agricultural gardens in schools as lifestyle changing points

Agricultural gardens can benefit the entire environment, a very critical factor in the face of environmental degradation in the age of climate change and ever increasing population pressure on the environment. The benefits can also be in the learning environment of schools, including their adaptability and use in other subjects other than the subject of agriculture itself (Ozer, 2007). Evidently, there are also lifestyle benefits from agricultural school gardens as they naturally enable learners to develop their soft skills such as interpersonal relationships, social skills, teamwork, leadership, and problem-solving skills (FAO, 2013). The garden is a free space that allows students to share their personal life stories with their peers as well as with their teachers as they do their tasks (Ozer, 2007). This helps in the development of their interpersonal skills. Also, the students interact and share ideas in working together on how best to solve the various tasks they have to do in the garden and this also helps in the development of their leadership skills while there is also an emerging tendency towards the development of lifestyle purposes for the learners (Ozer, 2007).

Even more pertinent to school agricultural gardens is that they promote parental involvement in the education of their children. More importantly, parental involvement has been linked to learners' higher academic achievement and lower dropout. In some cases, learning in agricultural gardens often rely on parent and community volunteers during weekends and school vacations (FAO, 2010). By and large, agricultural school gardens provide for the harnessing of skills from parents which may not necessarily be available in the classroom. The knowledge and physical strength of parents can be utilised in agricultural gardens. Undeniably, the involvement of the community in school programmes and projects school via agricultural gardens is healthy in developing progressive and mutually beneficial relations between the community and the teachers in whose responsibility the learners belong (FAO, 2013).

Conclusion

There are numerous benefits of agricultural gardens in schools. They impact the entire spectrum of communities involved with a school hence their integration into the education system. The agricultural garden is very paramount in the education of the learner. It goes beyond the teaching and learning of agriculture as a subject amongst many others, it becomes a place for the incubation of skills in agriculture that are critical for food production and for nutrition. The generative theory of rurality advocates for the connection of the agricultural garden to the whole matrix of community betterment by ensuring the involvement of all stakeholders including schools, the community and learners. If managed properly and synchronised in a progreesive way, this could help to improve levels of production of these gardens so as to meet the nutritional needs of both the learners and community members and above all, improve the teaching and learning of agriculture in Lupane rural schools.

References

Balfour, R. J. (2012). Rurality research and rural education: Exploratory and explanatory power. *Issue of Perspectives in Education, 30*(10), 9–19.

Balfour, R. J., Mitchell, C., & Moletsane, R. (2008). Troubling contexts: Towards a generative theory of rurality as education research. *Journal of Rural and Community Development, 3*(3), 100–111.

Brouwer, R. J., & Neelon, S. E. (2013). Watch me grow: A garden-based pilot intervention to increase vegetable and fruit intake in pre-schoolers. *BMC Public Health, 13, 363–363.*

Chitiyo, T., & Duram, L. (2017). Alternative agriculture characteristics in Zimbabwe: Experts views. *Journal of Geography and Earth Sciences, 5*(1).

Doerfler, H. A. (2009). *Using school gardens as a vehicle for health promotion for elementary school youth: A review of the literature.* Pittsburgh: University of Pittsburgh.

Food and Agricultural Organisation. (2010). *Setting up and running a school garden: A manual for teacher, parents and communities.* Rome: FAO.

Food and Agricultural Organisation. (2013). *Setting up and running a school garden: a manual for teacher, parents and communities.* Rome: FAO.

Mashozhera, F. and Pesanayi. F. (2016). Teaching and learning of 'Water for Agriculture' in primary schools in Lesotho, South Africa and Zimbabwe. *Southern African Journal of Environmental Education, 32*, 133–144.

Moletsane, R. (2012). Repositioning educational research on rurality and rural education in South Africa: Beyond deficit paradigms. *Perspectives in Education*, *30*, 1–8.

Ndlovu, C., James A., & Govender, N. (2021). Can IK and Western Science be complementary in an IK-SCIE agricultural curriculum? Theorising for an appropriate agricultural curriculum. In K. G. Fomunyam & S. B. Khoza (Eds.), *Curriculum theory, curriculum theorising and the theoriser: The African theorising perspective.* Boston: Sense.

Ozer, E. J. (2007). The effects of school gardens on students and schools: Conceptualization and considerations for maximizing healthy development. *Journal of Health Education Behaviour, 34*, 846.

Sherman, J. (2007). Learning from others: Synthesis of experiences in garden-based learning for school-age children in five Southern African Countries. *Workshop Report Part II.* Harere: FAO.

4. *Home involvement and Early Childhood Development (ECD) learning: Challenges and opportunities in Zimbabwean rural ecosystems*

NDONDO SEMKELISO & NDONDO SHEPHERD

Introduction

For decades, the world over, parental involvement in children's education has been associated with many benefits in education (Matshe, 2014; Duma, Kapueja, & Khanyile, 2011). The creation of a conducive learning home environment, an obligation for caregivers of children, that is, parents and guardians, is associated with a multiplicity of benefits towards the attainment of quality educational outcomes (Mukute, Francis, Burt, & Souza, 2020). Several research studies have recognized that a positive home environment manifests in the socio-emotional and cognitive development of learners (Matshe, 2014; Li & Fischer, 2017; Li & Qiu, 2018; Laura & Mahia, 2019). The home is the first socializing agent for children from which the school plays a complementary role (Ntekane, 2018). As such, the home creates a better learning environment through developing a good relationship with the school. Similarly, a review of the literature shows that a school can only achieve its goals in partnership with the home (Malone, 2017; Laere, Houtte, & Vandenbroeck, 2018; Laura & Mahia, 2019). Based on the preceding argument, parental involvement initiatives were made to create partnerships between the home and school. Through this partnership, both environments become ideal for the facilitation of quality educational outcomes societies are striving for. The provision of quality ECD is a necessity hence it is well stated in the Sustainable Development Goal number 4 Target 4.2 which underlines that all children should have access to quality ECD in preparation for primary education (Hannaway, Marais, Govender, & Meier, 2018). In this regard, the provision of quality ECD begins with a positive home environment which will be complemented by the school. Despite efforts by governments in creating and implementing policies that foster conducive learning environments for children, parents have not been involved in education as they should. A spate of literature has pointed to the lack of knowledge and resources as some of the major hindrances in creating positive learning environments by parents mostly in historically disadvantaged rural spaces in Zimbabwe (Musiyiwa & Chikwiri, 2017). The COVID-19 pandemic which brought a succession of lockdown measures further affected the already strained ECD delivery system in Zimbabwean rural ecosystems. To this end, the authors examined the role played by the home in fostering a positive learning environment, the challenges encountered in the process and the support needed in the Zimbabwean rural species.

Theoretical frameworks

The argument presented in this chapter is couched in Epstein (2009)'s model of parental involvement and the Ecological Systems Theory advocated by Urie Bronfenbrenner in 1986.

Epstein's model 2009

This model explores six types of parental involvement; parenting at home, communicating, volunteering, learning at home, decision- making and collaborating with the community. Epstein mainly focuses on what parents do at home and school that can fit into the goals of the school (Epstein, 2011). Parenting is helping all families establish supportive home environments for children as students (Epstein, 2009). Communicating is establishing effective two-way communication about school programs and children's progress (Keller, Miller, Dulce, & Wohrle, 2021). Volunteering is recruiting and organizing parent help and support at school, home, or other locations (Epstein, 2009). Learning at home is providing information and ideas to families about how to help their children at home with their learning (Epstein, 2009). Decision making is having parents serve as representatives and leaders on school committees (Humphrey-Taylor, 2015). Collaborating with the community is defined as identifying and integrating resources and services from the community to improve school programs (Epstein, 2011).

In the context of the current discussion, an understanding of Epstein's model will see a development of a warm learning relationship between learners and their parents through parents' show of interest and support in school work. Two-way communication between the school and home is enhanced thereby creating a positive learning environment that will make the school objectives achievable. Through volunteering, learning at home, involvement in decision making and collaboration, parents feel confident in taking part in their children's learning thereby creating positive learning environments for the achievement of quality ECD.

Ecological Systems Theory 1986

This theory stresses that the development of children is affected not only by factors within the child but also by their family and the surrounding world (Bronfenbrenner, 1979). The child is affected by social, political, biological, and economic conditions in his/her development (Bronfenbrenner, 1986). The ecological environment is pictured as a nested arrangement of concentric structures, with each of these structures contained within the next. Bronfenbrenner arrayed these ecological systems as micro-, meso-, exo-, and macrosystems. A microsystem is 'a pattern of activities, roles, and interpersonal relations experienced by the developing person in a given setting with particular physical and material characteristics' (Bronfenbrenner, 1979: 22). In this layer which affects the child most closely (Bronfrenbrenner, 1986), children experience a reciprocal face-to-face relationship with these immediate surroundings. The main settings and institutions involved are the family, school, teachers, peers, child health services, and the neighbourhood. Children's development is to the greater extent a function of a face-to-face relationship with these immediate surroundings. According to Bronfenbrenner, (1979), institutions in the microsystem influence each other through continuous interaction. For instance, the school affects the neighbourhood and neighbourhood affects the family members of the child. The exosystem consists of one or more settings that do not involve the child as an active participant, for example, the support from extended family members and parents' workplaces tend to have a more positive attitude at home (Bronfenbrenner, 1979). The mesosystem connects the microsystem and exosystem. This system includes the interrelations among two or more settings in which the child is an active participant. For example, the relations among school, home, and neighbourhood comprise the mesosystem. The development of a child is enhanced when the linkages among components of this system are strong and positive (Bronfrenbrenner, 1994). The macrosystem includes attitudes and ideologies of the cultures such as laws, morals, values, customs, and worldviews. The elements of culture can be very prominent in children's development. The influence of culture in child-rearing practices is unavoidable hence institutions must consider cultural norms and values in education. He inserted another layer known as the chronosystem. This refers to change or consistency over time in the life of a person. For example, changes in family structure over time, such as its demographic characteristics, have effects on a child's development (Bronfenbrenner, 1986).

Guided by this theory, institutions involved in ECD learning in rural ecologies should value the child's immediate environment as it is indispensable in his/her development. Similarly, some environments in which children are not directly involved need to be considered as they are also crucial in their development. More so, a warm interaction among environments that affect children's learning is very critical. Knowledge about children's cultural norms and values enhances their development and a record of their life history is important. For Bronfenbrenner a consideration of the systems/structures explained in his theory is a route to child development and quality education.

Home involvement and ECD learning

Literature has shown that support from a caregiver during the child's early years is critical in developing social competencies and enhances cognitive skills in schools (Mafa & Makuba, 2013; Laura & Mahia, 2019; Li & Qiu, 2018; Maša & Mila, 2017; Eccles & Davis-Kean, 2005). It is for this reason that positive home environments for ECD learners are indispensable in the acquisition of school competencies. The creation of positive learning environments is only possible if parents/caregivers understand and appreciate that their role is important in children's learning at school (Mawere, Nyaruwata, & Thomas, 2015). Learners' performance at school can be affected by different ways in which the concept of the home environment is understood by caregivers/parents.

A study by Chikutuma (2013) reveals that most parents feel that they are creating positive home environments through having a warm relationship with the school. This can be achieved through payment of fees, partaking in fundraising activities, attending meetings and consulting with ECD teachers on their children's progress. Chikutuma further points out that some parents buy toys for their children and some of them produce toys for learners in a bid to promote conducive learning environments for ECD learners. A large number of existing studies in education literature indicate that poor understanding and appreciation of the home environment has led to inadequate participation of parents in the education of their children (Mavuso & Duku, 2014; Mwinjuma, Kadir, Hamzah, & Basri, 2015; Ntekane, 2018). In this regard, parents feel that education is the domain for professionals hence home environment is not important in children's learning (Mavuso & Duku, 2014; Hannaway, Marais, Govender, & Meier, 2018). In most cases, the poor socio-economic background of rural homes coupled with high levels of illiteracy has hindered parents in understanding their role in creating positive learning environments for their children (Matshe, 2014; Malone, 2017; Plessis & Mestry, 2019). The deficiencies in understanding and appreciation of the role of the home environment have led to poor parental involvement in children's learning thereby affecting the achievement of quality ECD (Musiyiwa & Chikwiri, 2017). The foregoing literature review underscores the critical role played by the home environment hence the need for parents/caregivers in rural spaces, to get involved for the betterment of their children's education.

Challenges and opportunities for rural homes in ECD learning

The main idea behind early childhood education is to lay the foundation for the child's cognitive, personal, social, emotional and physical development at an early age (Musiyiwa & Chikwiri, 2017). This offers opportunities for children to be prepared for a meaningful school engagement and they also learn how to manage change in a positive way (Musiyiwa & Chikwiri, 2017; Williams & Mann, 2011). The implementation of ECD programmes presents children with new skills they will use to interact with the environment hence the need for rural homes to create positive learning environments. The ECD programmes are meant to make all teachers and learners enjoy the right to teaching and learning environments designed to enhance learners' early stimulation for optimal development (Madondo, 2021). If rural homes offer a positive learning environment for ECD, children's weaknesses and strengths are identified at an early stage and appropriate measures are taken. Literature reveals that young children with developmental delays and disabilities demonstrate better progress when intervention is offered early and in inclusive classrooms (Nyarambi & Ntuli, 2020). The Zimbabwean ECD curriculum shows great opportunities for learners by its inclusiveness and an emphasis on play-based, developmentally appropriate activities. Learners are welcome in their diversity, the school adapt to meet their learning needs (Musiyiwa & Chikwiri, 2017). Notwithstanding the opportunities ECD learning can offer, the teething challenges that characterize its implementation in rural settings keep the hope of quality ECD elusive. These challenges can be classified into two categories, that is, the home-based and school-based barriers. Considering rural home environments, most caregivers cannot meaningfully engage with ECD learners. Lack of resources and skills make parents reluctant to participate in their children's learning (Christenson & Sheridan, 2001; Plessis & Mestry, 2019). Furthermore, most rural parents are illiterate such that they find it difficult to assist their children in school activities hence rural home environments remain unsupportive to ECD learning (Wanke, 2008; Mwinjuma, Kadir, Hamzah, & Basri, 2015). The structure of the family may inhibit the creation of a positive home environment for ECD learning thereby impacting negatively on quality ECD (Mafa & Makuba, 2013). Some families are headed by children or grandparents because parents are dead or are working far away from home. These families, in most cases, cannot create positive home environments for ECD learning. The effects of the COVID-19 pandemic which left educational institutions closed for a long time had its toll on ECD learning in rural ecosystems (Shumba, Muntanga & Macha 2020). While the learning institutions in urban settings switched to online learning during the lockdown periods, the same did not happen in rural areas. The prolonged closure of schools increases the urban-rural divide in educational provision (Mukute, Francis, Burt, & Souza, 2020; Rundel & Salemink, 2021). Furthermore, the prolonged school closure exacerbated the existing vulnerabilities and inequalities among children, especially girls, children with disabilities, those in rural areas, orphans and vulnerable children, as well as those from poor households and fragile families (Shumba, Muntanga, & Macha, 2020).On the other hand, the school climate plays a major role in creating a positive home environment(Morisson, Storey, & Zhang, 2015). Owing to the lack of staff training on parental engagement most rural schools are unwelcoming to parents (Duma, Kapueja, & Khanyile, 2011; Masabo, Muchopa, & Kuoth, 2017). The school views education as its professional domain in which parents have no stake (Matshe, 2014; Duma, Kapueja, & Khanyile, 2011). This has led to a one-way communication system in which parents are excluded from school activities (Đurišić & Bunijevac, 2017) to the detriment of the home environment. In light of these challenges, the school and home must find strategies for creating a positive home environment for ECD learning.

Enhancing the positive home environment for ECD learning in rural ecosystems

Despite the barriers encountered by rural learners in accessing quality ECD owing to the unsupportive home environment, the right to quality education remains an imperative for all children. As such, measures to mitigate the barriers encountered in the process of creating positive learning environments in the rural home should be taken. This calls for a concerted effort from all stakeholders in education. Considering that socioeconomic disparities are the root cause of impoverished rural home learning environments (Lara & Saracostti, 2019), it is the duty of the government through its ministries to support the rural homes with suitable learning resources to enable them to meaningfully assist ECD learners. In most cases, parents fail to take part in the education of their children because they lack knowledge and skills (Chikoko, 2008). To this end, parents should be equipped with basic skills to participate in educational activities. This can be facilitated through adult education programmes, workshops and seminars so that they are enlightened on educational issues to enable them to take part irrespective of their social or educational background (Masabo, Muchopa, & Kuoth, 2017). By equipping parents with skills, the school will be boosting confidence in them such that they will in turn foster fertile ECD learning environments at home. The training of parents should be preceded by creating welcoming environments for parents at schools (Chikoko, 2008). If parents feel valued, they are likely to participate in educational activities (Ntekane, 2018). For this goal to be achieved, teachers should also be trained through workshops, pre-service and in-service programmes to prepare them for parental engagement (Antony-Newman, 2019). Teacher capacitation will give way to a two-way communication system between school and home hence the enrichment of home environments. There should be a commitment by all stakeholders to overcome the identified hindrances for quality ECD to be achieved particularly in rural Zimbabwe.

Conclusion

The implementation of ECD programmes presents a lot of opportunities in the achievement of quality educational outcomes. These opportunities can only be realized through the creation of positive home environments that will be supportive to the school. Through the ECD programmes, learners are stimulated to grasp concepts they are introduced to in later grades at school. The learning difficulties and strengths are identified at an early age and appropriate learning experiences are provided. Notwithstanding the opportunities, ECD learning provides to learners, a host of hindrances militating against its implementation abound. Among them, the creation of positive a home environment for learning comes dominant. This mainly results from Among the frequently mentioned are lack of knowledge and skill by parents and teachers in parental involvement in education, lack of basic human needs and learning resources, economic activities in the area of study which have created a phenomenon of child-headed families in which no child has a clue of creating a positive learning environment for his/her their siblings and a lack of role models in the community. To enhance positive home environments for ECD learning in rural ecosystems, a two communication systems between the school and home should be promoted. This would enable the home and school to share knowledge and skills for the attainment of educational goals. A multi-stakeholder approach to the creation of positive home learning environments is needed. Thus the government, non-governmental organizations, schools and parents should join hands in sourcing out basic human needs like food for needy families, learning resources including organizing for teacher and parent capacitation on parental involvement in education. A commitment by all stakeholders in this regard will see a move towards quality ECD in Zimbabwe's rural areas.

References

Antony-Newman, M. (2019). Parental involvement policies in Ontario: A critical analysis. *School Community Journal*, 29(1), 143–169.

Bronfenbrenner, U. (1994). The ecology of human development. *International Encyclopedia of Education*, 3(2), 1643–1647.

Bronfenbrenner, U. (1986). Ecology of the family as a context for human development: Research perspectives. *Developmental Psychology*, 22(2), 723–742.

Bronfenbrenner, U. (1979). *Ecological models of human development: Experiments by nature and design*. Cambridge, MA: Harvard University Press.

Chikoko, V. (2008). The role of parent governors in school governance in Zimbabwe: Perceptions of school heads, teachers and parent governors. *International Review of Education,* 54(2), 243–263.

Chikutuma, T. (2013). Quality of education of Early Childhood Development Class B learners in Zimbabwe: Case study of Gweru Primary Schools. *International Journal of Social Sciences and Education*, 3(2), 154–165

Christenson, S. L., & Sheridan, S. M. (2001). *School and families: Creating essential connections for learning*. New York: The Guilford Press.

Duma, M. A., Kapueja, I. S., & Khanyile, P. D. (2011). Educators' experiences on the role of parents in the school governing bodies of rural schools. *American International Journal of Contemporary Research*, 1(3), 44–52.

Eccles, J., & Davis-Kean, P. E. (2005). Influence of parents' education on their children's educational attainments: The role of the parent and child perception. *London Review of Education*, 3(3), 191–204.

Epstein, J. L. (2001). School, family, and community partnerships: Preparing educators and improving schools. Boulder, CO: Westview Press.

Epstein, J. L. (2011). School, family, and community partnerships: Preparing educators and improving schools (2nd ed.). New York: Routledge.

Epstein, J. L. (2009). *In school, family, and community partnerships: Your handbook for action* (3rd ed.). USA: Corwin Press.

Hannaway, D., Marais, P., Govender, P., & Meier, C. (2018). Growing early childhood education teachers in rural areas. *Africa Education Review*, 16(3), 1–20.

Humphrey-Taylor, H. (2015). Barriers to parental involvement in their children's education. *Journal of Initial Teacher Inquiry*, 1(1), 68–70.

Keller, J. G., Miller, C., Dulce, C. L., & Wohrle, R. G. (2021). Community-Based participatory research in a public school setting. *Children & Schools*, 1(1), 149–158.

Laere, K. V., Houtte, M. V., & Vandenbroeck, M. (2018). Would it really matter? The democratic and caring deficit in 'parental involvement. *European Early Childhood Education Research Journal*, 20(2), 187–200.

Lara, L., & Saracostti, M. (2019). Effect of parental involvement on children's academic achievement in Chile. *Frontiers in Psychology*, 10(1464), 1–5.

Li, A., & Fischer, M. (2017). Advantaged/Disadvantaged school neighborhoods, parental networks, and parental involvement at elementary school. *Sociology of Education*, 90(4), 355–377.

Li, Z., & Qiu, Z. (2018). How does family background affect children's educational achievement? Evidence from Contemporary China. *The Journal of Chinese Sociology*, 5(1), 1–21.

Madondo, F. (2021). Perceptions on curriculum implementation: A case for rural Zimbabwean early childhood development teachers as agents of change. *Journal of Research in Childhood Education*, 35(3), 399–416.

Mafa, I. O., & Makuba, E. (2013) Mainstreaming inclusion in teacher education in Zimbabwe. *The International Journal of Engineering and Science*, 2(5), 155–167.

Malone, D. (2017). Socioeconomic status: A potential challenge for parental involvement in schools. The Delta Kappa Gamma Bulletin: *International Journal for Professional Educators*, 20(4), 58–62.

Masabo, L. P., Muchopa, E. D., & Kuoth, W. B. (2017). Parental involvement in school activities in Kibondo District, Tanzania: Challenges and remedies. *International Journal of Education and Research*, 5(10), 89–96.

Matshe, P. (2014). Challenges of parental involvement in rural public schools in Ngaka Modiri Moleme District of North West Province. *International Journal of Humanities Social Sciences and Education (IJHSSE)*, 1(6), 93–103.

Mavuso, M. P., & Duku, N. (2014). Participation of parents in school governance: A case study of two Eastern Cape Schools: A View from Below. *Mediterranean Journal of Social Sciences*, 5(3), 454–460.

Mukute, M., Francis, B., Burt, J., & Souza, B. d. (2020). Education in times of COVID-19: Looking for silver linings in Southern Africa's educational responses. *Southern African Journal of Environmental Education*, 36, 1–16.

Musiyiwa, J., & Chikwiri, E. (2017). An assessment of quality issues in the provision of early childhood development B in Zimbabwe. *American Journal of Educational Research and Reviews*, 2(11), 1–16.

Mwinjuma, J. S., Kadir, S. b., Hamzah, A., & Basri, R. (2015). A review of characteristics and experiences of decentralization of education. *International Journal of Education & Literacy Studies*, 3(1), 34–41.

Ntekane, A. (2018). Parental involvement in education. *Research*, 2(2), 1–5.

Nyarambi, A., & Ntuli, E. (2020). A study of early childhood development teachers' experiences in Zimbabwe: Implications to early intervention and special education. *Open Journal for Educational Research*, 4(1), 49–66.

Plessis, P. D., & Mestry, R. (2019). Teachers for rural schools – A challenge for South Africa. *South African Journal of Education*, 39(1), 2–9.

Rundel, C., & Salemink, K. (2021). Bridging digital inequalities in rural schools in Germany: A geographical lottery? *Education Sciences*, 11(4), 1–18.

Williams, D. T., & Mann, T. L. (2011). *Early childhood education in rural communities: Access and quality issues*. Fairfax: UNCF/Frederick D. Patterson Research Institute.

Zhonglu, L., & Zeqi, Q. (2018). How does family background affect children's educational achievement? Evidence from Contemporary China. *The Journal of Chinese Sociology*, 5(13), 1–21.

5. *Potential of home involvement in creating learning spaces in rural areas*

Mkwananzi Dumisani & Cynthia Ncube

Introduction

Realising the need for isolated home learning, the opportunities for technology usage and the challenges bedeviling rural communities, this chapter is conceived. Guided by research into home learning experiences, the chapter presents a plethora of opportunities which are created by the home environment for learning purposes. It also brings to light, the challenges that learners experience while learning from home and the role of the parent and guardian for proactive action. Given access to education is a basic human right according to the Universal Declaration of Human Rights, this chapter highlights red flags with a view to ensuring learners are not left out, especially the rural learners in the adoption of modern technologies in teaching and learning.

Background

The Zimbabwean education system has been punctuated by the principle of classroom face to face teaching and learning in both urban and rural set-ups. Realising the learning environments have shifted from the traditional classroom to that of home through blended education, use of technological advancement and other alternative learning environments, it is incumbent upon both teachers and parents to embrace this change in order that our education system is in line with the current trends. The dynamism in curriculum overhaul and instruction has seen parents and teachers working hand in glove in an attempt to meet the curriculum demands so as to match the modern world standards. While education shifts to the home owing to isolations, the product of learning in particular, have been noted to mirror the productivity in factories for years (Chandra, 2012). The home is therefore a critical factor in determining the industry targeted by learning experiences. Parental involvement at the early stages of a child's acquisition of skills is of prime importance in setting the tone in order to fully transmit the curriculum using child friendly environments such as the home settings (Santrock, 2015).

Khan, Begum, and Imad (2019) noted the home is the first institution of a child that has significant relationships with learners' overall life. The home environment, according to the same, is made up of physical and psychological factors that entail the room spaces, provision of basic services like water, shelter, clothes, food and other physical needs of the child, as well as mutual interactions. The type of family, line of authority, status of family attitude of parents, their education history and financial position all affect the ability of a learner to learn. While significant efforts have been made to ensure the physical classroom at a school is within reach for each and every learner, through building of schools, the technology-guided classroom has become a far-cry for many learners and a threat to their right to a decent education.

According to Feeney, Christensen, and Moracvick (1983) the Ministry of Primary and Secondary Education has taken wide strides in ensuring that the home becomes a safe haven in influencing curriculum change through reviews and policy shifts towards technology integration and desire for relevant exit skills acquisition. This is being made possible through continuous activity learning assessment (CALA) and learner profiling. Learner profiling entails assessing competences on a continuous basis that includes knowledge, skills, abilities, values and traits (Education, Ministry of Primary and Secondary, 2016). This embraces what a learner is able to do and become so that the learner is directed to what best fits his or her capabilities. In line with this is the involvement of the home as an active base and catalyst in children's learning and development through partnering with educators and through use of various media platforms in imparting knowledge to the learners in different localities. The home environment has been found to be the child's first teacher through interactions that the child has with his or her surroundings, the child is able to learn through the various media platforms at his or her disposal. Magwa (2008); Kishindo (2000) and Obanya (1999) say at independence most African governments celebrated political independence, but did not see it necessary to review their education systems' curricula from primary to tertiary level. This observation brings about the gap in instruction that we experience today. The continued use of the classroom as an appropriate learning space is clear testimony that educators and other stakeholders do not acknowledge the importance of modern technologies and the role played by home environments in helping children acquire knowledge and skills. The rural learner is however faced with challenges which need both the parent and teacher's concerted efforts in order for them to partially overcome. Mumpande (2020) says, despite all this, Zimbabwe is counted among the many African countries who have seen it fit to engage in modern approaches to teaching and learning.

Drawing from the experiences of the COVID-19 period, most schools in Zimbabwe were considered digital-shy as the right to education was highly compromised by the forced closure of schools to control the spread of the COVID19 pandemic (Matimaire, 2019). While efforts have been made at electronic learning prior to COVID-19, it has been confined to some tertiary education institutions and well-up schools. The current landscape however demands that every learner, be it in rural or urban settings, needs to be connected. The non-availability of network connectivity infrastructure, and the low penetration of technology like computers and tablets, has made it very difficult for learners in the school system to benefit from online.

While learning is not by choice, but a right of every child, the right of each and every child to education, has been highlighted in a number of international agreements, which include the United Nations Convention on the Rights of the Child African Charter on Human Rights, the Millennium Development Goals (MDGs) of 2000–2015, and the Sustainable Development Goals (SDGs) of 2015–2030. While these frameworks advocate for every child's right to education, the social isolation as a result of COVID19 poses renewed thought on how each and every child will access education. How can education advance without threatening the right of the rural learner to education?

Theoretical framework

While thousands of philosophical thoughts have emerged on the subject of learning, there are five important theoretical orientations that form the foundation of and these include the Behaviourist Learning Theories, Cognitive Learning Theories, Humanistic Learning theories, Social Cognitive Learning Theories, and Constructivist Learning Theories (Chandra, 2012).

The chapter draws its theoretical framework from the Social Learning theory (SLT) which states that a child learns from his or her environment as he interacts and observes others at play (Santrock, 2008). The theory further contends that social learning guides a person's behaviour so that it is in accordance with social norms, values and beliefs. Such learning assists the child in becoming socialised. Mumpande and Barnes (2019) state that behaviour is learned, without necessarily being engaged in it and that such behaviour need not receive direct reinforcement. It should be noted therefore that adults should portray good moral behaviour for children to emulate. Learner and Hultsch (1983) say observational learning is important not only for learning but for survival. Teachers should therefore guide learners to adapt to new situations in order that they develop problem solving skills and also accept responsibility for their behaviour. Furthermore, the Curriculum Framework for Primary and Secondary Education (2015–2022) states the need to transform the structure and curriculum of the country's education system in order to adequately meet the evolving development aspirations. Education is fundamental to personal and national development as it provides a myriad of life opportunities. It also underpins the development of a highly skilled and innovative workforce which is critical for social, cultural and economic growth hence the potential of learners in our Zimbabwean schools should be fulfilled.

The Curriculum Framework (2015–2022) provides a long term policy direction to improving the status quo of every learner in both urban and home environments. The Curriculum therefore, aims to expose every learner to the disciplines of science and technology, engineering, mathematics and heritage studies such that the learner is exposed to life and work learning contexts through the life skills orientation programme (LOP) and access education from wherever they are. Through this teaching and learning turnaround strategy, the learner will learn to appreciate our unique identity as Zimbabweans at the same establishing strong scientific and technological bias within the curriculum. There has been high recognition that content mastery alone is not adequate as an exit attribute hence this turn-around strategy. The emphasis is now on developing higher- order thinking skills, leadership skills, technological skills, communication and teamwork skills and competencies.

The Presidential Commission of Inquiry into Education and Training (1999) offers a vision of the education system and the kind of graduates that Zimbabwe needs that is a graduate who is multi- faceted. The virtual learning systems have created unlimited access to information and teachers are no longer seen as the sole sources of knowledge and information. Teachers are now expected to assist learners develop competencies to access information independently and responsibly as well develop broader life skills. The understanding now is that there are many varieties in learning styles and the curriculum has both process and product. In order to empower Zimbabweans for effective citizenry and employment for the 21st century, the education system should educate well and educate all (being encompassing and inclusive). Education institutions should engage learners in Science, Technology, Engineering and Mathematics (STEM) bias so that learners thrive in a knowledge based economy and society (Wagner, 2012). Engaging learners in Science, Technology, and Engineering and Mathematics education empowers learners with critical skills for living and productivity like; taking initiative and being enterprising and being able to access and analyse information to name but a few. In this regard learners gear themselves in contributing meaningfully to the exciting world of economics.

Partnering teachers and parents in their children's learning provides a strong base for learners' aspirations. The Presidential Commission into Education and Training (CIET, 1999) underscores the need for the education system that is underpinned by a philosophy of 'Ubuntu/Unhu/Vumunhu that would see parents being the first teachers of children and laying firm foundations for learning. Consequently, such a system should offer learners experiences and opportunities that nurture self- actualisation and promote a sense of community belonging. This then provides a consolidated view of the curriculum through regulatory instruments like the Education Act of 1987 as amended in 2006, the School Development Committees Regulations (1992) that governs the activities of parent committees, Statutory Instrument 106 of 2005 governing the establishment and management of Early Childhood Development Centres, the Zimbabwe National Code on corporate Governance 2014, the Second Science Technology and Innovation Policy (Draft, 2012). The Curriculum Framework is also informed by International Conventions and agreements to which Zimbabwe is a signatory. For instance the Convention on the Rights of Children (1989), the SADC Protocol on Education and Training to mention but a few. A wholesome curriculum should incorporate policy provisions, international conventions and agreements as well as standard generic principles.

Review of literature

This study examined the potential of home environment in creating learning spaces. In view of the rapid shift towards online delivery strategies, influenced by technology advancements and forced on learners by COVID19-inspired regulations, which called for social distancing, learners in the global world found themselves learning from home. Realising the learning environment has shifted from the traditional classroom housed in the formal school environment to one that flips between school and home, the home has become a key centre for modern teaching and learning. While teachers have always given learners homework, to sustain their efforts at school, the need for home learning spaces is now a prerequisite for learners be it rural or urban.

The rural learner faces a multiplicity of challenges, which need parent community commitment for quality rural home environment space creation.

The potential of home to mould ideal learning spaces for learners is under spotlight in view of isolated learning spaces. While distance education and blended learning environments have existed for years, these have mainly serviced tertiary education students, the impetus is now on the school system to be formed out of a merger between remote instruction and home environment support. Where the instructional framework is dominated by school administrators and facilitator teachers, the home learning environment demands among other faculties, a commitment by the parent towards the provision of basic necessities According to Hussain and Naz, (2013) in Khan, Begum, and Imad (2019) the establishment of Parents' Teacher Councils/ Associations is an important step toward increased parent's involvement in the educational activities of children.

Home learning and the right to an education

Education is a basic human right that is recognized globally and documented in many education policies even among sub-Saharan African countries (Chakanika, Sumbwa, & Sichula, 2012). The 1984 convention held in Geneva by the United Nations Education Scientific Cultural Organization (UNESCO) declared that everyone has the right to education under Article 26 of the Universal Declaration of Human Rights (United Nations, 1948). Every child therefore has to have optimal chances of an education like every other child in society. In a study on students' home environment, it was discovered the home environment hinders or supports children overall development (Khan, Begum, & Imad, 2019). It was noted children's educational activities at home are based on the physical and the psychological environment of their home. The learning facilities at home thus, enable and restrain them in practicing educational activities in the home environment. Restraint on the child's education however is an infringement on their right to access education

While yesteryear learning implied going to school and being in a classroom, the modern learning environment has experienced vast modifications owing to technological advancements, chief among which is online learning. While debates on e-learning and the need for government to preserve the learner's right to education continue unabated, learning from home has continued to gain momentum in society. The need to set up power supply infrastructure, internet connectivity, computers and related information technology devices, and content for e-learning is now a basic education requirement (Singh, 2019). While learning from home demands the learner to connect with instructors, collaborate with fellow classmates, access library resources, engage different learning styles, and measure self-progression, there is also the need to evaluate the ability of each and every learner to access online material and participate fully in a home learning environment. The major task is to establish how connected learners are and what media should be used to reach out to all the learners.

Singh (2019) identifies the auditory, visual and kinaesthetic learners, and alludes to the use of appropriate media in order to reach out to each and every learner. Rolling back to March 1998, the Australian Human Rights and Equal Opportunity Commission noted, in a study on Australian rural human rights issues in rural and remote areas that education emerges as the major concern for people living in these areas. A Survey for the Human Rights and Equal Opportunity Commission (1998) established, availability and accessibility of educational services including technological support services needs to be addressed first if a technology–guided learning environment is to be adopted to avoid infringing on the right of the learner to learn. Passey (n.d.) suggested the creation of intranet hubs in which homes are linked to the school via modems allowing the teacher to interact with learners via electronic platforms.

Overview of the home learner

The home learner expected to take time to learn, have access to appropriate technology, plan for all learning areas, make choices about subjects, have strategies for the limitations related to home location, and adjust to education needs. Questions have over the years been raised on the quality of learning experienced by home learning particularly the rural home learners. Home learning also presents parents with the task of differently providing for their children. According to Stokes and Brunzell (2019), issues to do with time, cost, location and strategies need close attention to ensure learners are not disadvantaged by home learning. In a survey of education in rural and remote Australia

While in the physical classroom environment the generality of learners are given equal opportunities to learn, home learning creates new challenges for learners. Parents also need to be evaluated.

Rural home environment learning

In view of the COVID-19 pandemic, global nations turned to online environments as the most ideal alternative to continued learning while in isolation. Questions of vulnerability and the right to education have been raised with the rural learner the most affected. Matimire (2020) acknowledged African governments have a challenge of Infrastructure, personnel and resources for effective home learning. For the rural home learning environment, the challenges experienced go beyond just infrastructure and personnel.

The definition of rural has been linked to population size as well as location in relation to the city. Aziz (2011) referred to rural as an area that is outside the city, while Heeralal (2014) viewed 'rural' as a place characterised by isolation in different regards, distance from cities and services and smallness in population density. Kulkami and Mitra (2015) argued, rural is an area with economic dependence on agriculture and tourism activities, regardless of population density and location. It can be noted from these definitions that rural areas are characterised by remote geographical location, spacey populated areas and dependence on farming activities for survival. By virtue of being remote, Shikalepo (2019) indicated, rural areas are far from resources, services and facilities associated with urban life. This therefore means, such areas are not well connected to such services as electrical powerlines and service providers for computers, mobile devices, internet services and knowledge systems that promote online connectivity. Provision of basic necessities like primary healthcare, electricity supply, portable water, good roads, equipped schools, essential infrastructural facilities that promote home learning is a challenge for rural areas.

While frantic efforts have been made to ensure the learning process extends to the home, the rural home environment has complexities beyond the ordinary. In a case study of five rural schools to establish factors that characterise rural areas and their influence on teaching and learning, Shikalepo (2019) discovered rural areas posed unbearable experiences for teachers, like walking long distances, to access services, poor housing, unpredictable climatic conditions, poor hygiene conditions, lack of classrooms, libraries and laboratories, which creates a fertile ground for teacher exodus to urban schools where working conditions are favourable.

In view of extended learning to the home, the literacy levels of parents in rural areas is of concern, as the lifestyles do not depend on going to formal schools but rearing of animals and farming. So the learner experiences challenges of lack of understanding of the value of learning by the parent community. The ability to read and write may be considered ideal for instruction. By virtue of having attained low levels of education, the parent community may not value schooling.

Benefits of the home learning environment

Realising the learning environment has shifted from the traditional classroom housed in the formal school environment to one that flips between school and home, the home has become a key learning centre for modern teaching and learning. Such factors as technological advancement and the need to social distance, together with blended education, and advancements in distance learning, now require that the home be an alternative learning environment.

Technology and the home learning environment

The Zimbabwean education system has experienced numerous phases in the engagement of ICTs for learning purposes. Notable is the Open and Distance Education (ODL) programmes and the Blended learning environments, which primarily have been used by higher education institutions. The ODL programmes hinges on individuals, national and institutional structures, as well as students' willingness to undertake courses under this mode (Mhishi, Bhukuvhan, & Sana, 2012). Individual learners in particular pursue this approach for reasons that are diverse, and include personal fulfilment, upgrading of qualifications while engaged in some other initiative, and self-actualisation. While the ODL programme is guided by students' willingness to use it, the eLearning programme as a result of social isolation was not an option for the school going children as no other alternative was there for them.

The COVID19 lockdowns compelled teachers to adopt information and communication technologies (ICTs) to ensure there is learning beyond the traditional classroom settings. Teachers, mainly in urban setups have adopted various ICT approaches in ensuring teaching is not disturbed by frequent lockdowns. ICTs have stood the test of time ensuring they complement the teacher's efforts both at school and at home. Older technologies such as the telephone, radio and television, have a longer and richer history as instructional tools, mainly for open and distance learning, as well as being multimedia tools in the classroom. The computer, mobile phone and internet have become the backbone of modern technology usage in instructional practice

The use of eLearning is now central to instructional practice, not only in tertiary education and cooperate practice, but even in the primary and secondary school systems. Information networks like the Whatsapp platform, Google classroom, Microsoft teams, and Moodle, together with browsers like Firefox and Google.com have assumed key instructional roles owing to computer and internet availability. The use of print-based and online materials, combined with the traditional classroom has given birth to Blended learning, while learning opportunities characterised by separation has breaded Open and distance learning. Guided by the constructivism theory, the National

Research Council of the US has also come up with learner-centred curriculum, to ensure learners pay careful attention to the knowledge, skills, attitudes, and beliefs that learners bring with them to the classroom

The parent and the home learning environment

According to Passey (n.d.) if parental expectations for children are low, then mechanisms should be put in place to enable longer term vision by parents to be developed. Such mechanisms should include offering parents access to material which gives examples of long term vision and effects; providing tasks and educational practices which involve parents and pupils in longer term projects and coursework; giving ways for pupils and parents to link short term work outcomes to longer term intentions; and involving parents in less formal activity, but on a more frequent basis, in considering educational practice, directions, and outcomes. The current Zimbabwean education landscape supports the engagement of learners in projects under the CALA framework, and it would be ideal to map a strategy that compels the parent and teacher to collaborate in the education of children so that the parent and the teacher are together focused on the learner. In this way, the home will be better modified for learning and time slices will be created as well as material support by the parent.

Key technological demands of the home learning environment

Educational ICT tools have become focal as learners and teachers have come to communicate via mobile phones, over social media platforms and learning management systems, to cover up for the social isolation periods as a result of COVID19. Bonanati and Buhl (2021) noted the rapid technological development and self-efficacy in digital devices. Bonanati and Buhl studies six different qualities of parental support, and noted, family's cultural capital, parents' attitudes towards the internet, sharing of digital activities at home were leading in terms of promoting ICT-self efficacy in children. Today's learners have been noted to be tech savvy and requiring minimal support to gainfully engage digital devices. This is a plus towards ensuring the home becomes an ideal learning environment.

According to the International Computer and Information Literacy Study individual's ability to use computers to investigate, create and communicate is the starting point towards ensuring effective learner participation in learning from the home environment (Fraillon, 2014). This therefore means, ICTs should first be available, then used by both parents and learners to communcate, play, create and investigate, then focus be shifted to learning areas with full appreciation and support of the parent.

How learners can benefit from the home learning environment

Findings from a national sample of the National Institute of Child Health and Human Development Study of Early Child Care and Youth Development (2018) revealed an overall improvement in the home learning environment from 36 to 54 months of children's age, with 30.6 % of parents of pre-schoolers displaying significant improvement in the home environment (Seung-Hee & Frederick, 2010). Improvements have however been confined to language development and not academic performance. The need for learners from early childhood development up to advanced level to benefit from the home learning environment is focal given shifts in instruction in favour of isolated instructional practice. Son and Morrison (2010), noted children who read, write, and play board games with their parents at home may demonstrate better vocabulary and academic skills compared to those who have fewer occasions to do so with their parents. There is therefore a need to close the gap between the parent and the child for effective parent-learner engagement in learning from home.

Children's participation in learning activities, the quality of parent–child interactions, and the availability of learning materials are three key features of the home learning environment that help to support children's educational development (Simone, Evangelou, & Sammons, 2020). The authors thus, concluded that collaboration between parents and educators should bridge the two learning environments home and preschool to promote children's development adequately. It should therefore be noted that, the engagement of the parent's interest towards the learner child's education should form the starting point towards enriching the home learning environment.

A study to establish the experiences of parents during the COVID-19 pandemic revealed online learning is a tough routine for parents since they have to commit to their children's education on a daily basis (Bhamani et al., 2020). In view of the shift to Whatsapp, radio, television, cell phones, computers, network systems, and satellite systems, as alternatives to learning from home, the vulnerable and disadvantaged rural communities have bared the brunt as learning has continued in mostly urban communities. Bhamani et al. further noted, as much as these initiatives are found to be appropriate to address the need of the time, it has also given a tough routine to parents who are working from home and simultaneously taking the responsibility that their children's learning process continues seamlessly during the times of COVID-19.

Government and curricula demands on the home learning experiences

In an endeavour to promote progress in education, governments have come up with strategies to ensure learning progresses despite COVID-19 restrictions. Bhamani et al. (2020) indicated governments the world over have shifted to distance learning systems via internet and online platforms for continuous education. The massive open online course (MOOC styled lessons have dominated media as education ministries battle to keep education afloat amid social isolation. In the Zimbabwean context, radio lessons were introduced mainly for primary schools, but their effectiveness is still under scrutiny. To cement continued education assumptions, the Zimbabwe School Examinations Council (ZIMSEC) has ensured public examinations continue unabated. The challenge for the rural learner is an uncertain access to education resources, given poverty as a challenge.

Organisational demands on the home environment and possibilities for rural learners

The need for an interface to link the school and the home has been upped in view of increased participation of the home in the learning process. Such interface should facilitate increased flow of information between the parent and the school as well as engage the learner in the learning process. Pessey (nd) advocated for courses and workshops in which the parent can be involved.

Challenges of learning from home

The rural home presents learners with huge challenges that need multi-stakeholder commitment (Chakanika, Sumbwa, & Sichula, 2012). According to Du Plessis (2014), one of the greatest challenges facing rura communities is poverty. Most people in rural communities cannot afford the basics required to fend for their families. Bringing about the demands of education upon them becomes an extra burden on them. While parents may be relying on donations and other food handouts, they also need their children to be assisting them to get the much needed food on the table. The learner therefore faces the challenge of assisting the family raise food, and also attend to their school work. Another challenge for rural learners is access to services and facilities like water, electricity and sanitation. Technology is also another challenge, affecting rural learning. It may be unavailable, or available with little knowledge. Rural settings are also not attractive to school teachers who use every opportunity available to transfer to township schools. Another challenge facing rural homes is of marginalisation. In the Zimbabwean context, the economic meltdown and the devaluation of the local currency was a big blow which caused many rural parents to lose on years of investment as funds lost value overnight in towns as they were in rural homes.

Strategies that can be used to turn the home into a learning environment

The learning environment now calls for parents to take more responsibility for the academic engagement and achievement of their children. According to Sweet, Mandell, Anise, and Adamuti-Trache (2007), the home school partnership requires increased parental involvement in the extra-curricular life of the school as well as the establishment of a home learning environment that complements the work of the classroom teacher. Parents should therefore be engaged in discussions to identify needs of the learner in view of the tilting of the learning environment towards the home. Sweet et al. further note, the home learning environment calls for the promotion of a sense of autonomy in their children and also the incorporation of homework within established family routines. Autonomy is a self psychology concept that enables the learner to have a competence mentality, agency, self-efficacy, and more domain-specific terms like self concept and ability and self-regulation of behaviour. The incorporation of homework within established family routines allows learners to be responsible for their learning through managing the stress associated with home chores and the school tasks. Home learning presents conflicts between parents and their children as there is need to balance activities. Parents' beliefs about their children's development and learning shapes the relationships they establish with their children. As such, parents may want to be in control of their children's activities in the home and interfere with their learning, by denying them certain required resources like space, time and ICT gadgets, and derail their children's learning. Parents need to be strongly encouraged to be responsible for the success of their children's learning, by providing required resources and giving them the training for autonomy which will ensure the child is responsible for his learning.

The engagement of government, donor community, prolearner organisations like the UNICEF and United Nations, industry, church organisations, public and private sector support and individuals is crucial towards the establishment of home learning spaces for learners at a time when the physical engagement spaces are not readily available, and also because society wants to move with the times.

Conclusion

This chapter presented the home as a learning environment in a technology environment. Special attention was given to the rural learner and the writers pointed to the challenges and opportunities, given the changing learning landscape, where the yesteryear classroom with four halls is fast extending to the home, the role of the parent and relevant others in the home environment was presented as well as the ideal home learning environment.

References

Aziz, N. (2011). *Retaining high quality teachers in rural primary schools in Malaysia.* Harvard: Harvard University.

Bhamani, S., Makhdoom, A. Z., Bharuchi, V., Ali, N., Kaleem, S., & Ahmed, D. (2020, September 26). Home learning in times of COVID: Experiences of parent. *Journal of Education and Educational Development.* http://dx.doi.org/10.22555/joeed.v7i1.3260

Bonanati, S., & Buhl, H. M. (2021, July 8). The digital home learning environment and its relation to children's ICT self-efficacy. *Open Access.*

Chakanika, W. W., Sumbwa, P. I., & Sichula, N. K. (2012). The challenges of rural education in Africa. Retrieved August 23, 2021, from: https://www.researchgate.net/publication/336676604

Chandra, K. (2012). *Constructivist theories of ethnic politics.* Oxford: Oxford University Press.

Du Plessis, P. (2014). Problems and complexities in rural schools: Challenges of education and social development. *Mediterranean Journal of Social Sciences.* DOI:10.5901/mjss.2014.v5n20p1109

Education, Ministry of Primary and Secondary. (2016). *Curriculum framework for primary and secondary schools (2015–2022).* HArare: Government Printers.

Fraillon, J. A. (2014). Students' use of and engagement with ICT at home and school. Retrieved September 13, 2021, from https://doi.org/10.1007/978-3-319-14222-7-6

GovernmentofZimbabwe. (2005). *StatutoryInstrument106Of2005.* HArare: Government Printers.

Heeralal, P. (2014). Preparing pre-service teachers to teach in rural schools. *Mediterranean Journal of Social Sciences, 5*(20), 1795–1799.

Khan, F. N., Begum, M., & Imad, M. (2019). Relationship between students' home environment and their academic achievement at secondary school level. *Pakistan Journal of Distance & Online Learning, v*(II), 223–234.

Kulkarni, S., & Mitra, S. (2015). Access and quality in self organized learning environments formal education: Quality issues. Retrieved September 20, 2021, from http://wikieducator.org/images/c/cb/Suneeta_Kulkarni.pdf

Learners, R. M., & Hultch, D. E. (1983). *Human development: A lifetime perspective.* New York: McGraw Hill.

Matimaire, K. (2019). *50% of Zim schools connected to WiFi – Govt.* The industry and trade expect. Retrieved August 28, 2021, from . https://theindustrytrade.com/2019/09/20/50-of-zim-schools-connected-to-wifi-govt/

Mhishi, M., Bhukuvhan, C. E., & Sana, A. F. (2012, January). Science teacher training programme in rural schools: An ODL lesson from Zimbabwe. *The International Review of Research in Open and Distance Learning, 13*(1), 72–86.

Mumpande, I. (2020). *The revitalisation of ethnic minority languages in Zimbabwe. A case of Tonga.*

Nziramasanga. (1999). *Commission of enquiry into education and training.* HArare: Government Printers.

Passey, D. (n.d.). *Developing home-school links: Implications for learners, learning, and learning support.* Lancaster: Department of Educational Research.

Rural and Remote School Education. A survey for the Human Rights and equal Opportunity Commission. (1998). Melborne: Youth Research Centre, University of Melbourne, Vic 3010.

Santrock, J. W. (2008). *Children.* New York: McGraw Hill.

Seung-Hee, C. S., & Frederick, J. M. (2010). The nature and impact of changes in home learning environment on development of language and academic skills in preschool children. *Developmental Psychology, 46*(5):1103–1118.

Shikalepo, E. E. (2019). *Characteristics of rural areas and their effects on teaching and learning dynamics.* International University of Management, Namibia, Online.

Simone, L., Evangelou, M., & Sammons, P. (2020, January 31). The home learning environment and its role in shaping children's educational development. *An International Journal of Research, Policy and Practice, 31*(1). Retrieved September 20, 2021, from https://doi.org/10.1080/09243453.2020.1693487

Singh, R. (2019, June). Educational media in teaching learning process. *Bhartiyam International Journal of Education & Research, 8*(3), 7–14.

Stokes, H., & Brunzell, T. (2019). *Professional learning in trauma informed positive education: Moving school communities from trauma affected to trauma aware.* Melbourne: University of Melbourne.

Sweet, R., Mandell, N., Anise, P., & Adamuti-Trache, M. (2007). *Managing the home learning environment: Parents, adolescents, and the homework problem.* Retrieved September 10, 2021, from Https://Www.Researchgate.Net/Publication/242478415_Managing_The_Home_Learning_Environment_Parents_Adolescents_And_The_Homework_Problem

United Nations. (1948). Universal Declaration of Human Rights.

6. *Attainment of Sustainable Development Goal 4 (SDG 4): Teacher perceptions, readiness and practices*

Judith Musengi

Introduction

The concept of sustainable development has become topical at academic and United Nations platforms. Education has been identified as a vehicle sustainable development. Education is a human right which every child has to access. To this effect educational programs and curriculum innovations have been crafted to enhance effective learning of the learner. This in line with the United Nations' agenda to promote better living conditions for mankind through democratization of the Education system, pedagogical innovations that are learner-centered, embracing of Information Communication Technologies (ICT) inclusive educational models, lifelong skills and quality personnel to enhance these changes (UNESCO, 2017). While most Post-Modernist curriculum innovations are rolled out to promote Quality Education for the learner, attainment of that Quality Education depends on multiplicity of variables. These variables range from creation of conducive learning environment, learner-centered approaches, infrastructural development, learner welfare and teacher training. This discourse contends that there has to be more investigation amidst all these changes, there is a person on the ground, the teacher. Teacher readiness, perceptions and practices become critical for the success of any curriculum innovation programmer (Khunyen et al., 2020). Delving deeper into teacher attitudes is necessary as a monitoring and evaluation measure of the implementation process. Dolton et al. (2018) observe that teachers' jobs are difficult, their social status and remuneration are low in many countries. Zimbabwe is among such countries whose Education system has been struggling due to the political and economic challenges obtaining in the country. Teachers in the rural areas occupy a difficult position as they experience conditions which are different from those in urban areas. That is problematic as they are expected to demonstrate professional competence and efficacy just like their urban counterparts. Some teachers in the rural areas are detached from facilities such as electricity, safe water and health care and general remoteness impact on their practices and perceptions on enhancing Quality Education. Challenges teachers face have a bearing not only their living conditions but efficacy and motivation which directly impact on their execution of work and producing expected outcomes. In face of incapacitated disillusioned rural teachers, there is little doubt that concept of Quality Education as enshrined in UN SDG4 would be prolonged to materialize.

Concept of Sustainable Development Goal 4

The concept of Sustainable Development which has become a topic on world platforms was first projected by Brundtland (1987) where development is termed sustainable when it meets the needs of the present without compromising the ability of future generations to meet their own needs. FAO report (2011) reveals different development paradigms. It projects that human development which is people centred where focus is put on the various dimensions affecting the well-being of individuals and their relationships with society, health educators, settlements, capabilities and empowerment. Economic development, on the other hand is coined on the improvement of the way endowments goods and services provide investment opportunities. These paradigms are engrained in the various Millennium Development Goals (MDGs) set by the United Nations to promote economic, political and social stability in the world. Pro-poor growth envisage equitability and endogenous growth call for embracing of technology in the agenda of learning by doing. All these are interlinked in the UNESCO Sustainable Development Goal 4 on Quality Education. The concept of sustainability has to be understood as envisaging intergenerational equity. The foundation of Sustainable Development is the integration of environmental, social and economic aspects in all decision making (Dernbach, 2003; Stoddart, 2011).

The concept of Sustainable Development has to be understood from the integration vision and in practice it requires the elimination of fragmentation or inequalities. The United Nations, in its bid to pursue international stability among nations, published 17 Sustainable Development Goals. The Sustainable Development Goal number 4 (SDG4) is among the 17 Sustainable Development Goals rolled out by UNESCO in 2017 (UNESCO, 2017). SDG4 has the vision of promoting Quality Education through Inclusive and equitable quality education in order to promote lifelong learning opportunities for all. The major pillars of this Goal include Quality, Inclusive, Equitable, Lifelong and Opportunities. These have to be explored in depth and how they apply to rural learning ecologies. While the term sustainability may seem unclear, it literally means the capacity to maintain some entity, outcome or process over time. On the other hand Ben-Eli (2015) sees sustainability as a dynamic equilibrium in the process of interaction between the population and their carrying capacity of its environment such that population develops to express its full potential without producing irreversible adverse effects on the carrying capacity of the environment upon which it depends. This entails lifelong solution as projected by the UN SDG4. Education is a tool for social transformation in communities and promotion of sustainable development among learners is a strategy earmarked to equip the future generation to be active participants and not spectators in their country.

Themes of sustainable development have dominated conferences and academic papers as well as slogans of development and environmental activists. Quality Education as envisaged by UNESCO (2017) is concerned with creation of conducive learning environments that are learner centered and offer people with the right skills, attitudes and knowledge that go beyond narrowed outcomes of literacy and numeracy. It calls for a diversified approach where more competences are explored from the learner, in which case discourages the teacher from teaching to test a practice that would arresting the transformative potential of education. Quality content, environment and teacher would produce the intended outcome of a quality learner with the necessary skills. Inclusive Education as has been defined in the Salamanca Statement entails recognition of the need to work towards 'schools for all' Institutions that which include everybody, celebrate differences, support learning, and respond to individual needs (Boren, 2019). As Boren (2019) observes, inclusion in this context of education has foundation in the idea that all children learn together, regardless of differences disability (UNESCO, 1994). Inclusive Education commences with the realization that all learners have unique characteristics, interests, abilities and particular learning needs and further, that learners with special education needs and further, that learners with special needs must have equal access to and receive individual accommodation in the general education system (Chitiyo, 2019). However, though idealistic, this would promote tolerance by their peers without discrimination (although there is no guarantee of stigmatization). Inclusive Education therefore is the one that accommodates diversity. The whole concept of inclusion can best be summarized as encompassing acceptability, availability, accessibility, and adaptability. In the rural context, remote areas may be a hindrance to learners with disability if they have to travel for long distances to reach their schools. Filmer (2008) concurs by observing that disability has more probability of non-enrolment than gender or class. Inclusive Education is in line with the right to education as recognized in Article 11 of the African Charter on Human and Persons' Rights which has the provision that every child has a right to education. Equitable Education as engrossed in this SDG4 entails a just educational system that do not pose barriers to learners based on gender, status or disability.

Lifelong learning offers opportunities especially to adults who would not have had the opportunity to acquire education. At the same time to the youth it offers a chance for an ongoing process of acquiring knowledge and skills in order to solve problems in life. This would fulfill the inclusivity and sustainability of quality education agenda. However, in rural set ups it remains to be established if the elderly is aware of such programmers and if facilities are in place to cater for such. Sustainable development Goal 4 aims at ensuring that by 2030 all girls and boys complete free equitable and quality primary and secondary education leading to relevant learning outcomes. However, in Zimbabwe there is evidence of school dropouts due mainly to hardships experienced. The idea of 'All' is still yet to be realised as the rural communities still have patriarchal ideas deep rooted to such an extent that the girl child is still being prejudiced and access to education jeopardized. It is the vision of SDG4 to ensure that there is access to quality Early Childhood Development, care and pre-primary education so that they are ready for primary education. This vision is hindered by lack of infrastructure in the rural set ups and remoteness of some schools would not allow young learners to travel long distances every day. It aims to ensure that by 2030 there is equal access for all women and men to affordable and quality technical vocational and tertiary education including university. Many learners in the rural areas experience challenges in making it to tertiary education including universities due to hardships obtaining on the ground. Some still make it all the way despite unfriendly environments. SDG4 intends to substantially increase the number of youth and adults who have relevant technical and vocational skills for employment decent jobs and entrepreneurship. Whilst this is a noble idea their access is again compromised by the harsh environment. Of vital importance is the elimination of gender disparities in education and ensuring equal access to all levels of education and vocational training for the vulnerable, including persons with disabilities, indigenous people and children in vulnerable situations. In rural areas most parents are deep rooted in indigenous culture and elements of male dominance still affect girls' upward mobility in the Education ladder.

The sixth objective of SDG4 is to ensure that by 2030 all youth and a substantial proportion of adults, both men and women, achieve literacy and numeracy. This entails engaging in conventional and adult literacy to elderly in the communities including rural areas. Apart from gaining literacy, SDG4 aims at ensuring that all learners acquire the knowledge and skills needed to promote sustainable development, including among other things, through education for sustainable development and sustainable lifestyles, human rights, gender equality, promotion of a culture of peace and non-violence, global citizenship and appreciation of cultural diversity and of culture's contribution to sustainable development These values dovetail well with the philosophy of Ubuntu and responsible citizenship. Objective number 8 intends to build and upgrade education facilities that are child, disability and gender sensitive and provide safe, non-violent inclusive and effective learning environments for all. In rural settings there is still need to develop friendly environments as their schools suffer from lack of development generally. The UN SDG4 aims to substantially expand globally the number of scholarships available to developing countries, in particular least developed counties, for enrolment in higher education, including vocational training and information communications technology, technical, engineering and scientific programs, in developed countries and other developing countries. This would go a long way in assisting especially learners in the rural areas who are marginalized in accessing information and some are cut off from world links. Finally, this Educational goal aims to substantially increase the supply of qualified teachers, including through international cooperation for teacher training in developing counties, especially least developed countries and small island developing states. Adequate human resource is essential especially in some rural areas where teachers dread to be due to hardships and manpower retention is low.

Rural ecology and SDG4

Reports by United Nations have expressed concern over the gap between rural and urban schools in most developing countries. The marginalization of rural areas back date from the colonial period where development was mostly concentrated in the urban areas. In Africa most post-colonial governments are still struggling to bridge the gap. In Zimbabwe the demographical statistics show that 75 % of learners at Primary level, 70 % of secondary school and 81, 12 % of Early Childhood Development are in the rural areas (Zimstat, 2018). It means therefore that, in Zimbabwe more learners are in the rural areas. Educational programs are rolled out to schools in order to attain quality education irrespective of the conditions obtaining on the ground. Zimbabwe's rural schools are characterized by mostly lack of development. Most schools are experiencing acute shortages of resources, with inadequate or dilapidated infrastructure. Some of the schools are located in areas of low productivity and that affects flow of tuition payment by parents to enhance development. Other schools are characterized by geographical isolation and far from health and water sources. Most rural parents live in abject poverty and struggle to pay tuition for their children. Most learners in rural areas strive to have decent meals and many live under malnutrition, poor sanitation and have very low enthusiasm to undertake educational endeavors. Their capacity to learn is very low let alone accessing equal opportunities with their urban counterparts. According to UNESCO (2018) report rural areas being challenged by lack of access to internet and lack of electricity as well as electronic gadgets like computers to engage in digital learning. This is in concurrence with Zimstat (2018) which show that there is a wide gap between rural and urban schools. Consequently, promoting the use of Information Communication Technologies (ICT) in the rural areas may be insoluble.

The concept of quality education as enshrined in the UN SDG4 can be realised in environments where learners are health and well-nourished and ready to participate and supported in the learning process by families and communities Unfortunately, rural schools still have a long way to go to achieve quality education amidst these conditions. According to the UNESCO (2000), quality education can be enhanced in environment that are safe, protective and gender sensitive as well as provide adequate resources and facilities. However, with the conditions in rural schools revealed above it becomes evident that the learning environment is unhealthy and attaining UN SDG 4 would be a tall order. Quality learners do not need to have good health and nutrition only but to be physically and psychologically healthy in order to learn well. Unfortunately, most learners in the rural areas are badly traumatized by poverty, poor lighting and general backwardness. Quality education can be attained with consistent learner attendance which most rural children cannot afford due to difficulties. There has to be regular attendance for learning and exposure to the curriculum by learners (Fuller et al., 1999). Most rural areas are still rooted in culture that some of the parents' perception of gender awareness and responsiveness is still very low and patriarchy still dominates thus consequently leading to sidelining of female learners. Quality content has been considered as critical for attaining UN SDG4 in the education system with nondiscriminatory content and curriculum catering for individual differences (Glatthorn & Jailall, 2000). Ability to read and write is essential in the vision of sustainable development and many learners in the rural areas due to hardships incurred may end up not attaining literacy levels expected and may even drop out of school. This is in sync with the UNESCO (2017) report which indicated that there are drop outs both at Primary and Secondary rural schools of Zimbabwe generally.

Some of the learners in the rural areas are under child headed families of foster parents after parents succumbed to retrenchment or were HIV/AIDS victims. Such learners struggle to access education while others have challenges with paying tuition on their own. This explains why as UNESCO (2000) concurs, in Zimbabwe there has been inclusion of life long skills topic on HIV/AIDS in the curriculum. While the curriculum has to promote learner diversity, it has been noted that as compared to urban schools, rural schools have deficiencies in resources like laboratories, libraries and especially diversity in sporting activities. That has far reaching repercussions on the vision of quality inclusive education as learner abilities may not be realised without the necessary exposure. Inclusive education is nurtured in an environment where there are opportunities to benefit from learning and apply them to post school outcomes (Hehir et al., 2017). Unfortunately, the rural set up has limited facilities to enhance inclusivity and diversity. Few sporting facilities are offered by rural schools as mostly netball soccer and basket ball are popular while in urban areas some learners access a variety of sporting facilities with Sporting Academies to their exposure. These discrepancies impact negatively on enhancement of UN SDG4 agenda. Thus there are skewed opportunities in the rural areas and the vision of UN SDG4 has the potential to dismantle the inequalities in the rural areas. Learners in the rural areas are mostly drawn from low income families where guardians are self-employed as peasants or artisans. It is in these communal areas that parents struggle to meet tuition obligations on time. There are challenges in the Basic Education Assistance Module (BEAM) which accounts for a significant funding for rural schools. The funds are usually delayed so is the late reimbursement of the fund which covers for orphaned and learners with disability. Collectively these derail the potential of achieving sustainable development in rural schools. Quality and inclusive education is compromised even considering the fact that it entails that just like in urban areas, rural schools have to embark on non-formal education (adult literacy). Without electricity and internet, as well as other learning materials, the vision of 'no one should be left out' becomes a mirage. In some resettlements where bans serve as make do classrooms, conditions are worse as even furniture would be scarce as well as boards. Amidst these conditions is a rural teacher who is expected to execute quality education to learners in the best way possible.

Role of the teacher in enhancing UN SDG4

The success of any education system is anchored mostly on a good teacher who has sound pedagogical knowledge and skills and can deliver effective quality education in diverse learner populations, supporting them from different learning trajectories. The teacher has to have the capability to provide learners with opportunities that ensure sustainable learning with lifelong skills. Bhat (2020) observes the teacher shoulders the responsibility of enhancing sustainable development. In order to make the learners socially conscious citizens. It becomes the role of the teacher to sensitise the young generation by identifying the right ways and means for educating and preparing learners for sustainable development. The teacher as the creator of the future generation, has the mandate to assist learners to develop the necessary skills, knowledge, attitudes and values relevant for sustainable development. As Ansani (2005) notes, it's the role of the teacher to show the right direction and enhance social change and modernization in the society. The question is who best can ensure that no one is left behind in accessing quality education and learning if it is not the teacher. Unfortunately, the teacher in the rural area who himself/herself is entangled in the web of underdevelopment has to ironically forge the agenda of sustainable development to the future generation. Mishra (2017) identifies the teacher as the torch bearer of the society and has to assist in preparing learners to be responsible citizens. It has to be the duty of the teacher to plant the seed of sustainable development on the learners. The mentality of sustainable development has to be navigated by the teacher to the learners. The teacher in the rural areas, who is faced with mostly children of vulnerable conditions due to the conditions obtaining in the rural ecology, has the responsibility of implementing curriculum goals as they are rolled out to schools. He has to strategise and be more innovative than the urban teacher due to lack of resources. In the absence of laboratories, classrooms and furniture learning has to be conducted and achieve set goals from an almost impossible situation. The rural teacher is faced not only by pedagogical but also psychological challenges to enhance effective learning. The teacher has a role in enhancing in enhancing lifelong skills like leadership, critical thinking, problem solving and career guidance. Quality education entails learners to possess some unique skills which make them eligible for the tasks ahead (Pavel, 2012). Graduates from Higher and Tertiary Education need to have skills that will help learners acquire such skills and help them make decisions and come up with new ideas of doing things from a Post Modernistic perspective. British Council (2014) failure to invest in compromise on teacher efficacy and backwardness instead of fostering sustainable development.

Teacher perceptions, readiness and practices

Attaining Quality education depends on a multiplicity of factors but most important is ensuring that a quality teacher is in place. Teachers are a cornerstone for the betterment of education and their perceptions, readiness and practices determine the success of any educational programme including attaining UN SDG4. The UNESCO report observed that there has been slow pace in implementation of Sustainable Development in most developing countries and especially in areas that are marginalized. Slow progress may attest to challenges in teaching those populations that are left behind, the rural areas. Being in a school for learners is not adequate if they do not learn .and get the expected outcomes, the teacher's preparedness perceptions would determine their practices in ensuring the success of quality education. Professional training for teachers has to be a priority if high standards in education are to be maintained. Well trained and empowered teachers can afford taking up responsibilities ahead of them without much difficulty. This overshadows the opinion that teachers are made and not born teachers.

Key to ensuring implementation of quality education and lifelong skills is the quality of the teacher training prospective teachers acquire which is predicated on ensuring that the academic instructors are appropriately skilled and qualified. A vicious circle is created if teachers are ill-equipped for half baked teachers cannot bring the child's learning process to desired levels. There seem to be rolling out of programs to ensure realisation of UN SDG4 without giving serious investment in ensuring a quality workforce which would navigate learners to desired learning outcomes. Training should prepare teachers to real situations on the ground including hardships in rural areas and how teachers have to adapt to them. There is a high correlation between how teachers are trained for both general and special education and the success of inclusive education. The highest quality teachers are those most capable of assisting in both their subject matter and pedagogy (Darling-Hammond, 1997). The preparation that teachers receive before beginning their work in the classroom vary world over but is critical in attaining set educational goals. Teacher competence has to be a priority and lays a foundation for the success of any educational programme. It has been noted through available literature that there have been sins of omission and commission in teacher training. There is need for pedagogical overhaul by teachers to cater for the diversity enshrined in the concept of inclusivity. Lack of serious digital and innovative pedagogies, skills in special education and lifelong skills have been noted to be lacking in most teacher training courses. Despite a call to improve and be innovative in approaches, many teachers and educational systems continue to depend almost entirely on traditional methodologies which are not learner-centered but rigid and even authoritarian (Chou, 1996). In concurrence with this observation Colby (2000) states there is continued use of traditional methods even in assessment as there is reliance is on traditional paper and pencil tests of factual knowledge that tend to promote rote memorization rather than higher order thinking. Such practices in rural settings would jeopardise the agenda of inclusivity as not all learners are gifted in the same way. In addition, the rural teacher has the dilemma of inadequate resources and meeting expected outcomes leading others to mostly improvising sometimes from their meagre salaries to keep the vision of quality education on track. However, whether a teacher uses traditional or more current methods of instruction, efficient use of school time is of considerable importance to enhance meaningful learning.

Teachers' presence in the classroom has far reaching effects in ensuring quality education, the teacher has to be motivated to be in the classroom in order to deliver services. However, most rural teachers despite having or lacking necessary skills in Information Communication Technology and lifelong skills, have more challenges that hinder them from providing quality education. Most teachers in rural areas live in deplorable conditions and that affects their practices. In rural areas, some teachers are subjected to dilapidated houses with no electricity, running water, clinics, and no network connectivity. Because of lack of connectivity, both teachers and learners in the rural areas are sidelined in online learning activities especially in this coronavirus environment. In addition, rural teachers get subjected to social isolation and professional isolation, endangering their personal safety in those deplorable conditions. These conditions greatly impact on effective execution of quality education. Many aspects of school life and educational policy influence teachers' perceptions of their employment.

Low remuneration has a serious bearing in teacher practices and negatively affect learning outcomes. United Nations reports have revealed that teachers' salaries deteriorated in recent years forcing many to undertake other activities to supplement their meagre salaries. Teachers in rural areas seek transfers to urban or peri-urban where they can undertake some lucrative business activities. Effective teachers are highly committed and exhibit care towards their learners (Craig et al., 1998). What is needed is to ensure that teachers in rural areas receive supportive working conditions to maintain positive attitudes that would go a long way in promoting quality education. The complex equation to quality delivery service in the education sector entails teacher recruitment and retention. Teachers have to remain highly motivated to execute their duties especially in the rural areas with so much hardships. In Zimbabwe the payment of a Hardship Allowance to rural based teachers though inadequate, is acknowledging that the living conditions are deplorable. The teacher in the rural areas who has to provide psycho social services to the learner also need those services to be able to perform duties effectively and enhance lifelong skills. Bennell (2011) warns that the consequences of poor working conditions for teachers include low pass rate and higher rate teacher attrition. Therefore, there is need for prioritization of rural environment and welfare for the welfare of the rural teacher if the vision of UN SDG4 is to be realised. Zimbabwe in line with respecting children's rights affiliates to the 1994 Salamanca statement and Framework Action on Special Needs Education whose agenda is to promote inclusive education. As a matter of fact, therefore, training teachers in this area becomes a de facto.

Provision of necessary infrastructure to cater for learners with special needs is of necessity. However, in most rural schools there is serious deficiency in both learning materials and special rooms for learners with special needs. In Zimbabwe there are policies for Ministry of Primary and Secondary Education despite discrepancies, learners are catered for with the same inclusive education. There is however lack of special Education specific legislations (Chitiyo et al., 2019). Existing literature point to lack of resources such as braille and large print materials for the visually impaired learners. Research by Chitiyo et al. (2019) indicates that teachers acknowledge the need for Special Needs Education but projected possible barriers to successful implementation most important being lack of thorough preparedness. Learners' needs come in their multiplicity ways that sometimes teachers struggle to mitigate. In rural areas many learners suffer from various socio-economic deficiencies and need constant mitigation from a teacher who is were equipped to assist these learners meaningfully. Counseling in-service courses to cater for the multiplicity of situations as they surface. There is need for more up to date training for teachers. Neal and Crouch (2013) observe that, Tertiary institutions should raise their curriculum. A call for more skills in dealing with psychological and emotional situations teachers face with learners who thrive in rural areas. A challenge is experienced especially at secondary school where there seem to be disappearance of special classes and lack of trained personnel for special needs as teachers showed ignorance in how to deal with some learners with special needs. Nonreaders for instance were major concern from secondary teachers. It means attaining of quality and inclusive education in these rural areas is still imaginary.

Contrary to research by Chitiyo in which teachers demonstrated concern in assisting learners in special needs education, Singal (2004) observed that teachers feel that Inclusive Education is something they are told to do often without resources and it becomes a top down burden rather through a collaborative process. For teachers in rural areas its more burden in face of the unfriendly teaching environment. It becomes mandatory for teachers to have knowledge and skills to create meaningful inclusive classrooms in the rural settings. Whilst in-service programs are necessary, some scholarship have reservations alluding to the fact that they do little in terms of impacting on change. One off workshops or parachute trainings or continuing professional development are considered to be inadequate (Fullan, 2007). Schulka (2018) concurs with this assertion that inclusive educational techniques were being offered as professional development at one off workshops. For a long term solution to the education system that would be a plausible approach for the teachers already in service, there is need to appraise them with the necessary skills, especially in rural areas if quality education has to be achieved.

While most public schools in urban areas face challenges with double sessioning, teacher-pupil ratio in rural areas is low due to low enrolment. However, teacher to subject ratio is higher. Teachers in rural areas are forced by circumstances to attend to teach more than one subjects at secondary level. One teacher may undertake diverging learning areas like Science, Shona and Commerce. At primary one teacher may can be in charge of two classes or grades due to lack of adequate human and material resources. The situation is worse in remote and satellite areas where a lot of innovation and improvising has to save the day. Such a load affects quality and teacher may not attend to individual needs as the load can be overwhelming. A situation where teachers' conditions are not elevated is counterproductive to learning as learners would remain stuck in a deficient condition. There is a high correlation between teacher perceptions, attitudes and practices. Unianu (2012) projects that teachers' attitudes towards Inclusive education also determines successful implementation of inclusion practices and policies. This is important because positive attitudes enhance active participation. Teachers' active participation is an essential element for effective professional development (Desimore, 2011). If they have negative attitudes towards Inclusive education they may exhibit lack of will to see it through (Galore et al., 2014). Teachers in rural areas experience conditions that water down their enthusiasm to effectively deliver their duties. Attainment of sustainable development through quality education becomes problematic since there are reports on general teacher disillusionment in Zimbabwe.

Conclusion

There has been rolling out of Education programs to meet the 2030 Agenda for Sustainable Development and reinforcement of UN SDG4 on quality

Education in the Primary and Secondary schools of Zimbabwe with the focus on the learner. However, this discourse acknowledging the importance of the product(learner), has brought the attention of the teacher whose task is to enhance the successful implementation of any curriculum innovation programs. Teacher readiness, perception and practices are interwoven and if not looked into seriously have the vicious cycle of being counterproductive in promoting the intended curriculum outcomes. The training teachers get reflect their lack of readiness and proper empowerment which lead to unwillingness to implement intended curriculum. Their attitudes and perceptions are closely linked to preparedness and general working conditions, which if not seriously invested into, would seriously jeopardise the agenda for Sustainable Development in Zimbabwe. Some of the rural areas of Zimbabwe are seriously lagging behind in development and working conditions for teachers are deplorable, to expect rural teachers to carry out their duties with efficacy would be unrealistic. Implementation of UN SDG4 in rural areas without prioritizing the teacher's welfare would be disastrous to the whole vision of Sustainable Development.

References

Annual Zimbabwe Education Statistics Report 2018.

Ansari, M. S. (2005). *Teacher in emerging Indiana Society.* Meerut: International Publishing House.

Ben-Eli, M. (2015). Sustainability: Definition and five core principles a new framework the sustainability laboratory, NYinfo@sustainabilitylabs.orgwww.sustainabilitylabs. [Google Scholar]

Bennell, P. (2011). A UPEIS emergency programme for primary school teachers,Paris:UNESCO EFA Global Monitoring Report

Bhat, A. (2020, April 23). Secondary research –Definition,methods,and examples. *QuestionPro* https://www.questionpro.com/blog/secondary-research/

British Council. (2014). *can higher education solve African's job crisis?* Available on http://www.britishcouncil.org/sites/britishcouncil.nk2/files/graduate-employability-in-ssa-final-web-pdf. Accessed 07/08/21.

Boeren, E. (2019). *Understanding Sustainable Development Goal (SDG)4 on quality education from meso and macro perspective.* London: Palgrave-Macmillan.

Brundtland. (1987). Our common future World Commission in Environment and Development.

Chitiyo, M., Hughes, E. M., Chitiyo, G., Changara, D. M., Itimi-Phiri, A., Haihambo, C., Taukeni, S. G., & Dzenga, C. G. (2019). Exploring teachers' special and inclusive education professional development needs in Malawi, Namibia, and Zimbabwe. *International Journal of Whole Schooling, 15*(1), 28–49.

Chou, C. P. (1996). *A study on the state of Chinese comparative education:1949–1996.* National Cheng-Chi University Monograph, 71, 201–225

Colby, J. (2000). *Learning outcomes in international context.* Paper presented at the annual meeting of the comparative and International Education Society, San Antonio, Texas, March.

Craig, H., Kraft, R., & Du Plessis, J. (1998). *Teacher development and making an impact.* Washington, D.C.: Academy Educational Development, ABEL Cleaning House for Basic Education

Desmore. (2011). L.M A Prime on effective professional development. *Phi Delta Kappan. International Journal of Whole Schooling, vol.*1.5, no. 1, *92*(6), 68–71.

Dernbach, J. C. (2003). *Achieving Sustainable Development: The Centrality and Multiple Facets of Integrated decision making. Indiana Journal of Global Legal Studies, 10*(1), 247–285.

Dolton, D., et al. (2018). *Global teacher status.* Index Varkey, Foundation, London https://www.varkeyfoundation.org./media/u867/gts-index-13-11-2018pdf

Farell, P., & Ainscow, M. (2002). *Making special education inclusive.* London: David Fullon.

FAO. (2005). An approach to rural development: Participatory and negotiated territorial development rural development Division Food and Agriculture Organisation of the United Nations(FAO), April 2005. http://www.fao.org/sd/dim-pe2/docs/05040 2d1-en.pdf

Filmer, D., & Pritchett, L. (1999). The effect of household wealth on educational attainment,Evidence from 35 countries. *Population and Development Review, 25*(1), 85–120. http://dx.do.org/1o11111/J.72819999.00085.x-4457

Fulher, B., Dellagnello, L., et al. (2000). How to raise children literacy? The influence of family, teacher and classroom in northeast Brazil. *Comparative Education Review, 43*(1), 1–35.

Fullan, M. (2007). *The new meaning of educational change* (4th ed.). New York: Teachers College.

Glattthorn, A., & Jailall, J. (2000). Curriculum for the new millennium. In Brand, R. (Ed.), *Education in a new era: ASCD year book 2000.* Alexandria,Virginia: Assosciation for Supervision and on Development.

Hehir, T., Gnidal, T., Freeman, B., Lai more au, R., Borquayes, Y., & Burke. (2017). A summary of the evidence on inclusive education, Report prepared for institution Alana,in partnership with ABT Association.

Hammond, L. D. (2013). The importance of education: From start to end. Available on http:www.nie.edu.sg/nienews/sept13/?g=content/20/01

Khunyen, N. T., Van Belen, N., Lin, P. L. Lin, N. J., & Chang, C. Y. (2020). *Measuring Teachers' Perceptions to Sustain Stem Education Development,Sustainability, 12,* 1531.

Kuroda, K., Kartika, D., & Kit Amir, Y. (2012). *implications for teacher training and support for inclusive education in Cambodia: An* empirical case study in a developing country. JICA Research Institute working paper 48

Mishra, J. (2017). *Teacher education and sustainable development-Indian Scenario.*

Neal, A. D., & Gronch, W. (2013). *four ways to improve higher education* (online). Available on htttp://www.jewishpolicycenter.org/4660/improve–higher–education. Accessed on 10/09/2021.

Pavel, A. (2012). The importance of quality in higher education in an increasingly knowledge-driven society. *International Journal of Academic Research in Accounting, Finance and Management Sciences, 2*(1), 120–127.

Rieser. (2012). Implementing education https://tinyuri.com/ye4+6jyz all of the primary literature sources on implementing inclusive suggest that the first step in inclusive implementation is to help schools ushered their own challenges resource assets.

Shulka, M. J. (2018). *Implementing inclusive education K4D helpdesk report:* Brighton, UK: Institute of Development Studies.

Singal, N. (2009). Inclusion in the real world. Practitioners making sense of inclusive education in the Indian classrooms. In Almv, Timmons (Eds.), *Inclusive education across cultures, crossing boundaries sharing ideas* (pp. 200–219). Los Angeles: SAGE.

Stoddart, H. (2011). A Pallet guide to Sustainable Development governance, Stakeholders Forum.

Unianu. (2012). Teacher's attitudes towards inclusive education *Procedia –Social and Behavioral Sciences, 33*, 900–904.

United Nations. (2000). United Nations millennium declaration. AIRES/55/2 New York: UN https://sustainabledevelopment.un.org/content/documents/21252/030%20Agenda%20for%20sustainable%develpoment%20web.pdf

UNESCO. (1994). *Education inclusive education*, www.//portal.unesco.org/education

UNESCO. (2017). Education for sustainable development learning objective Paris: UNESCO https://www.unesco.de./sites/default/files/2018-08/unesco-education-for-sustainable-dvpt

UNESCO. (2018). Global education monitoring report 2019: Paris rural-compensation https://www.researchgate.net

7. *Use of ChiTonga language as a medium of instruction across the Early Childhood Development curricula in ChiTonga speaking Districts of Zimbabwe*

MUDIMBA COLLEN

Introduction

Developed countries, like the United Kingdom, America, Japan and China have reached these levels because of using their indigenous languages as mediums of instruction across curricula (Magwa & Mutasa, 2014; Magwa, 2008). In Zimbabwe, the Education Acts of 1987, 1996 and 2006 (Amended) respectively, recommend the teaching of Early Childhood Development classes using mother language. The 1999 Presidential Commission of Inquiry into Education and Training and the Constitution of Zimbabwe (Amendment No.20 of 2013) recommended the recognition of local culture and use of indigenous languages as mediums of instruction in early childhood development instruction in their areas of dominance. For example, the interpretation of the constitution is that, ChiTonga, as an indigenous language should be used in all ChiTonga speaking communities across the ECD curricula. Psychologists, such as the cognitivists, whose proponents are Jean Piaget, Levy Vygotsky and Jerome Bruner, all concur that cognition is facilitated by use of mother languages and that human beings think in their mother language (Kishe, 2003; Mazonde, 2014). This chapter gives reference to the Human Needs theory (Burton, 1990; 1997), which contends for the recognition of indigenous knowledge epistemologies. Though the earlier on mentioned government initiatives and policy guidelines recommend teaching ECD classes using mother language as a medium of instruction, the situation obtaining on the ground is different (Mumpande, 2006; Mumpande &

Barnes, 2019; 2020). This is so because all textbooks for other learning areas, except ChiTonga language are written in English language. This therefore compels teachers to use English language as a medium of instruction. Thus, the chapter seeks to establish possibilities of using ChiTonga language as a medium of instruction across the ECD curricula.

Background

Before the advent of colonialism, African societies depended on a traditional education curriculum whose emphasis was mostly hands on and oral literature, transmitted in African indigenous languages (Desai, 2001; Emeagwali & Dei Sefa, 2014; Nsamenang, 2006; Ukwuoma, 2015; Zvobgo, 1988). This period was hopeful, with socio-economic development since it was productive in nature. However, when the Europeans arrived on the African continent, they despised this education and introduced theirs, with the belief that everything by indigenous Africans was repugnant, backward and primitive. The imperialists introduced a curriculum, which digressed from the African peoples' ideology of practice to theory (Tanyanyiwa, 2019; Dube & Mashiri, 2007). This they did it in order to ensure Africans, stopped thinking, but remembered what they were taught (Emeagwali & Dei Sefa, 2014; Ukwuoma, 2015). The Eurocentric curriculum was deliberate and intended to produce labourers for whites, instead of self-reliance (Magwa, 2008; Ukwuoma, 2015). Depending on the coloniser, Africans were introduced to a curriculum whose medium of instruction is either English, French, Spanish or Portuguese (Magwa, 2008). This resulted in scholars, who knew very little importance of learning in their indigenous languages. They popularised foreign languages hegemony and ensured anyone who spoke in vernacular was punished (Magwa, 2008; Ukwuoma, 2015; Desai, 2001). The colonialists did this deliberately, since they knew that according to the psychological views, human beings think in their mother language, and this was meant to oppress thought (Emeagwali & Dei Sefa, 2014; Gudhlanga & Makaudze, 2005; Ukwuoma, 2015).

Batibo (2005: 18) and Magwa (2008) say, the value people put on other natural resources is not the same they attach to their indigenous languages. Accordingly (Batibo, 2005; Magwa, 2014) confirm that the colonisation of the African continent was multifaceted, though most people seem to be only aware of the political aspect. The precolonial period was characterised by Africans communicating and transacting using their indigenous languages (Shizha, 2013). However, colonialism resulted in the yoking of not only political and economic facets, but languages too (Brock-Utine, 2005; Brock-Utine,

& Hopson, 2005; Nsamenang, 2006). Africans, through Christianity and education started to shun their own mother languages and used foreign languages. Depending on the colonisers, such languages like English, French and Portuguese replaced African languages as mediums of communication and instruction in government business, administrative and education sectors (Dube & Mashiri, 2007; Shizha, 2013). According to Ukwuoma (2015), colonialism resulted in African indigenous languages being relegated to less prestigious functions like community forums and letter writing to parents in rural areas. To strengthen their hegemony and dominance, European governments formulated language policies, which forbid use of African indigenous languages from primary education to university level (Magwa, 2014; Ukwuoma Shizha, 2013; 2015). Unknowingly, Africans did not realise that learning in a foreign language meant a threat to their culture and traditions, which gradually faced extinction. Apparently, the few educated African scholars encouraged fellow African students to embrace these foreign languages of their erstwhile colonisers to an extent of outshining them (Magwa, 2008; Mutasa, 2002; 2005). The colonial settlers did not show that the elevation of their languages was a hidden economic agenda to get labourers who understood them (Nsamenang, 2006; Zvobgo, 1986).

The psychologists view that there is a relationship between learning in mother language and development seems to be true, especially if we look at how Africa has remained underdeveloped due to using foreign languages (Magwa, 2014). Today, developed countries like America, the United Kingdom and France are at that level because of their curricula which is derived from their culture. Their education systems are an extension of their traditional home experience (Magwa & Mutasa, 2014; Ukwuoma, 2015). These developed economies of the worldview language as a symbol of their culture (Dube & Mashiri, 2007; Shizha, 2013). The medium of instruction in these developed countries is their indigenous languages from ECD to university level (Magwa, 2008; Mukanganwi, 1992). They understand the relationship between using an indigenous language, comprehension and development. As if to give confirmation, other countries that have successfully developed through using their indigenous languages are Japan, Korea and most recently China. These have developed sophisticated technologies due to their education systems, which have been localised in terms of language use (Kishe, 2003; Mitchel, 2000).

It is so glaring that Asian countries that are using their local resources together with their indigenous languages, are competing well with the perceived super powers, America and the United Kingdom (Kishe, 2003; Magwa, 2008: 8; Ngara, 1982). However, the story is different with Africa.

The continent has remained the poorest in the world, despite her resources (Chimhundu, 2003). Most scholars have attributed this to using foreign languages.

Kishe (2003); Mutasa (2002) and Mutasa (2004) say that despite attaining political independence and enjoying decades of self-rule, Zimbabwe and indeed most African countries have continued to employ the diglossic approach to language use in their countries. The languages of their colonial masters are still being used as medium of instruction across curriculum. However, a few countries on the African continent, namely; Tanzania, Guinea, Somalia, Sudan and Ethiopia have managed to pursue an active endoglossic language policy (Magwa, 2008: 10). These countries have declared that, their indigenous languages are to be used in administrative and government business as well as mediums of instruction in the education system. They have reserved foreign languages for international relations and university education.

Ukwuoma (2015) and Shizha (2013) view the continued use of foreign languages as medium of instruction in African curricula as inability to articulate the relationship between language and development. African governments do not see the cultural value attached to indigenous languages and the development of indigenous communities. Magwa (2008) say it is not surprising to see African politicians addressing their electorates in foreign languages and seeking the services of translators. To African leadership, using African indigenous languages is a sign of primitiveness, lack of education and backwardness (Ukwuoma, 2015). African scholars are very comfortable in using foreign languages, as they associate them with high status, while their indigenous languages with low status.

As stated earlier on by Magwa (2008) and Shizha (2013), Africans do not value their indigenous languages in comparison to other heritage resources like; land, cattle and minerals. In addition, their engagement in liberation wars was only when European governments introduced draconian laws with regard to land tenure. Thus most African countries wedged protracted liberation struggles not to reclaim their language dominance, but to end the unfair laws pertaining land ownership. This resulted in them attaining political independence, which they never utilised to reverse language hegemony (Zvobgo, 1986). Independent African governments do not see the importance of their indigenous languages. They actually regard use of foreign languages in their day-to-day correspondences as a symbol of development and source of prestige. Nevertheless, to the colonisers, continued use of foreign languages in African school curricula was and continues to be seen as a tool of colonisation (Magwa, 2008, Chimhundu, 2003). Up to date, the use of African indigenous languages in Africa is relegated to a low status of subject and not medium of instruction across the education systems (Magwa, 2008). Language policies in existence all point to the teaching of African indigenous languages as subjects, not as mediums of instruction. Notwithstanding, even at ECD level, using indigenous languages as a medium of instruction is not possible because all textbooks, except ChiTonga in this case are in foreign languages, with teachers having to translate into their indigenous languages. This chapter interrogates possibilities of using ChiTonga across the ECD curricula in ChiTonga speaking districts.

Human needs theory (Burton, 1997)

An indigenous language is considered as a people's epistemology, which should be preserved for future generations (Masaka, 2018). This study therefore draws its theoretical framework from the Human Needs Theory (HNT) propounded by Burton (1997). This Human Needs Theory is premised on the underpinnings that language is a basic human need, which goes beyond those identified by Maslow's theory of physiological needs such as food, love, water, and shelter (Amoo & Odendaal, 2002; Mumpande & Barnes, 2019;). According to Burton (1997) human needs include both physical and non-physical elements, necessary for human development, protection and growth, which human beings are predetermined to achieve (Amoo & Odendaal, 2002: 4). Furthermore, Burton (1997: 31) says 'these non-physical human needs include; identity, security, participation, freedom and recognition in human lives as individuals or collectively'. Weighing in the argument are Mumpande and Barnes (2019), who say that these human needs which human beings are compelled to attain are a powerful determinant of human behaviour and social interaction aimed at satisfying own needs. Often than not, if these needs are not satisfied due to oppressive means, they lead to insurgency or protests (Mumpande & Barnes, 2019). It should be noted that, the universality of these needs has attracted immense debate, rendering them elusive. Various scholars have suggested own essentials deemed as driving human beings to achieve satisfaction. One such notable scholar is Burton (1997), who argues that every human being needs to belong to a clearly identifiable and distinguishable group to associate with (Mumpande & Barnes, 2019).

Burton (1997: 31) further says that, it is natural for every human being to gain confidence in that his language and culture is free from oppression from other cultures. This brings an element of security to human beings. The HNT theory also views the importance of indigenous cultures and languages, in allowing full participation of the owners in decision-making processes with regard to issues that directly affect their lives. Mumpande (2020: 64) says, '... the HNT, according to Burton (1997), popularises human beings' desire to be free from any form of oppression, domination and discrimination in the face of foreign cultures, while at the same time seeking reaffirmation, recognition and respect for their cultural differences'. Ordinarily, some scholars view other human needs as including; self-esteem, personal fulfilment, and distributive justice, among others as key to human beings' pursuit of completeness (Amoo & Odendaal, 2002). However, Maslow (1954) is arguably a leading scholar on the human needs subject, arguing that human needs can be organised into a hierarchy as evidenced by his commonly known theory of Maslow's Hierarchy of Needs (Mumpande & Barnes, 2019). But Burton (1990; 1997), who can be said to have developed Maslow's theory and its application seems to differ with his mentor (Maslow) by arguing that, true human needs considerably, differ, but this does not constitute their hierarchical classification for their fulfilment (Burton, 1997). Apparently, despite the notable differences of views about human needs, various scholars seem to converge that any government's failure to address a particular society or group of people's needs results in frustration and conflicts (Mumpande & Barnes, 2020). Thus, any form of omission or oppression of a people's culture often attracts disgruntlement and insubordination to the political leadership (Masaka, 2018; Mumpande, 2009; Mumpande & Barnes, 2020). In the same vein, any attempts to suppress or vilify the search for the satisfaction of these human needs, generates political conflicts, since these needs are sensitive to the owners, hence cannot be compromised (Masaka, 2019; Mumpande, 2009; Mumpande & Barnes, 2020). The continued dominance of minority cultures and oppression by the majority has been viewed as contributing significantly to most cultural conflicts in most multicultural societies (Masaka, 2018; 2019; Mumpande, 2009). The HNT theory pursues an idea of valuing original and majority cultures, while at the same time fighting against the suppression of ethnic indigenous minority groups and their languages (Burton, 1990; 1997; Mumpande and Barnes, 2020). The theory views language as a tool of colonisation, while the education system as a vehicle and possible avenue for the total unyoking of the country's development. Apparently, there is need to pursue the possibilities of using ChiTonga as a medium of instruction across the ECD curricula in ChiTonga speaking communities in Zimbabwe.

Medium of instruction explained

Chimhundu (2003), Masaka (2018), Ukwuoma (2015) and Mumpande and Barnes (2020) seem to concur on the definition of medium of instruction as referring to a language that is used to convey educational information in a learning situation. The colonial period in most African countries ensured all learning, except in indigenous subjects being conducted in the languages of the oppressor. Meaning that despite political independence, most African countries still use such languages like English, Spanish, Portuguese and French as their medium of instructions from ECD curriculum to University (Chimhundu, 2003; Masaka, 2019; Ukwuoma, 2015). Ironically, even those African countries which were not colonised by any of the above colonies, are actually recolonising themselves by using languages of these colonisers as their mediums of instruction. Government language policies have also missed the concept of medium of instruction. They state that indigenous languages should be used as medium of instruction when all literature and textbooks for various subjects of the ECD curricula are in English language (Constitution of Zimbabwe, 2013 Amendment; 1999 Presidential commission). To say an indigenous language is a medium of instruction means more than what is proclaimed by most African governments' policy documents. It means that all learning areas of the primary and secondary schools are taught in indigenous mother languages, with textbooks written in local indigenous languages across curricula (Dube & Mashiri, 2007; Tanyanyiwa, 2019; Ukwuoma, 2015). What is currently happening on the ground is code switching, where if learners fail to articulate a particular word or concept, the teacher switches to an indigenous language to explain. This is not the case with Asian countries, who have promoted their languages to medium of instruction status (Chimhundu, 2003; Ukwuoma, 2015). In the developed world, subjects like; Mathematics, Science, Arts, commercial subjects and indeed all learning areas are taught using their mother languages. Medium of instruction in ECD should constitute that from the syllabus, to individual subjects learning material, text books included, is in indigenous language. The ECD curriculum seeks to bridge the gap between home and school (Gatsi & Mamvuto, 2016). This therefore, should mean that all play activities, including games and materials are in mother language. Teachers should be qualified to handle these learners and should be fluent in the mother language of the dominant language of a particular area. It will be an omission to say a particular language is being used as a medium of instruction, when all school business emphasise the opposite (Batibo, 2005; Bodomo, 1996; Nsamenang, 2006). It means that comments in children's exercise books, reports and other correspondences between the school and community are in the local language (Chimhundu, 2003; Mutasa, 2004). It will be an understatement to say a particular indigenous mother language is a medium of instruction, when all labels, correspondences, meetings and other school business transactions are done in a foreign language (Batibo, 2005; Bodomo, 1996; Mutasa, 2002). Language is a symbol of culture, therefore, successful efforts to ensure a particular language has been identified as a medium of instruction, will mean understanding the culture associated with that particular language. The effort put by various African governments with regard to the introduction of indigenous languages as medium of instruction, is far insignificant. The major challenge is that foreign languages have been allowed to remain as major determinant for one to be employed, resulting in citizens having a negative attitude towards their mother languages (Eju, 2015; Nsamenang, 2009). Introducing mother language in ECD as a medium of instruction, calls for governments to invest in that regard. Teachers should be trained in particular local languages, so that they understand what constitute language as a medium of instruction (Mazonde, 2014; Ukwuoma, 2015). They need to develop an appreciation of the traditions and culture of particular languages so they can impart them to learners. The language issue, is an emotional one, because it is political, hence there is need to first instil a positive attitude in teachers so that they understand aspects of culture and identity.

Indigenous languages can only attain medium of instruction status, if respective governments enact acts of parliament and various statutes, which compels all government arms and communities to observe the urgent need to use local languages as medium of instruction across curricula (Mumpande, 2006; Mumpande & Barnes, 2020). For example, the language policy should be contextualised, but ensuring that no child remains learning using a foreign language. Allowing a section of children to remain using a foreign language can raise suspicion because they may be viewed as elites, with an advantage of job opportunity based on requirements for a foreign language. Adopting use of mother language as a medium of instruction, will call for a paradigm shift to policy, with total elimination of foreign language or simply learning it for communication purposes (Chimhundu, 2009; Ogutu, 2006). In fact the lower prestige accorded to indigenous languages in learning institutions, should be vice versa. Foreign languages should occupy that low profile. The current situation obtaining in learning institutions shows that there is serious lack of political will to redress this imbalance. African governments do not seem to understand that development and language are interconnected. Today despite the language policies that promote indigenous languages, schools actually punish children for using mother language (Chimhundu, 2009). Ukwuoma (2015) and Masaka (2018) believe use of indigenous languages as medium of instruction is possible on the African continent, from ECD to university, if governments commit themselves fully.

Nature of Early Childhood Development curriculum in Zimbabwe

The education of young children has evolved over time, showing a paradigm shift to the organisation of curriculum and learning areas. During the pre-colonial period, children were exposed to mostly a skills based curriculum, where they learnt various trades that included; pottery, curving, basketry, and weaving among others (Chimhundu, 2009; Eju, 2015, Ukwuoma, 2015). These were meant to ensure graduates had attained a source of livelihood, and some survival skills. Traditional education was popularised as problem solving and promoting self-reliance (Masaka, 2018; 2019). However, the advent of colonialism, led to the change of curriculum, with children learning a curriculum meant to produce labourers for the whites (Emeagwali & Dei Sefa, 2014; Nsamenang, 2006; Shizha, 2013). The curriculum changed so much that children spend most of their time learning numeracy and literacy. More subjects were introduced, congesting the curriculum. Learning digressed from skills based to purely academic (Gatsi & Mamvuto, 2016). Learning became more rote, with children memorising facts and learning European history that resulted in them knowing more about the European culture than theirs. The colonial curriculum, best known as the Eurocentric, used English language as a medium of instruction, from early childhood level to university (Eju, 2015). English was given a higher status over other languages. This resulted in the publishing of textbooks in English, with children being restricted from using their mother languages, which were referred to as vernacular. This curriculum developed an attitude in African learners, who viewed their mother languages as of less value to English (Magwa & Mutasa, 2014; Shizha, 2013; Ukwuoma, 2015). Employment opportunities favoured those who did well in English. It was therefore every parent and child's wish to be efficient in English.

The post-colonial periods did not give much attention to the issue of language (Magwa, 2008; Shizha, 2013). Subsequent governments, despite being of black leaders actually replicated the same attitude towards indigenous languages. Children in early childhood were said to be taught using mother language, but all subjects remained in English language. This distortion of facts resulted in teachers using English language as a medium of instruction. All activities, be it play, stories or dramatization, are dominated by English (Eju, 2015, Gatsi and Mamvuto, 2016). Children are drilled to recite poems in English, and most songs are in English, with children understanding very little if any about their meaning.

In independent Zimbabwe, the early childhood education and care program was first attached under the Ministry of Women's' Affairs. Old women were appointed to take charge of these classes (UNICEF, 2017). There was very little learning, with children mostly attending for feeding and play. Although, these caregivers were untrained, the curriculum was mostly emphasising use of English, with mother language being considered too. However, the situation in Private centres provoked everything, since those children were so fluent in English (UNICEF, 2018). Parents admired the use of English, which they view and continue to be view as occupying a higher status. Since these private centres were expensive, very few could afford them, until when the government introduced more centres. Nevertheless, parents were not happy about the use of mother language because they saw it as a disadvantage, since most subjects of the infant curriculum were taught in English. To parents, the language policy that encouraged use of mother language in ECD classes was off the hook, because it did not resonate well with the practical learning on the ground, where all subjects were in English with all textbooks written in English language. There was a distortion of facts because those children, who were taught in English language at ECD centres, did not have problems with learning others subjects of the infant class curriculum. This resulted in parents sending their children to those centres where the curriculum was taught in English language.

In 1999, the government of Zimbabwe appointed a commission of inquiry, The 1999 Presidential Commission of Inquiry into Education and Training, popularly known as the Nziramasanga Commission of Inquiry. The idea was to establish the type of education, which was prevailing, and possible improvement. Among the recommendations of the Commission, was introduction of a viable ECD program, where children were taught using mother language, with emphasis on skills based learning. The issue of a skills based curriculum cutting across ECD to university level intends to promote self-reliance and problem solving education (1999 Presidential Commission of Inquiry into Education and Training). Consequently, various administrative circulars and statutory instrument 106 of 2005 were enacted. Curriculum review was done to align learning to the new recommendations. This gave birth to the ECD 'A' and 'B' classes, which were attached to the main primary schools (UNICEF, 2018). The policy on medium of instruction in these classes remain mother language, but everything, including materials, books, play equipment and learning areas, depict a Eurocentric curriculum. In the absence of learning materials in indigenous languages, teachers had no option, but to use the available resources. Therefore, it remained mother language on paper, but English in practice.

It is now twelve years since the government of Zimbabwe, committed itself to implement the recommendations of the 1999 Presidential

Commission of Inquiry into Education and Training, but the curriculum still remains Eurocentric, with all subjects of the ECD curriculum still in English. Deployment of teachers to ECD classes is just random, with no consideration for ones' aptitude in the local language, making teaching using mother language as a medium of instruction unattainable, and a dream (Magwa, 2008; ZILPA, 2021). Nevertheless, this chapter interrogates ways of ensuring ChiTonga language is used as a medium of instruction across the ECD curricula in ChiTonga speaking districts and communities.

Benefits of using ChiTonga language as a medium of instruction across the ECD curricula

The benefits of learning in ChiTonga mother language to a Tonga child are overwhelming (Mumpande, 2006; Mumpande & Barnes, 2019; 2020). Beside improved comprehension of concepts, attachment to the language and self-identity are fostered. Learning in mother language has cultural gains, among them preservation of indigenous culture and passing it on to next generations (Eju, 2015, Gatsi & Mamvuto, 2016). A child who learns in mother language comprehends information faster than the other learning in a foreign language (Chimhundu, 1997; Magwa, 2008). The continued use of mother languages by Europeans, French, Portuguese and most recently the Japanese, Koreans and Chinese is an indicator that mother language is vital and is associated with development. Apparently, the exclusion of African indigenous languages as mediums of instruction in African education systems by colonial regimes serves to oppress the whole continent despite political independence (Miller, 2003: 36; Mutasa, 2002; Tanyanyiwa, 2019). Many people seem not to relate language and development. Batibo (2005) and Magwa (2008) say that indigenous languages should be treated the same way countries treat other natural resources like; gold, oil reserves, diamond and forests. Today Africans find it difficult to invent, because their curriculum is taught in foreign languages, which stifle imagination and creativity. This is even contained in the provisions of the 1951 UNESCO resolution, that children learn best when the medium of instruction is mother language (UNESCO, 2018). Mumpande (2006) and Mumpande and Barnes (2020) view the teaching of ChiTonga across the primary and secondary curricula as means to unlocking opportunities for the BaTonga child to contribute knowledge to the global knowledge systems. Africans have failed to compete with Europeans in research because; they are using borrowed language while the Europeans are using mother language (Nsamenang, 2006; Ukwuoma, 2015). Introducing mother language to young children will give them an opportunity to become self-reliant and engage in problem solving. According to Batibo (2005) and Mahochi (2003), indigenous languages are tools of development, because there is no way communities can develop, unless the facilitators of developmental programs use a language, which is part of their culture.

Probably the first and foremost benefit of using African indigenous languages as mediums of instruction across the education systems in African is identity, followed by easing comprehension (Chimhundu, 2009; Emeagwali & Dei Sefa, 2014; Nsamenang, 2006). Language is our pride and a symbol of cultural identity. It is what defines us as Africans and unique to Europeans (Magwa, 2008). Bodomo (1996), Chimhundu (2009), and Mahochi (2003) submit that learning using mother language has immense benefits especially in the development of confidence, self-esteem and abilities to express self. They believe that language wields power of authority, which one loses upon using the other's language. Language serves as a means of communication and carrier of culture (Mutasa, 2004). Magwa (2008, 15) says, "language is one of the indispensable features of the cultural systems of all societies and it penetrates into all aspects of social, economic, political and religious spheres". Kishindo in Magwa (2000: 15) says," There is no country anywhere in the world (except in Africa) where the most important, most prestigious and the most powerful activities of the nation are conducted in what is for most of the citizens, a foreign language". The scholars' submissions here show that the unsuspecting Africans have been colonised to think that foreign languages are the only means to survival, hence most government require them both in education and work places (Eju, 2015; Emeagwali & Dei Sefa, 2014; Ukwuoma, 2015). Magwa (2008: 16) wraps it up by saying, "The process of decolonising the mind can never be complete therefore without putting our own languages at the forefront of all our endeavours, be it educationally, economically, socially, politically or technical". This serves to say failure to use our indigenous languages across the ECD curricula is self-marginalisation and recolonisation. Mumpande (2006) and Mumpande and Barnes (2019; 2020) believe using ChiTonga as a medium of instruction across the primary school curricula will allow parents to participate in the learning of their children, as is the case with Europeans. Any learning that excludes the custodians of the culture and language, the elders, is doomed (Eju, 2015; Ukwuoma, 2015).

Challenges of using ChiTonga language as a medium of instruction across the ECD curricula

Change, whether, politically, educationally or developmentally is not easily embraced by people. Similarly, Magwa (2008) and Mukanganwi (1992) say, although there are efforts to ensure the currency of introducing African indigenous languages as mediums of instruction across curricula is getting stronger over time, scholars and other researchers admit that the process is tedious. Some researchers cite lack of political will, and inadequate resources as some of the major drawbacks to using mother language as a medium of instruction (Mitchell, 2000; Mukanganwi, 1992). They argue that for an indigenous language to be used as a medium of instruction, governments and other stakeholders, as the NGOs should allocate adequate funding to produce learning material. Magwa (2008: 14) says, 'Imperial forces against the idea of introducing African indigenous languages as mediums of instruction in African education systems; view the idea as divisive'. However, Batibo (2005: 105) views that there is a possibility of succeeding in using indigenous mother languages as mediums of instruction, despite scarce resources, if the process is introduced gradually. Those against the use of African indigenous languages as medium of instruction, cite the unavailability of African indigenous language literature in sciences and other subjects as militating against possibilities of using indigenous languages as medium of instruction. However, Magwa (2008) is of the view that language is an agreement, and developing local names for science cannot pose any challenges to the efforts of using African mother languages as medium of instruction. Ogechi (2003) views lack of clear language policies and omission of language issues in most African governments' constitutions clearly indicates challenges in achieving this desire. Magwa (2008) and Kashioki (1993) say that globalisation been used by imperialists and Neo-colonial forces as a scapegoat to stifle efforts towards the introduction of African indigenous languages as medium of instruction in African school curricula. To the former colonisers, using African indigenous languages as mediums of instruction in schools is viewed as self-isolation from the global education systems, where information is passed on in world languages namely: English, French, and Portuguese. Nevertheless, one can cite the Asians as having succeeded without English, with most technological gadgets being produced in their countries. Ogutu (2006) and Ukwuoma (2015) view that most Africans have been colonised to such an extent that they are very proud to see their children learning in foreign languages.

Strategies for using ChiTonga language as a medium of instruction across ECD curricula

The possibilities of using ChiTonga as a medium of instruction across the education curricula, primarily rests in the hands of the Zimbabwean government (Mumpande, 2006). The government can choose to promote indigenous languages by enforcing a language policy that relegates English language from medium of instruction to international affairs communication role (Magwa, 2008). As long as English language continues to be accorded a juxtaposed status with indigenous languages found in Zimbabwe, then English language will prevail as superior. On lack of adequate vocabulary for science areas and other technological fields, Magwa (2008) says that language is a constructed and a social agreement. Meaning that, African languages terminology can be developed for those scientific terms. Terminology should not be a barrier to the adoption of ChiTonga as a medium of instruction in ECD, because, just in recent years, the Asian countries were able to successfully use their indigenous languages in all spheres of life. Similarly, if a more robust approach is used, then English can be relegated to less prestigious role, that of international communication. Batibo (2005), Ogechi in Ogutu (2004) and Mutasa (2002) view the absence of literature and lack of human resources as requiring African governments to invest in their education systems to achieve this noble cause. According to Chimhundu (1997), African governments should come up with deliberate policy guidelines, which promote the introduction of these indigenous languages to the role of mediums of instruction. Another strategy is to deliberately enrol teachers who will undergo training in indigenous languages at various higher learning institutions, so that they spearhead the noble cause of introducing indigenous languages. Those already employed can also undergo in-service training to keep abreast with curriculum change and innovations. Mumpande and Barnes (2019), Nsamenga (2006), and Ukwuoma (2015) posit that there is need by African governments and donor community to invest in the development of African indigenous languages in order for them to enjoy the status of being mediums of instruction in African education systems.

The issue of negative attitude and pride by most scholars, especially, those who studied outside the African continent can act as a major drawback to efforts of promoting indigenous languages to the status of medium of instruction (Emeagwali & Dei Sefa, 2014; Nsamenang, 2006). The government should carry out awareness campaigns and sell the idea of popularising the once marginalised languages to that of higher status. If other African countries like; Somalia, Tanzania, Sudan, Sierra Leon and Guinea have successfully dislodged English through pursuing an endoglossic language policy, which promoted their indigenous languages to lingua franca status (Magwa, 2008: 10; Nsamenga, 2006), the same can happen with ChiTonga in the ChiTonga speaking communities. For example, languages like, Kiswahili, Kriol, Limba, Mende and Temne have been elevated to lingua franca statuses (Magwa, 2008: 11). This positive progression in the direction of self-unyoking by some African countries comes because of community awareness programs aimed at empowering the whole nation on the importance of African indigenous languages as mediums of instruction across education curricula.

Recommendations

In light of the numerous obstacles that hinder total use of ChiTonga language as a medium of instruction in the ECD curriculum, this chapter recommends that:

- The government of Zimbabwe changes its attitude towards English language, that of according it a supremacy status. English should no longer be a language of transacting government business. It should no longer be a determinant for one to get employment.
- All indigenous languages should be accorded equal status as enshrined in the Constitution of Zimbabwe of 2013 (Amendment No. 20). These indigenous languages should be a requirement for people to be employed. This will make people change attitude, and realise that government is serious about recognition of indigenous languages. Just like in Tanzania, Botswana, Guinea and Sierra Leone, English should be taught as a communication tool for international affairs.
- The government of Zimbabwe should come up with a clear policy on medium of instruction, than to leave it to the discretion of educators. The policy should pronounce the use of ChiTonga language across learning areas of the ECD curriculum, not only during ChiTonga lessons.
- All subjects like Heritage studies, Mathematics and science should be taught in ChiTonga language. Nevertheless, this can only be possible through investing in human capital.
- Teachers should undergo in-service and upskilling training to embrace the importance of local languages.
- Deployment of teachers should also consider the first language of the teacher and those who would have undergone education training, with specialisation in ChiTonga. Non-ChiTonga speaking teachers, with a component of professional syllabus 'B', the pedagogics of teaching ChiTonga can be considered.
- Curriculum Development and Technical Services, an arm of the government, which designs and reviews curriculum changes and innovations should clearly state that publishing houses should publish books

for the ECD curriculum in ChiTonga. Meaning that all learning areas, be it Mathematics, Heritage studies, Science and many others should be in ChiTonga. This paradigm shift towards the promotion of indigenous languages can motivate parents to have a positive attitude to indigenous languages, like ChiTonga.

- Indigenous communities contribute to curriculum design to preserve culture and promote problem-solving skills.

Conclusion

There is evidence that development is related to the language of instruction used in the education system of a country. First world countries have attained such status because their children learn in their mother language. Similarly, the lack of development in the developing countries, mostly those on the African continent is attributed to use of foreign languages in government business and education instruction. The recent development of most Asian countries has been identified as one indicator of the importance of using indigenous languages as medium of instruction. There is an understanding that development is closely related to language. Though most African governments, including our Zimbabwean government, have come up with policies to promote indigenous languages to the status of medium of instruction across the education curricula, more still need to be done. Possibilities of using ChiTonga as a medium of instruction across the ECD curricula in ChiTonga speaking districts and communities require political will. This can be done by investing in curriculum review and change, with teachers being trained in ChiTonga language and text books for various learning areas of the ECD curricula written in ChiTonga language. Finally, deployment of teachers in ChiTonga speaking areas should consider aptitude in ChiTonga language.

References

Amoo, S. G., & Odendaal, A. (2002). "The political management of ethnic conflicts in Africa: Human needs based approach." *Track Two, 11*(4). www.ccr.uct.ac.za/archive/two/11_4/index114.html

Batibo, H. M. (2005). *Language decline and death in Africa: Causes, consequences and challenges.* Clevedon: Cromwell Press Ltd.

Bodomo, A. (1996). *On language and development in Africa: The case of Ghana. Nordic Journal of African Studies, 3*(2), 54–67.

Burton, J. (1990). *Conflict: Human needs theory.* New York: The MacMillan Press Ltd. https://link.springer.com/content/pdf/bfm%3A978 1 349 21000-8%2F1.pdf

Burton, J. (1997). *"Human Needs Theory." In Violence Explained.* 32–40. Manchester: Manchester University Press.

Chimhundu, H. (2003). *The status of African languages in Zimbabwe.* SAPEM. October issue, pp. 57–59.

Desai, Z. (2001). *Multilingualism in South Africa with particular reference to the role of African languages in education. International Review of Education, 47*(3), 323–339.

Dube, B., & Mashiri, P. (2007). Zimbabwe colonial and post-colonial language policy and planning practices. *Current Issues in Language Planning, 00*(00), 1–38.

Ejuu, G. (2015). *Is this ECD Ours? Deciphering what African Parents want their Children to learn in ECD. New Zealand Journal of Teacher Work, 12*(1), 30–44.

Emeagwali, G., & Sefa Dei, G. (2014). *African indigenous knowledge and the disciplines.* Toronto: Sense Publishers.

Gatsi, R., & Mamvuto, A. (2016). *Early childhood development curriculum.* Harare: Global Journal of Advanced Research.

Gudhlanga, E. S., & Makaudze, G. (2005). *(Unpublished conference paper) Promoting the use of an African language as medium of instruction in institutions of higher learning in Zimbabwe: The case of Masvingo State University's Department of Languages, Literature and Music.*

Kashioki, M. (1993). Some thoughts on future language policy for South Africa with reference to language plan of action for Africa. *Africa Studies, 52*(2), 141–162.

Kishe, A. (2003). *Kiswahili as a vehicle of unity and development in the Great Lakes region. Language, Culture and Curriculum, 16*(2), 218–230.

Magwa, W. (2008). *Planning: Exploring possibilities of using Indigenous African Languages as Languages of Instruction in Education- the ZimbabweanExperience.* UNISA

Mahochi, E. S. (2003). *Language choice for development: The case for Kiswahili in Kenya. Journal of African cultural studies, 16*(1), 85–94.

Masaka, D. (2018) *The prospects of ending epistimicised in Africa: Some thoughts. Journal of Black Studies 2018, 49*(3), 284–301. SAGE.

Masaka, D. (2017). *Challenging epistimicised through transformation and Africanisation of the philosophy curriculum in Africa. South African Journal of Philosophy 2017, 36* (40), 441–455.

Mazonde, I. (2014). *Culture and education in the development of Africa.* Harare:UNESCO.

Mukanganwi, K. G. (1992). *Language planning in Southern Africa.* In *Democratically speaking: International perspectives on language planning* (pp. 6–11). Salt River: National Language Project.

Mitchell, D. (2000, October 22). *School curricula must not allow degeneration of local languages. The Sunday Mail*, pp. 28.

Mumpande, I., & Barnes, L. (2020). *"The Revitalisation of Ethnic minority languages in Zimbabwe: The case of the Tonga." UNISA*

Mumpande, I., & Barnes, L. (2019). *"Revitalisation of the Tonga Language in Zimbabwe: The Motivational Factors." Language Matters, 50*(3), 46–69.

Mumpande, I. (2006). *Silent voices.* Harare: Silveira House.

Mutasa, D. E. (2004). *People speak: Language policy and language use in South Africa.* Pretoria: S. G. Publishers.

Mutasa, D. E. (2002). *The renaissance of African languages: An inevitable enterprise? South African Journal of African Languages, 22*(3), 239–247.

Nsamenang, A. B. (2006). *Human ontogenesis: An indigenous African view on development and intelligence. International Journal of psychology, 41*(4), 293–297

Nziramasanga Commission Report. (1999). *Report of the Presidential Commission of Education and Training.* Harare: Government Printers.

Ogutu, E. A. (2006). *Mother tongue amidst other languages: Playing roles in the classroom and outside.* Pretoria: S. G. Publishers.

Shizha, E. (2013). *Reclaiming our indigenous voices: The problem with post-colonial sub-Saharan African School Curriculum. Journal of Indigenous Social Development, 2*(1), 1–18.

Tanyanyiwa, V. I. (2019). *Indigenous knowledge systems and the teaching of climate change in Zimbabwean Secondary Schools.* SAGE Open, 1–11.

Ukwuoma, U. C. (2015). *Educational development of Africa: Changing perspectives on the role of indigenous knowledge*: Original scientific paper Botswana International University of Science and Technology.

UNESCO. (1998). *Report on the intergovernmental conference on language policies in Africa.* Harare: University of Zimbabwe.

Zimbabwe Indigenous Languages Promotion Association. (2021). Report.

Zvobgo, R. J. (1986). *Transforming education: The Zimbabwean experience.* Harare: College Press.

8. *Changing home environments to learning centres: An alternative pathway to improved learning outcomes in rural ecologies*

Samkeliso Mathe & Christopher Ndlovu

Introduction

It is becoming increasingly obvious that students' learning is largely influenced by the conditions that exist in the home environment. The home environment, as the first social institution with which the student interacts, should equip its physical and social structures with Yandex.quilbots that allow and motivate learning. The physical structures to be found in the home environment include the following: a defined learning space with suitable sitting equipment, a library and learning facilities (Webre, 2005). Social structures should, among other things, include a peaceful environment, good systems of values and norms, as well as a supportive family.

For a long time, people have always imagined urban areas as places where only high-quality learning outcomes can be obtained. Best and Shucksmith (2006) posit that in rural areas it's difficult to achieve settings that motivate teaching and learning. The object of this chapter is to explore ways of transforming rural home settings into effective learning centres. The chapter further demonstrates that where home settings support learning, learning outcomes are significantly improved. The chapter concludes by urging parents and guardians in rural areas to take the lead in ensuring better learning outcomes in rural learning ecologies.

Children's learning space

A conducive home environment, such as one with comfortable study room set-up, a peaceful environment, loving and supportive family members, relevant sources of information and a variety of daily leaning experiences plays a pivotal role in the quality of education (Duncan, Miller, & Jiang, 2012). The quality of education should not only be dependent on the teachers but on the home environments as well. The home learning environment is the combination of everything found in the home that can be used to enhance learning (Shin & Albers, 2015). This includes the opportunities the learner has to play and interact with books, objects and everyday experiences that influences their world views. Duncan, Miller, & Jiang (2012) state that children's participation in learning activities, the quality of parent to child interactions, and the availability of learning materials are three key features of the study space that help to support learners' educational achievement.

Ordonez (2011) believes that learners in rural like their counterparts in urban areas need home environments that support their educational endevours for better learning outcomes. Parents in rural areas can use available materials in villages such as mud, poles and grass to construct and equip conducive study rooms. Well-designed rooms and adapted to the rural contexts are adequate for the children's usage. Parents in rural areas can make wooden tables, shelves and chairs for their children at home to use when studying and doing their work. In such a supportive environment the learners are likely to do better in school as they will develop a positive learning culture from the home environments. Learning space can be stimulating through the use of pocket boards with word cards, pictures cards, numbers, alphabets, story outlines on the wall and low or no cost teaching and learning aids in the study room. Sithole and Lumadi (2013) state that optimal use of locally available resources is encouraged as a way to make study rooms stimulating in rural learning environments. Parents and the community members can work together to transform the drab learning spaces of their children into stimulating environments through making well designed wooden furniture for learners. The study room floor can be made smooth and clean with layers of plaster and floor paint (Ogbeba & Muluku, 2013). A clean study room gives learners in rural areas an understanding of the importance of hygiene and cleanliness, even in an environment with little or no resources.

Mini library

Each home in a rural area can have a mini library where books for reading are kept. It doesn't need to be having all features of a library. The reading material in the home library should depending on availability compromise of religious materials, fictions, bedtime stories, magazines, newspapers and school textbooks. Books that were used by the other family members can be collected and placed in the mini library. Old newspapers can be part of the reading materials. These can give the children latest development in many aspects of life hence making rural learners aware of their surroundings. Erikson and Markuson (2007) stress that this home library should be made attractive for the young children as to foster a reading culture among them at an early stage. A child should be encouraged to read at least one book from the home library every week. The parents and all other family members should lead by example in reading the books from the home library to show the importance of reading. Jena (2013) urges parents in rural areas to come up with the most affordable type of libraries in their contexts for the benefit of their learners ... The setting of a library home library conveys a message that reading is an important aspect of the lives of all people. Even though some schools lack libraries in their schools rural parents can assist their children by having well some established home mini libraries (Cartledge and Keesey, 2016).

Display of learning media

A common, effective way of learning is through the use of visual presentations. These tools are especially useful in elementary school, where children tend to have shorter attention spans. Having charts or diagrams at home can help reinforce the information that the children are learning or have already learnt at school (Webre 2005). Jena (2013) avers that visual tools can help the process content appreciation and to make connections with daily experiences more easily. Parents in rural areas should make a deliberate efforts to have these materials as to improve the educational outcomes of their children. These can be displayed in the home mini libraries thus making the libraries colorful and attractive for the children to spend time in them. Charts and diagrams are especially helpful, as they enable children to see ideas visually laid out in an organized way. Webre (2005) added that ideally, the charts should be displayed at the students' eye level or just above eye level. When displaying media in the mini library, the charts should have clear images and large text. Parents at home can keep charts that have information throughout the year on display so their children can refer to them when they need to for example, parents can keep a chart on multiplication tables on the wall until their children master it.

Provision of electronic media

Erikson and Markuson (2007) define media as resources materials that help to facilitate teaching and learning. For Jena (2013) media means all available human and materials resources that which appeal to the learners' sense of seeing, hearing, smelling, tasting touching or feeling and which assist to facilitate teaching and learning. Cartledge and Keesey (2016) weigh in outlining that electronic media is as any device with instructional content that is used for teaching purposes audiovisual and other sensory materials, scripts for radios and television instruction, smart phones, computer-managed sets of materials for construction and manipulation. As a way of educational investment parents in rural ecologies should be encouraged to have a variety of learning media for the sake of their children. While there are prohibitive costs in acquiring most of the electronic learning media, there are some that are now readily available in rural area like a radio and a smart phone. The normal radio can be used as a learning media with parents helping their children in selection of programs to listen to. Programs like daily news, reading of books, farming discussions are among programs that assist the children to learn better and are to be followed at all possible times children should be encouraged to make summaries of these programs with the parents and older siblings marking or checking on them.

In the 21st century the use of digital technology has increased reaching millions of people even many in rural settings. The use of smart phones has also increased, making it one of the mostly used gadgets in the world. While a smart phone is a communication gadget it can be effectively used as a teaching and learning in rural settings where network connectivity is available rural children can enjoy the full use of the smart phone just like the urban children. The rural parents should make smart phones be available for their children for learning purposes. Children learn faster and better by using smart phones as they are naturally attracted to the phones. Smart phones also have programs that combine learning with games this increases the concentration span of the children. The availability and use of smart phones can enable the rural learners to engage on online learning, a development that can improve the education quality in rural learning ecologies. Parents in rural settings are therefore encouraged to acquire smart phones for their children as to improve the quality and appreciation of learning by their children.

Secure environments

Safety of human beings is of paramount importance to their survival and wellbeing. Most of the human activities will flourish when the lives of human beings are at a safe and secure environment, where no dangers are evident. To maintain a safe and secure home environment, homes should be well constructed and away from dangerous environments. The houses should be visibly strong having little or no chances of falling apart. It is in such homes that children will find peace. These safe home environments provide conducive areas for children to excel in their studies. Cartledge and Keesey (2016) note that children have some psychological needs for order and security, love and belonging which should be found in the home settings. Stranko, Hilderbrand, and Palmer (2012) explain homes designed to meet these needs allow children in rural areas to experience the sensation of privacy without foregoing the need for adult supervision. Children feel more control in protected spaces with walls at their backs than exposed in the middle of a large open space that frustrate their concentration in doing activities including studying. Parents in rural areas should create homes that are both safe and secure using the available resources in rural settings. The homes should be strong enough to resist the natural hazards like heavy storms and floods.

A quiet and stable home environment

Creating a stable home environment that is organized and that is characterized by mutual respect makes it a lot easier for the children to learn effectively. One of the most important things parents can do to promote learning is to create quiet and stable home environments where all family members are relaxed and at peace (Stranko, Hilderbrand, and Palmer, 2012). The home environments should be free of domestic based violence that threaten the home tranquility. Children and parents should work together freely without fear of abuse or ridicule. The difference of opinions should be tolerated and judgmental attitudes should not have place. In such a home environment children readily concentrate in their learning at schools and continue learning freely in their homes. A well-organized home environment helps children feel confident to share their ideas, values and attitudes without fear of negative feedback from their siblings or parents. Quietness in their study rooms or mini libraries help the children to understand their studies better and brings out the meaning of the lessons taught, helping them to think deeply and broadly (Ordonez, 2011).

Parents in rural areas should create stable home environments that encourage hands-on, interactive learning that sparks the imagination and unlocks creativity of their children. According to Karatas and Baki (2013) the home environment should be created to support free and critical thinking that allows the growth of new ideas. If the home environments are not conducive gaining new knowledge or skills become difficult in the rural homes and children lose interest in their school work.

Sense of self-esteem

The home environments should foster a sense of self-esteem and belonging. Belonging is the feeling of being accepted and loved, and it comes after security. Dodge, Colker, Heroman, and Bickart (2002). explain self-esteem as a sense of one's worth. Self-esteem comes from daily experiences that confirm who we are and what we are capable of doing. Jena (2013) acknowledges that a positive environment will recognize children's achievements and build on these for further growth of the child. When children have positive experiences, their self-esteem grows and they see themselves as people who can do things successfully and attain good achievements on their studies thereby improving the quality of education on the rural learning ecologies. Dodge et al. (2002) believe that children's sense of self-identity and self-esteem is rooted in their culture and ethnic background which are both direct products of stable home environments. Rural and indeed all parents must value and respect the need of peaceful home environments that promote self-esteem in children and improves their academic achievements. It is the duty of parents to make sure that all children feel accepted and loved in their home environments.

Conclusion

Quality education involves and encompasses critical thinking, learning to work with others, work independently, good grades in school and acquiring of social skills which equip the child with innovative ways of improving ones livelihood. Ordonez (2011) says quality education is the one considers on the holistically enhancement of the child in all facets of life. Quality education does not necessarily mean just scoring higher grades in public examinations it's far deeper than that. When a student fails to acquire social skills but obtains a high grade in the examination that does not translate quality education. Quality education speaks to a set of skills necessary in our individual, academic and social life and academic attainment is only a portion of that. Webre (2005) advocates that quality education ensures how to face the realities of life applying the things learners learn in their academic life. The values that the school passes on to students, both boys and girls, are as important as the official curriculum. This learning helps equip students to exercise their rights and overcome obstacles on their path to living the lives they choose. Quality education will certainly make the students from rural areas be creative and develop their thinking process thereby improving their livelihoods and improve the living standards in their communities.

For children to learn better and attain quality education, their homes should be an extension of the school and a place where they experiment and put into use all the things that they have learnt in school (Best & Shucksmith, 2006). In a home learning environment, parents should create study spaces or build study rooms. The study room is an important factor at home when a child starts school or is at school. In their home environment there should be a provision of a mini library within their study area. Erickson and Markuson (2007) state that in a home set up a library can be set in a small corner where books are kept and the children are encouraged to read. The learning space should be full of learning media displayed in the wall. Children learn most of the things when seeing, so to enhance this the homes should display various learning media both projected and non-projected. If all this happens then children in rural learning ecologies are likely to improve on their school work and the quality of education (Ogbebe & Muluku, 2013).

References

Best, R., & Shucksmith, M. (2006, April). Homes for rural communities. In *Joseph Rowntree Foundation: Rural housing policy forum.*

Cartledge G., & Keesey, S. (2016). Culturally relevant literature: What matters most to primary-age urban learners? *Reading & Writing Quarterly*, *32*(5), 399–426.

Dodge, D. T., Colker, L. J., Heroman, C., & Bickart, T. S. (2002). *The creative curriculum for preschool* (p. 540). Washington, D.C.: Teaching Strategies.

Duncan, I., Miller, A., & Jiang, S. (2012). A taxonomy of virtual worlds usage in education. *British Journal of Educational Technology, 43*(6), 949–964.

Erikson, R., & Markuson, C. (2007). *Designing a school library media center for the future.* NewYork: American Library Association.

Jena, P. C. (2013). Effect of smart classroom learning environment on academic achievement of rural high achievers and low achievers in science. *International Letters of Social and Humanistic Sciences*, (03), 1–9.

Karatas, I., & Baki, A. (2013). The effect of learning environments based on problem solving on students' achievements of problem solving. *International Electronic Journal of Elementary Education*, *5*(3), 249–268.

Shin, J. H., & Albers, P. (2015). *An analysis of the effect of a cyber home learning system on Korean secondary school students'* English language achievement and attitude. *TESL Canada Journal*, *32*(2), 45–45.

Sithole, B. M., & Lumadi, M. W. (2013). Improvisation and the use of community resources in business studies teaching. *Journal of Social Sciences*, *34*(1), 1–7.

Stranko, S. A., Hilderbrand, R. H., & Palmer, M. A. (2012). Comparing the fish and benthic macroinvertebrate diversity of restored urban streams to reference streams. *Restoration Ecology*, *20*(6), 747–755.

Ogbeba, J., & Muluku, A. (2013). Influence of clean school environment and standard class room size and facilities on students' achievement in biology in Gwagwalada Area Council of Fct-Abuja. *International Journal of Case Studies.*

Ordonez, V. (2011). *Rural education: Changing environments; emerging challenges, policy Perspective and option.* Shangai: UNESCO.

Webre, E. C. (2005). Enhancing reading success with collaboratively created progress charts. *Intervention in School and Clinic, 40*(5), 291–295.

9. *Quality curriculum for rural learning ecologies in Zimbabwe*

MANDLENKOSI NDLOVU

Introduction

It is crucial that, whether in the rural or urban areas, young people are equipped with knowledge, skills, competencies, values, and attitudes that enable them to contribute meaningfully to national and local development as well as to their upkeep in a sustainable way. This could be achieved through an effective and relevant education system that is needs-based and culturally-grounded. Once governments and communities embrace such an education system, it is envisaged that the struggles against poverty, hunger, disease, and marginalisation in most rural areas of Zimbabwe, and the global South in general would be successfully fought.

At present, high failure rates at all levels of Primary and Secondary education where there is certification, that is, in Grade Seven (7), Form Four (4), and Form Six (6) are recorded in Schools that are situated in the rural areas (Ncube, 2004). This implies that, learners in rural Schools, especially those completing Form four, have limited opportunities of enrolling for higher education or entering the job market as a full Ordinary level certificate ('O' level) with passes in five subjects or more, including English Language is a pre-requisite for both. Ncube (2004) observes that although the national pass rate at 'O' level is usually between 20% and 30%, that of rural Secondary Schools is even lower. The fundamental questions that should be asked are: Can learners that fail to pass the required academic subjects at whatever level of learning fail to do anything meaningful to sustain themselves and their immediate communities? If so, Why? The other question is: Are learners in rural areas different from those in urban areas? If so, How? If not, what then contributes to them failing more than their counterparts in urban areas?

Quite a number of researchers and authors have written on what could be the possible factors that contribute to poor performance by learners at rural Schools and subsequent dearth of job opportunities for those learners (Mandina, 2012). According to Bauch (2001), most schools in the rural areas lack basic infrastructure and amenities. As a result, most competent and qualified teachers shun rural schools. Besides, some of the schools in the rural areas are located in some of the remotest parts of the country and are inaccessible. As a result, Education Officers (EOs), now referred to as District Schools Inspectors (DSIs) rarely visit remote schools for purposes of supervising teachers to ensure quality education (Mandina, 2012). With specific reference to rural Day Secondary Schools, Ncube (2004) notes that learners walk long distances to the schools and they would be tired at school and not concentrate much. Lack of screening at Form One level also militates against high quality results at 'O' level for learners at most rural Day Secondary Schools.

What partly contributes to the concern among researchers about learning and teaching in rural ecologies in Zimbabwe in particular is that the majority of schools and learners at Primary and Secondary levels are found in the rural areas, yet the performance of learners in academic subjects in rural schools is poorer than in urban settings (Ncube, 2004). This means that a lot of youth remain stranded after failing in their studies, and face a bleak future. According to the Intercensal Demographic Survey, 2017, 68% of Zimbabwe's population resides in rural areas. The same survey revealed that, 84.46% (5 311) of all Primary Schools are in rural areas. As for Secondary Schools, 78.86% of them are in rural areas. In terms of absolute numbers, 756 884 (69.71%) of all Secondary School learners were enrolled in rural schools in 2018, while 328 944 learners were enrolled in urban schools during the same year (Ministry of Primary and Secondary Education Statistics Report, 2018). The meticulous concentration on these enrollment statistics is meant to demonstrate that, indeed, most of the learners in Zimbabwe are found in the rural schools. If the quality of performance of learners is poor, it means that the majority of youth are adversely affected. They lack opportunities and as a result, their future is compromised.

Since the challenge of poor performance in rural schools continues unabated despite numerous recommendations and interventions to rectify the situation, it becomes pertinent to ask fundamental questions about the relevance and suitability of the curriculum in the first place. Is it feasible to implement similar curricular to different learning ecologies and expect similar results? Is the current academic curricular appropriate to the needs and challenges of learners in rural areas? What kind of curricular is suitable and relevant to rural learning ecologies? In its quest to answer the above questions, the chapter is divided into three sections. The first section introduces a Theory of Change (TOC) as an analytical tool. In the second section, the discussion centres on conditions experienced by learners and teachers in rural schools. The third one interrogates what is meant by a quality curriculum that is relevant to rural ecologies.

Theory of change

The purpose of engaging in any research and that pertaining to the conditions of learning and teaching in rural environments in particular, is to stimulate change in order to alter existing negative conditions and outcomes for the benefit of key stakeholders, especially the learners. A TOC is relevant as an analytical tool in this study because it asks that we identify initiatives that seek to induce positive change so as to achieve success and development. In other words, a TOC asks that we identify those things that need to be done or changed that will lead to the desired change that is sought (Valters, 2015). It (TOC) seeks to explain why and how we think certain actions and interventions will produce desired change in a given context. In its simplest form, a TOC can be expressed in the following form: 'If we do **X**, **Y** and **Z**, it will lead to **W** or if we do **X**, it will lead to **Y**, which will lead to **Z** which might possibly lead to **W**' (Woodrow & Oatley, 2013: 8).

The issue of context is critical in a TOC. Any intervention process or change should be preceded by serious contextual analysis. How change can be delivered in one context does not necessarily mean that it can be directly transferred to another setting. This is the reason why Woodrow and Oatley (2013) say that a TOC is context-specific and not universal. In our context in the education sector, this implies that any changes or interventions that can be implemented in rural learning ecologies cannot necessarily mean that they can produce similar outcomes if applied to urban learning ecologies. An advantage of a TOC in transforming rural learning environments is that it helps to build an evidence-based, clear, and practical theory that focuses on identifiable pathways. It is in this regard that Rogers (2014) states that a TOC should begin with a sound situation analysis. Research findings are the crucial evidence that guide a TOC.

In this particular research, the starting point is a discussion on conditions prevalent in rural schools, i.e. what local resources are available, what is in short supply, cultural values, lived experiences of learners as well as what is needed in general to eke a living in rural areas. This is the evidence that would be used to proffer recommendations on what to be done to design and implement a relevant, needs-based, and effective curriculum in rural schools. An improper diagnosis of a problem would always result in inappropriate intervention measures. So, we need to clearly identify that which is problematic in rural learning ecologies that militates against high achievement or good performance by learners. In simple terms, a TOC is a tool that is intended to strengthen the quality of design and implementation of a programme such as a curriculum. As such, it is intended to be practical and helpful.

Conditions and experiences in rural schools

Generally, conditions and experiences in rural schools throughout the global South, and in Zimbabwe in particular are the same. Variations only appear among different countries depending on the state of that country's economy as well as on the remoteness or proximity of rural schools to urban centres or mining areas (Mandina, 2012). The stronger the national economy, and the closer the rural school is to an urban centre or mining area, the better the working conditions, including infrastructure and general amenities (Mandina, 2012). Conversely, in countries with fragile economies, working conditions, including infrastructure and general amenities are in a bad state. The same applies to rural schools that are furthest from urban centres and mining areas.

Among the most pressing challenges that affect teachers in rural schools in Zimbabwe is how to recruit and retain qualified teachers. This challenge, according to Mandina (2012), affects both Primary and Secondary Schools. The main reason for this challenge is due to poor socio-economic background, lack of basic infrastructure for teaching and learning, and inadequate accommodation for teachers among many others (Zvavahera, 2015). This challenge result in high teacher turn over in most rural schools in Zimbabwe. Many teachers prefer to teach in urban schools or in boarding schools even if they are in the rural areas because they have good infrastructure, including accommodation, water, and electricity (Ncube, 2004). High teacher turnover in most rural schools leaves learners unattended for some time before some replacement is found (Zvavahera, 2015). As a result, learners in rural areas lose most of their learning time when compared to their counterparts in urban or boarding schools.

Linked to the above point, Bauch (2001) recognizes that educational inspectors hardly visit rural schools due to their remoteness. Besides the fact that teachers would not be fully exerting themselves in their duties of teaching due to demotivation over poor infrastructure, non-supervision also means that they relax (Zvavahera, 2015). This also contributes to poor performance in written examinations. Due to the shortage of teachers in most rural schools, there is the prevalence of what are termed multi-grade classes in some resettlement areas in Zimbabwe. A multi-grade class is one that comprise learners from two different grade levels (Dube & Jita, 2020). For example, grade three and grade six in the same class and being taught by one teacher.

The above scenario could also contribute to poor performance as teachers that take multi-grades would be overwhelmed and tired most of the time. It is not surprising therefore that some rural schools have recorded successive zero percent pass rates for a number of years. This could be as a result of unfavourable working conditions on the side of teachers. Between 2001 and 2008, the highest percentage pass rate ever reached in Gokwe North district, in the Midlands Province, at Grade Seven level was 42.27 in 2001, while in 2008, the percentage pass rate plummeted to as low as 12.08% (Mandina, 2012). Gokwe North district is one of the most remote rural districts in the Midlands Province, and qualified teachers shun it.

Another challenge that negatively affect effective learning and teaching in some rural schools is the lack of classroom resources and equipment. One of Dube and Jita's (2020) participants in their research, Nonki, a teacher, lamented the dearth of resources. She explained the challenges she faces in this way:

> Policies are failing us, for example, we are forced to teach Information Communication Technologies (ICTs), yet we do not have resources in the form of computers and electricity. Our students continue to fail examinations. The exam does not consider conditions which teacher and students operate under (context), such as lack of resources and multi-grade classes (2020, p. 3873).

When faced with a situation where essential resources are unavailable or in short supply, teachers only dwell on the theory part of the subject where a lot of practical work is needed if resources permit (Dube & Jita, 2020). As Nonki aptly put it, they are 'forced' and not consulted on the best curriculum that would suit their teaching and learning environments. The issue of shortage of resources is not only confined to human resources in the form of teachers, and the issue of computers. In most rural areas, there is an acute shortage of textbooks, furniture, classrooms, chalk, and chalkboards (Ncube, 2004). Some of the learners use makeshift buildings like former farm houses as classrooms, while others conduct lessons under trees.

These and many other factors not mentioned here constitute the conditions and experiences of teachers and learners in many of the rural schools in Zimbabwe. In spite of these and many other debilitating conditions that militate against quality education in the rural areas, the issue that comes to the fore is that intervention measures are urgently needed from a different angle, that is, a contextualized curriculum so as to improve on the learning and teaching conditions and outcomes in the schools in rural areas (Stabback, 2016). It is believed that if the curriculum is relevant and needs-based, it could help to off-set some of the perennial challenges that afflict the delivery of education in the rural areas and make the lives of both the learners and teachers much better. The following section looks at what is deemed to constitute quality and relevant curriculum.

What is quality curriculum that is relevant to rural environments?

Quality is an elusive concept and therefore difficult to precisely define. It means different things to different people. In simple terms, the quality of something is its worth or usefulness. Goddard and Leask (1992) posit that quality is simply meeting the requirements of the customer. In this case, who is/are the customer (s) in the context of rural learning ecologies? The answer is simple. The main customers are the learners and surrounding communities that have basic requirements that they need to be fulfilled. Their requirements are to lead better lives and to solve problems that confront them where they live.

Put differently, quality curriculum should be anchored in a problem-solving approach that enables learners to solve their own problems and those of surrounding communities in order to make those communities better places to reside in. It is in this light that Bhurekeni (2020) suggests that any education system should be heritage-based, that is, it should utilise locally-available resources in order to foster meaningful development. Otherwise, any curriculum that leaves its customers stranded at what level of education, that is, with nothing to lean on for survival purposes after completing the learning process is not the best. A curriculum that produces stranded students is worthless, irrelevant and of poor quality.

In other words, researchers in the education sector should be asking themselves questions like: What kind of knowledge, skills, attitudes, competencies, and values are necessary learners to survive before after school. It is not important to be obsessed with the question of how many learners have a full 'O' level certificate, that is, passes in five subjects and above, yet even those with the so-called full certificates are stranded and cannot fend for themselves (Ncube, 2004). Commenting on the quality and relevance of the curriculum in Zimbabwe, Bhurekeni (2020) criticised it in that even forty years after independence, the curriculum still bears strong and indelible marks of the former colonial education system. The colonial curriculum was by all purposes, theoretically and pedagogically disengaged from the life worlds of the learners it intended to educate.

With that in mind, Bhurekeni (2020) argued for a contextualized curriculum that is heritage-based. He justified his views on the grounds that heritage-based education has the capacity to develop a sense of ownership, identity, responsibility, and innovation in learners, schools and communities. Instead of complaining about the shortage of resources, teachers that embrace a heritage-based curriculum would utilise locally-available resources in the vicinity in teaching subjects like Agriculture, Building, Music, Art and Design, Science, Culture and Heritage Studies, Physical Education and Sport. Unlike academic subjects like History, English Language, Geography, and Mathematics, to name only but a few, subjects with a practical orientation equip learners with life-long skills that enable them to cater for their needs in a sustainable way (Ncube, 2004).

One of the participants, a Mr. Ncube, recommended that the curriculum should be eighty percent vocationalised and contextualised in rural schools in Zimbabwe. His reason for that recommendation was that even if learners fail to pass five 'O' level mandatory subjects, they would still acquire enough practical skills that would help them to survive on their own without necessarily seeking formal employment (Interview with Mr. Ncube, 20.09. 21). Mr. Ncube's sentiments were echoed by another participant, a Mr. Tshabangu, an educationist by profession.

Besides suggesting that more practical than theoretical/academic subjects must be taught in rural schools, Tshabangu went on to say that the assessment criteria in most of the subjects taught in rural schools should have more weight on the practical than theoretical component. When asked to further clarify his thoughts, Mr. Tshabangu argued that most of these learners in rural schools spend the rest of their lives in rural communities around the schools where they learnt. So, it would be prudent to equip them with practical skills so that they till the land productively, build houses for themselves and for other members of the community, repair roads, dig wells and drill boreholes and do many other practical jobs for their own survival and for the development of their communities (Interview with Mr. Tshabangu, 15. 09.21). It is pointless to teach learners knowledge and skills that they would not utilise.

The issue of culture is also critical in developing relevant and quality curriculum. UNICEF (2020) report on improving the quality of education for vulnerable children everywhere recommends that in order for a curriculum to be considered relevant and of high quality, it should be framed through culturally relevant, meaningful, and responsive content and examples that respond to students' local context and lived experiences. Learning that is incompatible with a people's culture is less relevant. It is note worth that for rural and indigenous peoples, local knowledge and culture informs decision-making processes about critical issues of day-to-day life.

It means therefore that, if the curriculum is culturally-grounded and context-specific, learners would benefit through connecting curriculum content to indigenous practices, indigenous decision-making processes, social interactions, rituals, and spiritual beliefs (UNICEF, 2020). In that way, learners would realise that learning is not only confined to the four walls of the classroom, but also take cognizance of their environment, culture, and experiences. In other words, they would notice that learning extends to the real world they experience on a day-to-day basis outside the classroom. In order to have buy-in from learners and local communities, local beliefs, attitudes, perceptions, and worldviews should be acknowledged, respected, and integrated into the school curriculum (Stabback, 2016). That could be done through teaching Culture and Heritage Studies. In that way, the curriculum becomes relevant, acceptable and supported. This is different from despising local beliefs and worldviews, and then going on to impose alien beliefs and world views on local communities and learners.

After considering a number of issues that should be considered to come up with a contextually-relevant curriculum, Stabback (2016: 8) emphasizes that, 'a principal objective of a quality curriculum is, in a fair an inclusive manner, to enable students to acquire and develop the knowledge, skills, values, attitudes, and associated capabilities and competencies, to lead meaningful and productive lives.' What is emphasized here is the aspect of inclusivity. No learner should be left out of the learning process, be it in the rural or urban areas. The point that Stabback (2016) is putting across in other words, is that at the end of the course, students should use their learning for their personal, social, physical, cognitive, moral, psychological and emotional development. The same point is held by Tedesco, Opertti, and Amcidio (2013), where they say that quality curriculum should promote social justice and be relevant to society and individuals' needs.

Conclusion

Any curriculum at whatever level of education should enable students to produce goods and services after completing their studies so as to satisfy their needs and those of communities where they live. If the curriculum does not equip students with survival skills, then it is irrelevant and worthless. Students should not be stranded after completing their studies. Put differently, students should be equipped with knowledge, skills, values, and competencies that would help them to put food onto their tables, found families, and take care of their relatives even if they fail written examinations. For students in the rural areas, for example, the curriculum should be more inclined towards practical subjects that would enable them to employ themselves after school and escape the trap of poverty. The curriculum should be heritage-based, that is, it should utilise local resources and environment to avoid the challenge of the so-called shortage of resources for teaching and learning. In other words, even though infrastructural conditions in most of the rural areas are not attractive for the recruitment and retention of competent teachers, if the curriculum is of high quality and relevant, students in the rural schools would still benefit from the limited contact they have with teachers.

References

Bauch, P. A. (2001). School-community partnership in rural areas: Leadership renewal, and a sense of place. *Peabody Journal of Education, 76*(20), 204–221.

Bhurekeni, J. (2020). Decolonial reflections on the Zimbabwean Primary and Secondary school curriculum journey. *Educational Research for Social Change, 9*(2).

Dube, B., & Jita, L. (2020). The rural child and the ambivalence of education of education in Zimbabwe: What can Bricolage do? *Universal Journal of Educational Research, 8*(9), 3873–3882.

Goddard, D., & Leask, M. (1992). *The search for quality: Management in education.* London: Paul Chapman.

Mandida, S. (2012). Quality rural Secondary School education in Zimbabwe: Challenges and remedies. *Journal of Emerging Trends in Educational Research and Policy Studies, 3*(5), 768–774.

Ministry of Primary and Secondary Education. (2019). *2018 Primary and Secondary Education Statistics Report.* Harare.

Ncube, N. J. (2004). *Managing the quality of education in Zimbabwe: The internal efficiency of rural day Secondary Schools.* Unpublished Doctor of Education thesis, University of South Africa.

Rogers, P. (2014). *Theory of change: Impact evaluation 2.* Florence: UNICEF Office of Research.

Stabback, P. (2016). *What makes a quality curriculum?* UNESCO International Bureau of Education.

Tedesco, J. C., Opertti, R., & Amcidio, M. (2013). *The curriculum debate: Why it is important today?* Geneva: UNESCO International Bureau of Education.

UNICEF. (2020). *The learning passport: Curriculum framework adaptation guidance: Improving the quality of education for vulnerable children everywhere.* Cambridge: Cambridge University Press.

Valters, C. (2015). *Theories of change. Time for a radical approach to learning in development.* London: Overseas Development Institute.

Woodrow, P., & Oatley, N. (2013). *Practical approaches to theories of change in conflict, security and justice programmes.* Harvard: Department for International Development.

Zvavahera, P. (2015). Human capital problems in Zimbabwean rural schools: A case study of Mazowe District. *Journal of Case Studies in Education, 5*, 45–52.

List of Interviewees

Mr. Ncube. Date of interview (20. 09. 21).

Mr. Tshabangu. Date of interview (15. 09. 21).

10. Online instruction during COVID 19 pandemic: Excluding the already excluded rural learner

MLUNGISI MOYO & MUDIMBA COLLEN

Introduction

Coronavirus disease 2019 (COVID 19) has recently become one of the topical issues world-over. The disease has continuously claimed the lives of millions of people in both developed and developing countries, resulting in leaders of different countries being left with no options but only to close down all human activity (Zhao & Xu, 2020). As a result, there have been prolonged lockdowns in various sections of business and industry including the education sector since March 2020 in almost all countries, which was meant to address the spread of the pandemic. Mukute, Francis, Burt, and De Souze (2020) thus observe that by mid-April 2020, the alarmingly rapid spread of COVID 19 has paralysed schools, colleges and universities resulting in 1, 58 billion students being affected across the world.

Save the Children (2020) Report has also revealed that in Africa, 262, 5 million primary and secondary school going children have been closed out of the school. As a result, the COVID 19 pandemic has seriously affected the implementation of all the 17 Sustainable Development Goals, and this has a serious impact on children's rights to quality and inclusive education (INEE 2020, UN-Zimbabwe 2020). This has also affected many nations such as Zimbabwe in their endeavours to realise Vision 2030. Despite challenges faced because of the pandemic, nations have continuously made efforts to ensure that sections of education, industry and commerce were not on permanent closure (Education Cannot Wait 2020; Save the Children, 2020). As a result, digital learning has been found to be the only possible means to replace the notably unpragmatic face-to-face classroom instruction. United Nations (UN) 2020, UNDP (2020) and UNESCO IESALC (2020) however concur that in Africa COVID 19's significant impact on education has been on the gaps that it widened between the already marginalised and excluded learners and their counter-parts. Zhang et al. (2015) have established that in developing countries, educational inequalities still exist between rural and urban areas. Litheko (2012) expounds that income disparity, various institutional barriers and different parenting styles, among others, are regarded as potential causes of education inequality. As a result, there is a lot of evidence in research to suggest This theoretical chapter hence looked at how online instruction as a result of COVID 19, has led to more exclusion in equality educational opportunities of the already excluded rural school learner.

Background to COVID-19 and online instruction

The last three months of the year 2019, marked the advent of a virus disease associated with flue, called Corona Virus Disease, later to be known as COVID-19. The outbreak of COVID-19 was first noted in the city of Wuhan in Hubei province, China (Mulenga & Marban, 2020; Basilaia & Kvavadze, 2020). Since the disease is easily contracted airborne, through sneezing and contact, it could not be contained in China, and thus it quickly got out offhand, spreading to many countries, continents and later the whole world. Efforts to contain it were futile, with the World Health Organisation (WHO) suggesting different ways of reducing its alarming rate of spreading. Scientists the world over recommended various measures to lessen its impact, but all was in vain (Roy, 2020; Agnoletto & Queiroz, 2020). People died in big numbers in countries like China itself, Italy, Spain, France, America, Brazil, the UK, India and South Africa, just to mention a few. Medical doctors and traditional healers to control the number of people who were flocking to hospitals in search of medication prescribed different home remedies, both traditional and modern. The major problem was oxygen and ventilation machines since the disease made it difficult for patients to breathe. As all this was happening, intervention measures were being sought. The first recommendation was social and physical distancing, as it was established that proximity was one of the major agents for transmission (Basilaia & Kvavadze, 2020). This was followed by masking. People were advised to wear facemasks, especially those of four layers, the surgical, and of course, any other since the situation was becoming direr. In the preceding stages of trying to find a long-lasting solution, amid continuous dying of people across the globe, WHO came up with other guidelines of containing the outbreak, among them; sanitizing, vaccination, quarantine and closure of country borders

(Agnoletto & Queiroz, 2020; Basilaia & Kvavadze, 2020). In Zimbabwe, the first casualty to COVID-19 succumbed to it in 2020, with many reports of new cases being recorded, mostly from people who were coming outside the country. As all this was happening, learning was still in progress in most countries.

However, the month of March saw a sharp increase of cases, globally, which prompted most governments, including Zimbabwe, effecting lock-downs, a measure mooted to restrict the movement of people in towns and rural areas (SADC and UNESCO, 2020 Reports). Law enforcement agents were romped in to assist the government in ensuring people adhered to the new regulation. This eventuated into curfews, where people were not allowed to move from one location to another. Intercity travelling was banned as another effort intended to curb the rate at which COVID-19 was spreading (SADC and UNESCO, 2020 Reports). Learning all over the world was affected, with various governments introducing online learning as means to ensure children's right to education was not breached. Developed countries, whose technologies are advanced, like South Korea, North Korea, America, China and the United Kingdom, responded timeously by providing learning opportunities online (Zhao & Xu, 2020). These countries have sophisticated internet and network connections, which are accessible to both rural and urban learners. Network data bundles in the developed world are either free or the tariffs are affordable by everyone (Sintema, 2020). The developed world also has free Wi-Fi zones, which make it easy for learners to surf information.

Furthermore, developed countries like Australia, have a variety of optional e-learning and virtual platforms, which include; teleconferencing facilities, like skype, zoom, Facebook, Twitter, and other Google applications like google drive, drop box, cloud, Moodle cloud, Edmodo, Instagram, Yahoo and many others (Roy, 2020). China introduced Sina Microblog, which facilitated e-learning (Zhao & Xu, 2020). This gave birth to the much-popularized digital learning. Children in the developed world did not see much difference between the period before COVID-19 and during the pandemic because their learning was not much affected by the new 'normal' of doing business. They continued learning in the comfort of their homes digitally. The subsequent closure of schools did not spare African countries; hence, they also followed WHO measures of closing learning institutions to protect learners, who are well known to play with surfaces like tables, desks, doors and toilets, which are main sources of contracting COVID-19 (Mulenga & Marban, 2020; Basilaia & Kvavadze, 2020).

COVID 19 and classroom instruction

The COVID-19 pandemic has resulted in the closure of all learning institutions, globally in an effort to contain it (Sintema, 2020). The closure of schools has been considered specifically as a response to adhere to the World Health Organisation and recommendations from health ministries and task forces in respective countries. Therefore, the implications meant that there was no more traditional face-to-face instruction, which is the norm globally, and hence nations had to find other means of conducting instruction to ensure children continued to learn amid the threat of the COVID-19 pandemic. Such developments gave birth to a paradigm shift of instruction. Distance education and remote instruction became ubiquitous with various online platforms being utilised. Burke (2020) and Zhao and Xu (2020) and observe that the paradigm shift in classroom instruction did not affect most developed countries whose technologies are advanced. For example, China, Japan, America, North and South Korea, among others, had permitting infrastructure that made it easy to facilitate students' learning. Mulenga and Marban (2020) thus observe that it is the African continent that had hardest hit, especially those countries in Sub-Saharan region, due to poor network infrastructure. Thus, the poor who are mostly rural children and those living in high-density suburbs in urban areas cannot afford learning online. This is due to lack of digital gadgets to access learning instruction since it is conducted through expensive smartphones or laptops and desktops, which are a privilege of the rich and mostly urbanites (SADC and UNESCO, 2020 Reports). The researchers' observations can further confirm that COVID-19 has affected learning in many ways, with teachers themselves failing to access the network to communicate with learners. As if this is not enough, most teachers do not have the same digital gadgets like cellphones which they are required to use to send learning instruction to their learners (SADC and UNESCO, 2020 Reports). Where they have relevant gadgets, teachers cannot afford required data bundles which are very expensive to send remote instruction. This in turn has affected the quality of instruction and learner feedback, where at some point parents do all the school tasks for the learners.

Mulenga and Marban (2020) posit that the governments in various countries, for instance, Zimbabwe, have tried radio lessons, which only benefitted mostly children in urban areas, where there is radio transmission. This means the rural child has not benefitted from these efforts. The above authorities further confirm that in some families, children are orphans and vulnerable and hence having a radio, cellphone or laptop is an imagination. This, therefore, means that children in this category especially in rural area are not learning (SADC and UNESCO, 2020 Reports). In this regard, online learning has further divided learners according to social status, with those from the rich, emerging as the main beneficiaries, because they can hire teachers for extra lessons or utilise international platforms like YouTube (Agnoletto & Queiroz, 2020; Burke, 2020; Mulenga & Marban, 2020). In this scenario, it is clear that COVID-19 adversely affected rural learners, who cannot not afford the technological gadgets and data bundles, doubled by limited network or none at all. This suggests that the poor, who had been struggling to learn in the traditional face-to-face instruction, are the same who are now not benefitting from online instruction. Mulenga and Marban (2020) hence concluded that it is indisputable that some children are learning using various e-learning platforms such as Skype, zoom, Facebook, Twitter, and other Google applications, which include google drive, drop box, cloud, Moodle cloud, Edmodo, Instagram, Yahoo, YouTube, e-granary, and many more. Instead, access to knowledge has remained a privilege for the elite. In this regard, COVID-19 has worsened the learning opportunities for the poor and mostly rural areas learners.

The excluded learner in the classroom through online instruction during COVID 19

Singh and Thurman (2019) posit that, exclusion in education is an elusive concept that is not easy to define and conceptualise. Sewnet (2020) goes on to say that, the concept may refer to a number of relative situations of which an excluded learner may encounter. In the practical aspect, exclusion may occur because a learner has been unable to pay tuition and levies at school. In this case, the learner might not be granted permission to be at school. On a different note, exclusion can be in the form of lack of access to educational resources and meaningful learning experiences, which all of it has a bearing on the quality of the product. Hence, an excluded learner in educational circles is one who is underprivileged in terms of access to quality educational provisions. According to UNESCO Report (2020), children in rural Zimbabwe have been identified as a disadvantaged group, even before the advent of COVID-19, because of long distances they walk to and from school. The current researchers also observed that children from rural school set-ups walk very long distances and hence reach school late and already tired.

This has been seen as marginalization in terms of accessing quality education as compared to their counterparts in urban areas, who attend schools in their locations, a few metres from their homes. In addition, the rural child is regarded as the excluded learner due to exposure to poor infra-structural development, poor staffing of the schools, lack of teaching/learning material and lack of ICT gadgets, among other things. Clark (2000) posits availability of learning materials, such as books, computers and other stationery is a prerequisite for learners to realise quality education. On an equal note, the absence of such digital gadgets as laptops and computers means that children found in such educational centres are left out of modern learning technologies. This is notably to be the reality on the ground regarding the rural learners during the advent of COVID-19 lockdowns and the closure of schools. The rural learners are defined as excluded learners during COVID 19 pandemic since no online instruction was given to them. Despite the efforts by various education ministries in developing countries to engage online radio lessons, the general overview also shows that this arrangement had its multiple challenges. For instance, not all rural families have the radio as a gadget (Zimbabwe Education Cluster, 2020). In some cases, very poor network connectivity has been a cause for concern. In situations where radios are a privilege with good network connectivity, the reality on the ground has shown that both the boy and the girl-child have no time to sit and listen to the radio lessons (Zimbabwe Education Cluster, 2020). The situation is worsened by the value in which their parents place in education. Hence, the absence of face-to-face interactions especially with the rural learner has meant zero schooling since these learners would engage in household chores and other outdoor activities. It is hence reality that the majority of the rural learners especially boys have resorted to illegal gold panning in Zimbabwe whilst teenage pregnancy is quite alarming world-over during this COVID19 pandemic (SADC and UNESCO, 2020 Reports). Government and schools would come up with means to ensure children continued learning despite the pandemic. The rural learners in all scenarios have been most affected, thereby classified as the 'excluded learner' due to online instruction during the COVID 19 pandemic (Sewnet, 2020).

Online instruction during COVID 19: Opportunities and realities

The closure of learning institutions, owing to the COVID-19 pandemic meant that other avenues should be found to ensure children did not miss education, which is a human right according to the Convention on the right of children 1989. This, therefore, resulted in resorting to other means like remote instruction to embrace the new 'normal' (Agnoletto & Queiroz, 2020; Mulenga & Marban, 2020). Learning during COVID-19 has been characterised by the utilisation of various digital platforms, which include the common WhatsApp platform videos and notes, radio programs, and sending notes via emails (Mulenga & Marban, 2020). Children have been required to download PDFs and other soft wares for learning. Learners with access to Wi-Fi and internet services have been surfing information and researching on their own, while asking teachers on various platforms for explanations. According to Agnoletto and Queiroz (2020) and Burke (2020), the implementation of online learning resulted in learning being done both synchronously and asynchronously. Synchronous learning occurs through live videos, zoom platforms, tele-conferencing and other virtual forms with instant feedback (Burke, 2020). However, in contrast, asynchronous instruction occurs when learners can choose their own time to respond to given tasks through different tools such as email or discussion boards. Learners can log into the online learning platform like google class platforms, communicate and complete tasks at their convenient times (Burke, 2020; Mulenga & Marban, 2020).

In Zimbabwe, COVID-19 resulted in learners learning using mostly WhatsApp platforms, which are deemed cheaper by most teachers, parents and learners. Teachers are sending audios, notes and downloads on these WhatsApp platforms and learners respond accordingly for feedback and the process is reciprocal (Zimbabwe Education Cluster, 2020). However, data bundles are not affordable to all families due to high costs. As a result, learners from poor rural families are not participating. Mulenga & Marban (2020) posit that, learners from poor families are being excluded from this only possible way of learning amid the continued lockdowns world-over. The situation as observed by Mulenga and Marban (2020) is rather dire in rural areas, where only a significant section of learners would participate in this remote learning. The government to transmit radio lessons has put efforts, but lack of transmission in most parts of the country has made the exercise to be in vain (Zimbabwe Education Cluster, 2020). Others have been utilising the WhatsApp platforms to cope with their counterparts in urban areas, but the lack of gadgets like smartphones has rendered the whole exercise a nullity (SADC and UNESCO, 2020 Reports). This means that those without these gadgets find learning difficult as it means that they have to rely on others. However, the most affected learners are those in early childhood development classes, since most of them are at a stage where they require the teacher's assistance to read. These can also be said to have been excluded from learning unless their parents and siblings are helping them.

Online instruction and its effects on the already excluded learner

Wang (2013) expounds that there is a 'digital divide' between rural and urban students to access to technology and opportunities to learn ICT skills. According to Wang, there are no hard and software gargets, internet connectivity and technology support within public schools. He argues that there is also a huge difference in how frequently students and teachers use technology within the classroom. The rural-urban infrastructure disparities indicate that urban areas can boast of electricity and telecommunications capabilities, but rural areas remain unconnected and hence disadvantaged (Gulati, 2008). Hence, the lack of ready access to technology is a key barrier to technology integration for developing areas.

Clark (2000) in his studies established that both teachers and students in rural are disadvantaged in technological facilities, with regard to teachers, the study showed that urban teachers in the U.S. have positive reactions towards technology integration. The findings of the study were that urban teachers feel confident about their ability to use technology and they believe that technology is an integral part of their classroom. Furthermore, the study concluded urban teachers want more software and equipment in their classrooms. On the other hand, research findings by Clark (2000) indicate that rural schools do not have teachers with the same qualifications and confidence levels in technology integration as urban schools do. Herselman (2003) asserts that the lack of experienced and skilled teachers and technical training has been an ongoing problem for rural schools.

Wang (2013) further indicates that students from rural schools score lower on all the Internet inequality indicators (digital access, autonomy of use, social support, Internet use and self-efficacy) and are therefore more disadvantaged in comparison to their urban peers. Researchers have also argued that students in low-income areas often use computers for repetitive activities, whereas students in high-income areas often use technology for higher-order thinking, problem solving, and other intellectually challenging activities (Songer, Lee, & Kam, 2002 in Wang, 2013).

According to UNESCO (2020), the rural community learner has been most affected in the digital world. Mulenga & Marban (2020) note that the COVID-19 pandemic caught many countries in the African continent off guard since a lack of preparedness in providing online services was glaringly seen. Basilaia & Kvavadze (2020) also note with concern that the proposed radio lessons and use of the internet were not possible since, the connectivity in most, if not all rural areas is non-existent. In this regard, COVID 19 era has worsened the digital divide between the rural excluded learner and his/her urban counterparts. A survey made by Moyo & Mudimba (2021) has also indicated that the rural girl child has continued to be the most greatly affected fellow in the case of Zimbabwe. Thus, due to the challenges in accessing classroom teaching, the rural learner has continued to lack exposure to quality education. In the case of the girl-child in rural communities, COVID 19 pandemic and continued school lockdowns have made her the most vulnerable species. For instance, the majority of these girls have become victims of child labour, sexual abuse and teenage mothers. It is critical to note that their counterparts in urban setups have continued to be exposed to online and house schools where they have continued to learn and hence widening the gap between the two. Whilst the rural child is seemingly left behind, Moyo and Mudimba (2021) have concluded that online instruction during COVID 19 pandemic has also contributed a lot to the value of ICT in the rural school. For example, rural teachers have been empowered on the ICT to embrace the 'new normal'. This on its own has become a positive step towards attaining Sustainable Development Goal 4 and realizing Vision 2030.

Towards including the excluded learner in online classrooms during COVID 19

According to UNICEF (2010), education is not only a fundamental human right. It is an enabling right with a direct impact on the realization of all other human rights. It is a global common good and a primary driver of progress across all 17 Sustainable Development Goals as a bedrock of just, equal, inclusive peaceful societies. Thus, when the education systems of both developed and developing nations collapse, peaceful, prosperous and productive societies cannot be sustained. Huang et al. (2020) observe that as the COVID-19 pandemic continues to spread, many countries have been left with a mammoth task of ensuring that their education systems do not collapse. Using China's strategy of 'School's Out, But Class On', UNESCO has designed a 'handbook on facilitating flexible learning'. UNESCO has designed a flexible learning approach that can offer choices in the educational environment, as well as customizing a given course to meet the needs of individual learners (Huang et al., 2020). The handbook has provided a comprehensive guide on how to use online teaching flexibly. Though the handbook noted the limitations of the Chinese experience of not addressing distance learning in areas with no internet connectivity and TV cables, it did not address how the disrupted class can proceed in such disadvantaged situations.

Wiki (2019) expounds that, to bridge the digital divide, local and regional governments need to adequately understand the gaps and needs of their communities through data. In addition to addressing the community's needs, closing the digital divide also means ensuring that technology is non-discriminatory and accessible to all people in the community including internet access, devices, and information. Wiki (2019) further posits that digital technologies should not leave anyone or any territory behind or widen existing inequalities, particularly in the rural communities. In this regard, therefore distance learning should be embraced as they aim at making learners more self-determined and independent, while teachers become more of learning facilitators. Huang et al. (2020) say learners can be afforded opportunities to study during evenings or weekends. Hailu (2020) and Tiruneh (2020) have also concurred that following the school closures due to COVID 19, response plans set by the Ministries of Education in respective Southern African regional countries have been to make use of various media, which include educational radio programmes and television learning programmes.

Challenges in including the already excluded learner during COVID 19

According to Cheng (2020), online teaching cannot achieve face-to-face emotional communication between teachers and students and lacks real-time feedback of information and classroom constraints. Moreover, if the closure long lasts, achieving the objectives of the course will be very difficult (IESALC, 2020). This, therefore, implies that, the excluded learner in the rural school set-up is continuously denied quality service delivery in education. In addition, as stated in World Bank (2020), while digital technologies can offer a wide set of capabilities for distance learning, most education systems in low- and middle-income countries, including schools, children and/or teachers, lack access to high-speed broadband or digital devices needed to fully deploy online learning options. As such, education systems need to consider alternative ways for students to continue learning when they are not in school, as is the case with the current COVID-19 crisis. Thus, online libraries, TV broadcasts, guidelines, resources, video lectures, online channels are important alternatives of face-to-face learning (Basilaia & Kvavadze, 2020; World Bank, 2020b).

In their studies Huang et al. (2020) established that several challenges have been experienced during the application of online learning in the global wide. For example, internet connection can be unreliable if there are thousands of learners learning simultaneously. In addition, some instructors can find it difficult to find online resources that are the most suitable in their teaching contexts because thousands of resources are published online. Furthermore, several instructors and learners do not have the appropriate digital skills to teach and learn online. Thus, all the above have seemingly contributed to failure of the educators to take online the already excluded rural learners during the COVID 19 pandemic. Basilaia & Kvavadze (2020) have also noted that several learners lack crucial learning competencies, such as adaptation, independent study, and self-regulation, which are key factors for successful online learning. The above authorities also note that several instructors simply use direct instructions without considering important features of online learning, such as interactivity, social presence, and cognitive presence, resulting in boring learning experiences. This also has a widening effect in excluding the already excluded rural learner especially during COVID 19 era. IESALC (2020) also observed that the number of students who have access to online learning but are not willing to use it is another challenge that has affected educators in their endeavours to address the digital divide amongst learners of varied backgrounds.

Conclusion

This chapter has reviewed and analysed the literature on online instruction, with special reference to how this has contributed to exclusion during the COVID 19 pandemic. The chapter outlined how online instruction during COVID 19 affected access to quality education service delivery to the rural schoolchild. From the reviewed and analysed literature, online instruction has been noted to be the panacea in facilitating teaching and learning to both the urban and the rural learners. This is despite the fact that the rural learner continues to be negatively affected in terms of getting full access. This being the case, all nations worldwide have continued to find best online practices during COVID 19 pandemic that may equally accommodate the rural school child so that he/she is not totally excluded. Online instruction strategies to accommodate the excluded rural learner were notably to be inclusive of the radio and television lessons. In addition, staff development with ICT skills for online instruction is a prerequisite for rural educators so that their learners are not excluded. This is despite the challenges that have been associated with this online during the COVID 19 pandemic.

References

Agnoletto, R., & Queiroz, V. (2020). *COVID-19 and the challenges in education.* Retrieved from https:// www.Researchgate.net/Publication/340385425

Basilaia, G., & Kvavadze, D. (2020). Transition to online education in schools during SARS- COV-2 coronavirus (COVID-19) pandemic in Georgia. *Pedagogic Research, 5*(4), em0060. https:doi.org/29333/pr/7937

Basilaia, G., & Kvavadze, D. (2020). Transition to online education in schools during a SARS-CoV-2 coronavirus (COVID-19) pandemic in Georgia. *Pedagogical Research, 5*(4), 1–9. https://doi.org/10.29333/pr/7937

Burke, J. (2020). COVID-19 practice in Primary schools in Ireland Report. April.

Clark, K. D. (2000). Urban middle school teachers' use of instructional technology. *Journal of Research on Computing in Education, 33*(2), 178–193. https://doi.org/10.1080/08886504.2000.10782308

Education Cannot Wait. (2020). *COVID-19 and education in emergencies.* Retrieved from: https://www.educationcannotwait.org/covid-19/

Gulati, S. (2008). Technology-enhanced learning in developing nations: A review. *International Review of Research in Open and Distance Learning, 9*(1), 1–16.

Hailu, B. H. (2020). *Education response to COVID-19: How can basic education be implemented in Ethiopia?* Retrieved from https://riseprogramme.org/blog/COVID-19-ETH-Basic-Education

Herselman, M. E. (2003). ICT in rural areas in South Africa: Various case studies. *Proceedings of Informing Science, June 2003*, 945955. https://doi.org/10.28945/2680

Huang, R. H., Liu, D. J., Tlili, A., Yang, J. F., Wang, H. H., et al. (2020). *Handbook on facilitating flexible learning during educational disruption: The Chinese experience in maintaining undisrupted learning in COVID-19 outbreak.* Beijing: Smart Learning Institute of Beijing Normal University.

IESALC. (2020). *COVID-19 and higher education: Today and tomorrow.* Impact analysis, policy responses and recommendation.

INEE (Inter-Agency Network for Education in Emergencies). (2020). Technical Note: Education during the COVID-19 pandemic. INEE, New York, USA.

Litheko, S. R. S. (2012). The difference in performance between schools situated in the urban areas and those in the rural areas of Lesotho. *Electronic Journal for Inclusive Education*, *2*(9), 2.

Mulenga, E. M., & Marban, M. J. (2020). Is COVID the gateway for digital learning in mathematics education. Open Access 2020, 12(2), pg 269. Online Learning (1988–2018). *American Journal of Distance Education, 33*(4), 289306. https://doi.org/10.1080/08923647.2019.1663082

Roy, D. (2020). Trying to homeschool because of Corona Virus: Here are 5 tips to help your child learn. https://the conversation.com

SADC & UNESCO. (2020). *SADC &UNESCO sign agreement to ensure learning never stops.* Press Release. Gaborone, Botswana/Harare, Zimbabwe: SADC & UNESCO.

Save the Children East and Southern Africa Regional Office & Save the Children West and Central Regional Office. (June 2020). COVID-19 impacts on African Children: How to protect a generation at risk. A Pan-African Policy Paper. Nairobi, Kenya/Dakar, Senegal: Save the Children International.

Save the Children. (2020). Save the Children: Outbreak could cause millions of children to suffer for years to come. Retrieved April 16, 2020 from: https://www.savethechildren.org/us/about-us/media-and-news/2020-press-releases/outbreak-could-cause-years-ofsuffering-for-millions-of-children

Sewnet, Z. (2020). *In Ethiopia: Keeping children learning during COVID-19.* UNICEF, Addis Ababa, Ethiopia. Available at: https://www.unicef.org/ethiopia/stories/ethiopia-keeping-children-learning-during-covid-19

Singh, V., & Thurman, A. (2019). How many ways can we define online learning? A systematic literature review of definitions of online learning (1988-2018). *American Journal of Distance Education*, *33*(4), 289–306.

Sintema, E. J. (2020). Effect of COVID-19 on the performance of Grade 12 students: Implications for STEM education. *Eurasia Journal of Mathematics, Science and Technology Education*, *16*(7), em1851.https://doi.org/10.29333/ejmste/7893

Tiruneh, D. T. (2020). *COVID-19 school closures may further widen the inequality gaps between the advantaged and the disadvantaged in Ethiopia*. Retrieved from https://www.riseprogramme.org/blog/COVID-19_ethiopia_school_closures

UNDP. (1997). *Human development report.* New York: Oxford University Press.

UN (United Nations). (2020). Policy brief: Education during Covid-19 and beyond. Retrieved from https://www.un.org/sites/un2.un.org/files/sg_policy_brief_covid-19_and_education

UNDP (United Nations Development Programme). (2020). Human development perspectives Covid-19 and human development: Assessing the crisis, envisioning the recovery. Retrieved from http://hdr.undp.org/sites/default/files/covid-19_and_human_development_0.pdf

UNESCO (United Nations Educational, Scientific and Cultural Organisation). (2020a). COVID-19 educational disruption and response. Retrieved from: https://en.unesco.

UNI CEF. (2020a). *Ethiopia COVID-19.* Situational Report No. 5, 11–16 April 2020.

UNICEF. (2020b). *Promising practices for equitable remote learning emerging lessons from COVID-19 education responses in 127 countries.* Innocent Research Brief.

Wiki. (2019). *Open learning.* Retrieved from https://en.wikipedia.org/wiki/Open_learning.

World Bank. (1994). *Poverty reduction in South Asia.* Washington, D.C.

World Bank. (2019). *International Bank for reconstruction and development.* 2019-Tracking SDG7-The Energy Progress Report.

World Bank. (2020a). *Guidance note on education systems' response to COVID19.* 25 March 2020. Retrieved from http://pubdocs.worldbank.org/en/450881585235950757/COVID19-Education-Sector-Guidance-Note-March26.pdf

World Bank. (2020b). *The World Bank Education Global Practice Guidance Note: Remote Learning & COVID-19.* Updated April 7, 2020.

Zhang, D., Li, X., & Xue, J. (2015). Education inequality between rural and urban areas of the People's Republic of China, migrants' children education, and some implications. *Asian Development Review*, *32*(1), 196–224.https://doi.org/10.1162/ADEV_a_00042

Zhao, Y., & Xu, H. (2020). Chinese public attention to COVID-19 epidemic based on social media 2021.08.13 20038026

Zimbabwe Education Cluster. (2020). Humanitarian response and COVID-19 situation report. Retrieved May 14, 2020 from: https://www.humanitarianresponse.info/en/operations/zimbabwe/education

11. *Online learning opportunities for rural learning ecologies*

Nkosilathi Sibanda & Mpumelelo Ncube

Introduction

Online Learning encompasses a range of technologies such as the worldwide web, email, chat groups and texts, audio and video conferencing delivered over computer networks to impart education (Kwon & Park, 2017). Anderson (2008) defines online learning as a subset of distance education that has always been concerned with providing access to an educational experience that is at least more flexible in time and space than campus based education. It helps the learner to manage their learning at their own pace and convenience. Online Education requires a great deal of resources and careful planning. In this, educators act as facilitators rather than transmitters of content knowledge and Information Communication Technologies (ICTs) are regarded as a resource reservoir that enhances the learning experience of students (Loannou, Demetriou, & Mama, 2014). Learners learn by using e-learning tools which are available to all. The internet is a key resource utilised by the students to aid their study as well as a means for delivering learning material.

Online learning has changed the face of learning through its innovative and interactive content delivery and is proving to be relatively appealing to students (Kwon & Park, 2017). These systems enable students to determine and process their learning styles, content, aim, current knowledge and individual skills. Online discussions carefully monitored by instructors promote constructed knowledge through activities such as sharing, negotiating, elaborating, evaluating, (Loannou, Demetriou, & Mama, 2014) and facilitates students' higher order thinking (Kwon & Park, 2017).

The interaction in online forums helps students to exchange different points of view on a subject (Duran, Cornejo, & Flores, 2017). One of the advantages of online forums following Arasaratnam& Northcote (2017) is having time for reasoned comments, which in the face-to-face sessions may not always be possible. The interaction among the various components is essential to promote mediated learning (Bates, 2019).The learning platform opens a new stage which exceeds the traditional space-time to motivate and make available to students, colleagues and various groups, a set of instructional options. The interaction in online forums helps students to exchange different points of view on a subject (Duran, Cornejo, & Flores, 2017). One of the advantages of online forums is having time for reasoned comments which in the face-to-face sessions may not always be possible. E-Learning platforms seek to exploit the most valuable aspects of the training scenarios to become open spaces for the intellectual and the communication resources available. It is a self-directed activity, and is a learner centred approach, which enables learners to develop autonomy and independence in their study habits. It also shifts the responsibility for learning them.

Integrating Information Communication Technology (ICT) in learning

Technology is used more widely especially for the purposes of learning and teaching. This is simply because it offers many tools that can be used in classrooms to improve teaching and learning Hussain, Morgan, and Al-Jumeily (2011). Rosnaini and Mohd (2008) define ICT integration as the process of determining where and how technology fits in the teaching and learning process.

Chigona and Chigona (2010) argue that the benefits of using ICT in teaching are yet to be realised in developing countries. According to Chigona and Chigona (2010), insufficient training on the use of ICT in teaching, inadequate technical support for teachers were some of the factors that limited teacher integration of ICT in teaching. This is supported by Balume, Edmore, and Simbarashe (2018) in their studies done in South Africa concluded that poor training, negative attitudes among others affect integration of ICT. Rok (2018) notes that teachers should have ICT competencies and pedagogical abilities to integrate ICT effectively in teaching and learning. Palagolla and Wickramarachchi (2019) argue that teachers' ICT competency, ICT infrastructure, leadership support and school planning are critical elements for effective integration of ICT in Learning. United Nations Educational, Scientific and Cultural Organisation (UNESCO) (2011) concludes that successful integration of ICT in teaching and learning depends on teachers' ability to structure the learning environment.

State of Online learning in Africa

Africa is in various stages of development hence there is no reliable data on the state of internet learning in Africa. Many countries have made a lot of investments in training teachers, equipping schools with internet and related computer technology. This has not helped a lot as Kanyemba, Nhongo, and Kanyemba (2021) note that promotion of technology in the school system especially in Zimbabwe is one area which has not been moving fast enough. This might be a result of lack of resources and absence of an integrated vision or strategy.

There is need for government to advance inclusive knowledge societies taking into account internet universality principles adopted by UNESCO General Assembly that advocates for human rights based Open and accessible internet for all (World Bank, 2020). Progress varies from one country to another. Improved broadband connectivity in countries like South Africa and Egypt has enhanced learners and teachers access to the internet which is a positive step towards attaining (SDG4) Sustainable Development Goal number 4 (Oroma, Wang, & Fredrick, 2012). Despite the promises and significant penetration of mobile phones across the continent, mobile learning did not take pace in Africa because of high communication costs, low bandwidth, low penetration of smart phones and absence of locally relevant applications on mobile phones (Oroma, Wang, & Fredrick, 2012). Education around the globe has taken a new trajectory it is upon schools to embrace new learning methods and enhance access to education. Oroma, Wang, and Fredrick (2012) show that for African countries in general, ICT infrastructure is poorly developed and is unevenly accessed. Internet access must be right for learners and their lecturers in this kind of environment.

State of online learning in Zimbabwe

E-learning has become the main teaching and learning modality (Gora, 2020). According to Gora (2020) the impact of the lock down has necessitated e-learning as a good option if everybody is able to access it. Major problems are access to internet network and data costs hence it is only good when everybody is able to use it or access it. Many students residing in rural and other remote areas find it difficult to access e-learning platforms. They have to travel long distances to do so, endangering their safety and wellbeing in the process (Gora, 2020).

According to Gora (2020), a sizeable proportion do not have smart phones and laptops which are needed to access internet and to utilise e-learning tools.

Online is imposing the social differences between students. Being financially unstable is now a hindrance to most students exercising their right to education. Erratic power supply was cited as another major challenge (Gora, 2020). Electricity is seldom available during the day. Students have to study during the night and are often unable to keep up with their academic workloads.

Gora (2020) implores that students living with disabilities argue that e-learning is inaccessible for many of them as Students that have impaired vision often cannot access and use content provided through WhatsApp or other e-learning platforms. The Ministry of Higher and Tertiary Education, Innovation, Science and Technology said that institutions are working with service providers to come up with long lasting affordable solutions to network costs (Gora, 2020).

They have also received offers for free access to Wi-fi in Telecom Edu Zones as well as cheaper Wifi solutions for students across the board and lecturers and teachers at home from Liquid Telecom (The Herald June 9 2020). Net One also offered to provide data access to all institutions. According to Mudzingwa (2020), solutions to the education crisis posed by COVID-19 must ensure two key human rights, which are learners' right to education with equal measure applied to their right to health.

Telecoms giant Econet Wireless Zimbabwe has taken the lead as it introduced online learning tailor-made for Zimbabwe's education system TecZim, l. (2020). Through its subsidiary Cassava Smartech, Econet launched Akello Digital Classroom8 and Akello E-Library, which allow students to have online classes and access to hundreds of school curriculum books online approved by the Zimbabwe School Examinations Council and international examination boards (TecZim, l., 2020). According to TecZim, 1. (2020) rural schools can make use of Skype and email to foster distance learning, which can be adopted to further learning. Zoom and Google Classroom are also among the many platforms recommended by UNESCO.

The Parliamentary Portfolio Committee on Primary and Secondary Education has also recommended basic e-learning initiatives readily available and already in use such as the WhatsApp Messenger application, where a parent can help a child follow through educational modules (Mudzingwa, 2020).The government urges people to look at the opportunities brought by e-learning with or without COVID-19. Investing in information technology helps children, even those who have been walking long distances to school (Mudzingwa, 2020). Mudzingwa (2020) argues that several school teachers have opened classes through WhatsApp Messenger groups with parents, in which work is given to pupils through their parents. At secondary schools, classes are conducted either directly with students or through their relatives via the same social media platform. These services should be extended to rural communities with the help of the government and relevant ministries.

In Zimbabwe everything has changed due to corona virus. All services have gone on-line hence the need for government and all stake holders to come up with sustainable pricing for data and internet access in Zimbabwe (TecZim, l. 2020). According to TecZim, l. (2020), the profit pricing by network providers produces in-equality which does not do good for the public and the marginalised learners who barely have no physical teaching instructions are completely shut out from learning. Teacher organisation such as Amalgamated Rural Teachers Union of Zimbabwe (ARTUZ) say that on-line is fuelling in-equality among learners. UNICEF is working extensively with the Ministry of Primary and Secondary Education to develop alternative learning platforms which include the development of radio and television lessons (Matimaire, 2019). The scholar further assert that Econet introduced an e-learning service with discounted data bundles for teachers and learners to continue learning in the comfort of their home.

Online learning comes as another burden to students who are already in an impoverished state and suggestions have been made for zero rating for websites. This is noted by Zinyemba, Nhongo, and Zinyemba (2021) who argues that both learners and teachers have challenges with maintaining online platforms as this was something that both parties were not prepared to make use of. Mandoga, Matswetu, and Mhishi (2013) posited that online learning has a number of challenges in many African countries that needed to be addressed at national level. This will help the learners and teachers to comfortably make use of the electronic platforms for educational purposes.

World Bank and other corporates are trying free education through remote learning via radio, television, internet and social media. According to UNESCO (2020), 89 % of learners in Sub Saharan Africa do not have household computers and 82 % lack internet access. Traditional tools such as radio and television can be difficult to access for many. The government is encouraging the use of digital platforms to provide remote learning services, for example Higher Life Foundation has provided free access to its online Ruzivo learning platform, though uptake has been limited (World Bank, 2020). In its Education Sector Response Strategy, the Ministry of Education plans to focus on the continuity of learning by providing remote learning services via radio programming, digital online resources and the distribution of supplementary learning materials (Zimbabwe Education Custer, 2020).

Though radio and television ownership are wide spread, learning via these channels would exclude significant portions of the population especially in rural areas where there is no connectivity thus Machingura (2016) is of the view that most rural schools in Zimbabwe are marginalised. Faced with these challenges, there is the need to understand and effect change of attitudes of both students and tutors or teachers. The persistence of these challenges and lack of knowledge about the use of ICT in education hinders readiness and utilization of online learning. This view is supported by Zinyemba, Nhongo and Zinyemba who argue that online learning is possible where there is enough infrastructure that is used for ICT like electrification and internet connectivity which is a thing not found in most Zimbabwean schools. There is need to expedite online learning, which was recommended by Dr. Caiphus Nziramasanga back in 1999. The Nziramasanga Commission, recommended the need to digitalise education (Nziramasanga, 1999).

Former president Robert Mugabe launched the National Schools Computerisation Programme. Since then, the Ministry of Primary and Secondary Education has only managed to install internet facilities in 50 % of the country's primary and secondary schools (Matimaire, 2019). The government signed a memorandum of understanding (MoU) with three contractors, namely ZARNet, e-Learning Solutions and the country's third-largest mobile operator TelOne Zimbabwe. ZARNet was tasked to install internet facilities and services to 1,300 schools at a cost of USD1.1 million, while TelOne was allocated 2,500 schools (Matimaire, 2019). All this was done in an effort to bridge the digital divide.

Learner perspcetives

Online earning has given learners a flexible working environment where most of the learning is self -paced as compared to physical learning. This view is supported by Berge and Giles (2008) who argue that online learning has the potential to deliver learning tailored to the specific needs of learners. Students can access online materials anytime and can use the internet to access up to date and relevant materials (Anderson, 2008). Such a scenario helps learners as they are able to research from their peers and other platforms. Zinyemba, Nhongo, and Zinyemba (2021) argue that learners do not have necessary gadgets for online learning. As a result, learners have not been keen on exploring digital platforms to their benefit.

Content delivered is devoid of irrelevant material that is synonymous with face-to-face teaching. Efforts by teachers is to provide understandable concepts that are broken down into simple segments that can be understood with minimum explanations. This view is supported by Anderson (2008) who posits that online learning systems can be used to determine learners' needs and to assign suitable materials for learners to select from and achieve their learning goal. The tendency by some teachers to compel learners to copy a textbook as notes has no place. The push factor to synthesise learning material by teachers is the time factor, especially for examination classes.

Online learning does not limit a learner to one instructor especially for senior learners who are revising for examination. Coman et al. (2020) allude that online learning enables learners to easily share information, state their challenges and receive feedback. Therefore, they have more options that simplify the learning process. What is more intriguing with this kind of learning is parental involvement. Parents become part and parcel of the academic development and the experience of the learning environment assisting and in relating to the challenges of school as well as appreciation of their role as parents together with other stakeholders in the education sector.

Teacher observations

Online learning gives teachers time to refine their teaching materials as well as skills because of the nature of the platforms. This view is supported by Anderson (2008) who posits that tutoring can be done anytime, anywhere and online materials can be updated. This means educational material is refined to relevancy so that it does not become bulky or too heavy for learners. There is also the cost factor to consider. The result is refined material that can be stored electronically to be retrieved as and when required.

Besides the financial rewards that come with e-learning, WhatsApp platform enables a teacher to multi-task. This is supported by Anderson (2008) who argues that in online learning there is no time zones thus students can access online materials anytime. This is facilitation to a number of classes at the same time, significantly reducing time spent on teaching. With the emergence of Information Computer Technology (ICTs), a lot of information is available on finger tips and thus Anderson (2008) posits that it is easier for teachers to direct learners to appropriate information based on their needs. Since most schools use hard copy textbooks, the textbook sharing ration is high, soft copies are easily obtained, cheaper and accessible to learners. Note writing on boards and dictating notes to learners was a cumbersome task that has been replaced with sharing notes on soft copies. It has enabled innovation and ingenuity from facilitators with the best tools to use with learners of diverse backgrounds, technological understanding as well as tying to adapt to a learner's disposition or environment at home (Anderson, 2008).

According to Zinyemba, Nhongo, and Zinyemba (2021) teachers complained that the internet bundle is beyond the reach of many and learners depended on night bundle that was affordable. This make it difficult for learner-teacher interaction. However, online teaching is costly hence most teachers resort to WhatsApp which is relatively cheaper as compared to other online learning platforms like Google Classroom and Zoom. Evaluating learning progress then becomes a challenge when there is a gap in feedback. When online learning is optional, it is a challenge to a teacher because a learner may choose to sit at home or due to financial challenges, this supports Moore (2000) who noted that in Africa most of people use basic internet service such as email and WhatsApp due to lack of financial resources. It will mean that when face to face lessons are conducted to compliment online learning, learners are at different levels.

Most teachers in Zimbabwe do not have the adequate knowledge on how to use the online learning programmes. This view is supported by Zinyemba, Nhongo, and Zinyemba (2021) who argue that teachers reported online learning to be a challenge as they did not know how to make use of learning platforms that were being used for online learning. In other words, they lack appropriate computer skills. Based on the responses from the questionnaires, the challenges identified by teachers were: poor infrastructure, constant power outages, inadequate computer laboratories, and poor Internet services (Zinyemba, Nhongo, and Zinyemba, 2021). Some teachers felt that availability of computers at home is an issue, hence most learners will depend on free school resources.

Online learning and human rights

The COVID-19 pandemic has critically affected the global education sector, potentially compromising the right to education of over 1.2 billion children (Daniels, 2020). The right to education has been infringed following school closures to combat the spread of COVID-19. Majority of developed countries have turned to online or electronic learning aided with digital technologies, hence preserving learners' human rights to education and health. Daniels (2020) cites Japan, Italy, China and the United Arab Emirates as some of the countries that are arguably doing well in education delivery. However, in Africa, the situation is different. In Sub-Saharan Africa, Zimbabwe is a typical example where debate is raging over the need for government to set up human and financial resources to address affordability, access and availability of infrastructure, devices, internet and content to aid e-learning (Mudzingwa, 2020). As Mudzingwa (2020) notes, the COVID-19 outbreak forced schools to prematurely close. Technically, both teachers and learners lost teaching and learning time. As much as it is a bid to ensure the right to health, Covid-19 induced lockdowns are being done at the expense of the right to health.

The principles of the African Declaration give Zimbabwe a solid model to adopt when it implements Online-learning, considering that various shortcomings have been identified.

Mukomama, Chimhenga and Mpofu (2021) note that the current situation, Zimbabwe can't fully embrace online learning, as it would prejudice and be discriminatory to persons without internet access or those who cannot afford access to the internet. They allude that students in rural and marginalised communities do not have the capacity in terms of hardware (mobile phones or other devices that facilitate access to the internet), infrastructure and finances to access the Online learning portals. Some cannot even afford to purchase the subsidised or discounted data offered by the internet service providers for online learning (Mukomama, Chimhenga, and Mpofu 2021). In light of the above, students' access to information continues to be infringed during this time. Data charges, internet coverage and technical skills required by teachers and students to utilise digital platforms and tools for online learning remains a stumbling block towards the advancement of the education technology revolution (Mukomama, Chimhenga and Mpofu 2021). MISA Zimbabwe as a lobby and regulatory body does spearhead campaigns such as a #DataMustFall campaign against telecommunication companies that peg data charges beyond the reach of many.

Other than WhatsApp, online-learning is out of reach for many students due to challenges with internet connectivity, let alone affordability. It has limited applicability due to limited power in rural Zimbabwe coupled with incessant power cuts in major cities (Matimaire, 2020). According to Matimaire (2020) more than 65 % of secondary schools are not electrified, while more than 75 % of primary schools are not electrified. Several schools have no single computer or laptop.

The Zimbabwean Constitution has a declaration of rights, which suffices as a foundational basis for digital rights. With reference to Article 19 of United Nations Human Rights Charter, there should be no demarcation as to rights that are exercised online and those that are exercised offline (World Bank, 2020). In terms of a resolution by the UN Human Rights Council, the same rights exercised and protected offline should also be exercised and protected online. Taking note of the supremacy of the Constitution, the foundational framework is present for the exercise of digital rights in Zimbabwe. Runyanga (2020) highlighted the need to address challenges to do with Online learning from a legal and administrative perspective, taking advantage of the recently gazetted Cybersecurity and Data Protection Bill that must give direct impetus to the protection and promotion of human rights online. The objective is therefore to ensure that online spaces are safe for communication and for transactions as posited by Runganga (2020). Seeing that children or students will be resorting to the internet for their learning, research included, there is definitely a need to ensure that the online space is safe.

Strategies to improve online learning in rural learning ecologies

Rural communities in Africa have little or no access to online education hence the government should provide internet services to rural areas especially in schools. The provision of internet services will enable the introduction of online learning to the disadvantaged rural learners (Dube, 2020). It is the mandate of the government through the ministry of education to improve quality of education in rural learning ecologies. This can be done through partnership with other stakeholders. Dube (2020) asserts that online learning is hampered by the unavailability of connectivity in some rural contexts. According to Dube (2020) this is a serious challenge which African governments address and invest a lot so as to improve the quality of education in rural communities.

According to World Bank (2020), students who are able to benefit from online learning are those who are competent in gadgets used in online learning and who have enough financial resources to support their online learning. It is against this background that the governments should strongly support online learning with support from stakeholders like UNICEF. Computer literacy campaigns should be vigorously carried out in most rural communities as this will minimise challenges associated with computer literacy (World Bank, 2020). These campaign activities should be coupled with the distribution in rural communities of online learning tools like laptops and desk top computers.

To improve quality of education in rural learning ecologies, there is need to provide learners with online education services like web conferencing. Rao et al. (2011) posit that web conferencing when incorporated into the education system will address challenges experienced by rural learners. According to Rao et al. (2011), web conferencing consists of a virtual meeting room with white board on which the online learning instructor can make presentations. The system allows participants to communicate with others in the virtual room by clicking on an icon that activates their microphone. The learners can communicate through text messages since the facility has a text-chat feature and this makes interaction of learners and the learning instructor possible. Rao, Eady, and Edelen-Smith (2011) allude that learning instructors can also place learners in online breakout icons making it possible to make sizable group discussions. These groups can be put back together after clicking a button.

There is also need to introduce online schools in rural communities to cater for rural learners. These online schools can be administered at provincial or district level. There should be funding for this type of online service. The teachers or instructors who provide teaching service should be employed by the relevant ministries. The assessment of learners should be done nationally through responsible examination boards. This idea of online schools is supported by Gemin et al. (2018) who assert that online schools are accountable for learners' academic achievement in the same ways as all other public schools. Online schools are imperative for rural communities because at times learners have no alternative because of limited number of schools (Gemin et al., 2018).

In areas where there is internet challenges, television and radio online learning can be adopted as a strategy that will improve learning process in rural ecologies. Policy makers should establish special television and radio stations with good reception at provincial or district centres which will broadcast learning lessons. This is supported by Urdan and Weggen (2000) who argue that online learning can result in a higher retention rate due to learning materials being personalised and reflecting different learning styles. These media gadgets (televisions and radios) are widely accessible and less expensive and most learners can have access to lessons. Also of importance is the establishment of community libraries equipped with internet which will enable learners to do their research. The libraries should be free of charge or made more affordable so that the majority of learners access these facilities (Urdan & Weggen, 2000). Internet cafes can also be established in rural communities and these should be government subsidised so that learners afford accessibility. This will enhance the learning process in these disadvantaged communities.

The government must scrap duties on ICTs in order to lower the prices of digital devices such as desktop computers, laptops, tablets and smart phones to make them available at affordable prices, considering that they play a key role for one to connect to the internet (Runganga, 2020). There must be a relevant Online-learning course that aligns with the syllabi. The scholar further notes that there is the need to develop digital literature accessible online and offline as well as methods that enable students to access that material on-line. Mutisya (2020) recommends training support for teachers on subject specific ICT technologies and their use in teaching and learning in order to influence their attitude to use them positively. The scholar further recommends that School Heads should be trained on how to monitor and support the use of ICT in teaching and learning.

Lastly and most importantly, there is a need to align laws that infringe internet use to the 2013 Constitution and ensure that the Cyber security

Bill conforms to Southern African Development Community (SADC), African Union and African Declaration principles (Runganga 2020). The scholar further suggests that in order to improve online learning there is need to enhance and improve the availability of internet networks and power across the country and bring necessary infrastructure to rural and remote areas. There is again need to develop remote learning solutions for students living with disabilities and engage students through surveys and consultations to find ways to fully embrace online teaching and learning in the rural ecologies.

Summary

Online learning has become the global face of education. It has presented a plethora of educational interventions that have simmered the effects of Covid-19 in Africa and Zimbabwe in general. The government has come up with legislative support as well as policy guides for the development of online learning through creating a conducive environment for stake holder participation. To achieve holistic online education, there should be a bridge to close inequalities propagated by online education and socio-economic factor as well as inclusion of the disabled. Gapes in rural spaces should be covered by ICTs and face to face learning and as well as blended education in Zimbabwe. Technology is evolving and with globalization, massive investment in infrastructure and education has to be accelerated so that no child is left behind. In addition, innovation is imminent for online learning in rural ecologies.

References

Anderson, T. (2008). *The theory and practice of online learning.* Second edition. AU Press. Canada. Athbasca University.

Arasaratnam, L. A., & Northcote, M. (2017). Community in online higher education: Challenges and opportunities. *The Electronic Journal of E-learning, 15*(2), 188–198.

Balume, A., Edmore, N., & Simbarashe, M. (2018). *Teaching and learning of physical education in South Africa.* A case of Johannesburg East Cluster primary schools in Gauteng Province. *International Journal of Sports Exercise and Health Research, 2*(1), 88–92.

Bates, A. W. (2020). *Advice to those who are about to online because of corona virus.* March 9. https://www.tonybates.ca/2020/03/09

Berge, Z. L., & Giles, L. (2008). *Implementing and sustaining learning in the workplace. International Journal of Web-Based Learning and Teaching Technologies, 3*(3), 44–53.

Chigona, A. and Chigona, W. (2010). *An investigation of factors affecting the use of ICT for teaching in the Western Cape Schools.* 18th European Conference on Information Systems: ECIS 2010.

Chinenga, S. (2017). *Transforming digital learning and teaching in Institutions of Higher Learning in Zimbabwe.* The case of Zimbabwe Open University. Bulawayo. ZOU.

Coman, C.,Tiru, L. G., Mesesan-Schmitz, L., Stancu, C., & Bularca, M. C. (2020). Online teaching and learning in higher education during corona virus pandemic: Students' perspective.

Daniels, L. (2020, May 20). Reopening of schools during Covid-19: *How other countries have fared. IOL.* https://www.iol.co.za/news/politics/reopening-of-schools-during-covid-19-how-other-countries-have-fared-48212849

Dube, B. (2020). Rural online learning in the context of covid 19 in South Africa: Evoking an inclusive education approach. *Multidisciplinary journal of educational research, 10*(2), 135–157. doi 10.4471/remie.2020.5607.

Gemin, B., Smith, B., Vashaw, L., Watson, J., & Harrington, C. (2018). *Digital learning Strategies for rural America: A scan of policy and practice in k 12 education.*

Gora, P. (2000). Students say online learning is not accessible to everyone. University work news. Africa. World news,com.

Hussain, A. J., Morgan, S., & Al-Jumeily, D. (2011). *How does ICT affect teaching and learning within school education.* In Developments in E- Systems Engineering. (DESE), 2011. 250–254.

Kwon, K., & Park, S. J. (2017). Effects of discussion representation: Comparisons between social and cognitivediagrams. *Instructional Science, 45*(4), 469–491. doi:https://doi.org/10.1007/s11351-017-9412-6

Loannon, A., Demetriou, S., & Mama, M. (2014). Exploring factors influencing collaborative knowledge construction in online discussions: student facilitation and quality of initial postings. *The American Journal of Distance, 28*, 183–195.

Mandoga, E., Matswetu, V., & Mhishi, M. (2013). Challenges and opportunities in harnessing computer technology for teaching and learning. A case of five Schools in Makoni East District. *International Journal of Humanities and Social Science, 3*(1), 105–112.

Matimaire, K. (2019, September 20). 50% of Zim Schools Connected to WiFi – Govt. *The Industry and Trade Expert.* https://theindustrytrade.com/2019/09/20/50-of-zim-schools-connected-to-wifi-govt/7

Matimaire. (2020). Digital-shy Zimbabwe's schools feel the brunt of COVID-19. *Internet Governance Forum,* 2020 June 3.

Matimaire, K. (2020). *Interview with Takavafira Zhou, president of the Progressive Teachers Union of Zimbabwe,* 2020 May 28.

Mudzingwa, F. (2020, May 28). Covid 19 lockdown and higher education. Time to look at a unpreparedness as a governance issue? https/www.ukfiet.org/2020/access to digital learning during Covid 19 closures compounding educational inequality.

Mukomama, S., Chimhenga, S., & Mpofu, J. (2021). Zimbabwe in Covid-19 lockdown: The benefits and shortcomings of online learning in open distance. *International Journal of Research and Innovation in Social Science. IJRISS, 5*(3), 2021 March, ISSN 2454–6156. www.rsisinternational.org.141.

Mutisya, S. M. (2020). Integration of Information Communication Technology (ICT) in teaching: The underpinning factors among Kenya's Primary School Teachers. *Journal of Learning for Development, 7*(2), 174–189.

Nziramasanga, C. T. (1999). The Presidential Commission for inquiry into education and training. National Report of the Republic of Zimbabwe. Harare: Government of Zimbabwe.

Oroma, j, O., Wanga, H., & Fredrick, N. (2012). *Challenges of e-learning in developing countries.* The Ugandan experience. In proceedings of INTED conference, 2012 March 5th–7th. Doi: http://dx.doi.org/10.13140/2.1.47.54.1448

Palagolla, W., & Wickramarachchi, R. (2019). *Effective integration of ICT to facilitate the secondary education in Sri Lanka.*

Rao, K., Eady, M., & Edelen-Smith, P. (2011). *Creating virtual classrooms for rural and remote communities. Phi Delta, Kappan, 92*(6), 22–27.

Rosnaini, M., & Mohd, A. H. I. (2008). Factors influencing ICT integration in the classroom: Implication to teacher education. EABR and TLC Conference Proceeding, Austria.

Runyanga, N. (2020, June 6). Cybersecurity Bill: Joining global cybercrime fight. *The Herald.* https://www.Herald.co.zw 2020/6/6/cyber-security-bill-joining-global-cybercrime-fight.

TechZim, l. (2020). EducationContentFor1stMonth. *Techzim* https://www.techzim.co.zw/2020/05/cassava-launches-akello-digital-classroom-with-free-education-content-for-1st-month

The Herald. (2020, June 9). Boost for learners as Cassava Edutech launches an e-library. *The Herald.* https://www.herald.co.zw/boost-for-learners-as-cassava-edutech-launches-an-e-libraryhttps://en.unesco.org/covid19/educationresponse/solutionsZimbabwe

UNESCO. (2011). *UNESCO ICT competency framework for teachers.* Paris: UNESCO.

Urdan, T., & Weggen, C. (2000). *Corporate e-learning: Exploring a new frontier.* Washington: Hambrecht and co.

World Bank. (2020). *Remote learning and Covid 19. The use of educational technologies at scale across an education system as a result of massive school closings in response to the Covid 19 pandemic to enable distance education and online learning.* Revised draft 2020, March 16. Retrieved from. https://documents.Worldbank.org/curated/en/266811584-657843186/pdf/Rapidresponse-briefing-note-remote-learning-and-covid19.outbreaks.pdf.

Zinyemba, L., Nhongo, K., & Zinyemba, A. (2021). Covid-19 induced online learning: The Zimbabwean experience. *African Journal of Social Work, 11*(4). 223–230.

12. *Digitalization and learning opportunities in Zimbabwean rural ecologies*

NDONDO SHEPHERD, CHRISTOPHER NDLOVU &
NDONDO SAMKELISO

Introduction

Even before the COVID-19 era which gave the digitalization of educational provisions an impetus, the world was gradually drifting into the technological mode of operation (Mhlanga & Moloi, 2020; Mukute, Francis, Burt, & Souza, 2020). The multiplication of technological gadgets in homes and institutions in recent years heralds the approaching Fourth Industrial Revolution (4IR) (Francis, Burt, & Souza, 2020; Ndung'u & Signé, 2019). While previous revolutions focused on the liberation of the mind and made mass production possible, the 4IR is characterized by the fusion of the digital and biological worlds, as well as the growing utilization of new technologies such as artificial intelligence, cloud computing, robotics, 3D printing, the Internet of things and advanced wireless technologies, among others (Xu, David, & Kim, 2018). These technologies impact all disciplines, economies and industries, bringing a new way of thinking and doing things (Ndung'u & Signé, 2019; Xu et al., 2018). The unforeseen effects of the COVID-19 pandemic made the use of technological devices in education more urgent than before. A succession of lockdown measures made the use of online learning pedagogies the most viable option (Mhlanga & Moloi, 2020; Mukute et al., 2020). Though there was reluctance in the use of digital platforms by teachers and learners in anticipation of going back to the traditional face to face pedagogies after the containment of COVID-19, the prolonged presence of the pandemic made digital learning a reality. As the world is turning technological, the use of digital platforms in education is merited for preparing the young generation for the digital world. The use of digital technologies allows for easy sharing of content, student-centeredness, convenient teaching and learning settings, flexible assessment procedures among other merits (Khan & Khan, 2019; Rapanta, Botturi, Goodyear, Guàrdia, & Koole, 2020). Though digital learning pedagogies are showing some positive results in some urban schools which are well supported in terms of technological devices and skilled teachers, the same is not happening in the historically disadvantaged rural ecosystems owing to a host of hindrances. The rural-urban divide in educational provision is felt globally but it becomes more pronounced in developing countries (The Foundation for Blended and Online Learning, 2018). Most schools in rural Zimbabwe are poorly resourced, teachers and learners have neither the gadgets nor the knowledge to interact on digital platforms (Msila, 2013; Daimary, 2020; Mukuna & Aloka, 2020). Given this scenario, this chapter, therefore, endeavoured to explore the opportunities that can come out of adopting digital technologies. The experiences of teachers and learners in using digital platforms in rural areas were examined and finally, teacher and learner support was recommended for the enhancement of quality digital learning in rural spaces.

Opportunities of adopting online teaching and learning

The fast-approaching technological age is affecting the way people communicate, work and govern (Erickson & Smallc, 2013). The Internet has brought a magnificent change in the use of computers and communications thereby creating greater learning opportunities by having access to a large amount of information with benefits in terms of time and cost savings (Hussain, Wang, & Rahim, 2013). To get maximum benefits from this new digital environment, citizens need to possess not only skills and abilities related to the use of technological tools, but also knowledge regarding the norms and practices of appropriate usage (Erickson, & Smallc, 2013). The dawn of the digital era is expected to improve human life in many aspects, as such, benefits abound for embracing online teaching and learning platforms. Digital learning platforms are associated with a revolution in pedagogy and assessment procedures, easy sharing of discipline content and preparing learners for the technological world. Furthermore, online platforms offer a lot of opportunities to reach out to the public and give way for learner and teacher interaction (Muhtaseb, 2015).

Digitalized teaching and learning are credited for learner centeredness in education, a popular approach in education that focuses on the needs of the learner (Rapanta et al., 2020; Adedoyin & Soykan, 2020). Unlike the traditional face to face mode of delivery, online teaching and learning allow active participation by learners through navigating online platforms. This participatory learning approach quickly enhances the technical skills needed in the digital world. These skills of the 'information age' acquired by learners will help them effectively use digital resources to resolve gaps in knowledge (Erickson, & Smallc, 2013; Okon, 2015). Child-centred learning goes together with individualized learning, an approach in which learners are not treated under one blanket but rather as individuals with their unique strengths and weaknesses. Through digital learning platforms, the teacher understands his/her learners on a one to one basis giving way to immediate remediation and extension work. In support of the foregoing argument, results of the study by Ramraj and Marimuthu (2019) revealed that digital platforms were largely favourable in facilitating the learning process, with constructive feedback on the use of technology-enhanced tools, especially surveys, journals, videos, discussion forums, blogs, concerning and ensuring interactivity as well as an enriched learning experience for all. In addition, meaningful interaction among learners can easily be facilitated using online teaching and learning platforms, which may include group activities and pair work (Muhtaseb, 2015).

The use of online teaching and learning platforms facilitates easy sharing of different subject content for learners as they connect to a global community of students, professionals, institutions, and organizations hence their experience is broadened (Muhtaseb, 2015; Lawless, 2014). It should be noted that technological devices can be used with different modes of educational delivery and management of educational activities for learners. This could be face-to-face in a classroom, online, or a combination of both (Hussain et al., 2013). Of great importance to note is that digital learning platforms facilitate distance learning and provide means to learners to access learning material any time and at any place (Hussain et al., 2013; Maatuk, Elberkawi, Aljawarneh, & Rashaideh, 2021). This becomes critical especially in times of natural calamities like the COVID-19 situation in which we are today. This period is characterized by a succession of lockdown measures that prohibit the traditional face to face mode of education delivery.

During the COVID-19 lockdown periods, various technologies were used in educational delivery hence educational activities switched to remote learning (online learning) thereby enhancing the potential of driving the education sector into the 4IR era (Mhlanga & Moloi, 2020). The use of digital learning platforms, therefore, allows meaningful teaching and learning to go on even during the COVID lockdown periods as they offer convenience in terms of the setting where teaching and learning are taking place. In addition, many digital technology tools have been adapted to support learning activities with discussion forums, wikis, websites, and newsletters being some of the information tools employed (Muhtaseb, 2015) while emails, video conferencing, instant messaging and newsgroups are used as communication tools. The use of online learning offers opportunities for interaction not only among learners and teachers but among various communities and also managing other aspects of the educational process; educational staff, employees, and researchers can easily share ideas and resources encouraging collaboration and interaction across geographical locations (Muhtaseb, 2015; Lawless, 2014).

Assessment of learners' performance is a critical aspect towards the achievement of quality education hence the need for monitoring learners' performance during and after the learning program. A revolution in pedagogy leading to the use of online platforms would mean a corresponding change to digital assessment procedures. The most distinct forms of assessment are formative and summative (Oldfield, Broadfoot, Sutherland, & Timmis, 2013; Blundell, 2021). Formative assessment is done during the programme so that remedial measures can be instituted while summative assessment comes at the end of the programme usually inform of a written examination. The COVID-19 pandemic has made it difficult to accomplish these two types of assessment, especially summative assessment. To this end, continuous assessment procedures began to gain popularity in some parts of the world. This is a way of assessing learners without waiting for the 'traditional examination'. Academic performance is continuously recorded for each student or pupil in various cumulative folders for future use (Obi & Obineli, 2019). Digital continuous assessment has been commended for its flexibility and capacity for immediate feedback provision (Khan, 2019; Rapanta et al., 2020; Adedoyin & Soykan, 2020). This form of assessment brings high prospects of achieving the whole process of teaching and assessment online. The world is in a state of transition, the 4IR is imminent hence the induction of learners into the new culture is critical.

Using digital platforms in teaching and learning prepares learners for the new world of technologies. To be 'digitally literate' entails the acquisition of some basic aspects needed for human function. This includes issues of cognitive authority, safety and privacy, creative, ethical, and responsible use and reuse of digital media, among other essentials. On the other hand, a lack of digital literacy increasingly implicates one's full potential of being a competent student, an empowered employee or an engaged citizen (Erickson & Smallc, 2013). It is evident that during this time of COVID-19, digital learning platforms have played a major role in cushioning the effect of this pandemic on educational activities by serving as the only platform for instructional design, delivery and assessment (Adedoyin & Soykan, 2020; Mhlanga & Moloi, 2020; Daimary, 2020). As the world is moving towards the 4IR, citizens need to be abreast with new technologies through the exposure to the digital world that facilitates information sharing, citizens gain the capacity to engage in meaningful community projects. Furthermore, in rural communities, people communicate to keep their values alive and relevant in a society that is constantly changing (Okon, 2015). A habit of holding on to past practices may be a barrier in the use of digital platforms but through continuous support, teachers and learners will end up realizing opportunities presented by online learning platforms.

The utilization of online teaching and learning platforms in rural Zimbabwe

As the 4IR is engulfing the world, nations are positioning themselves to embrace this new form of life. The digital world is coming with a lot of benefits to human life, however, these benefits are difficult to obtain for people in marginalized geographical spaces. Furthermore, the effects of the COVID-19 pandemic led to an abrupt shift to the digital world exposing a lot of deficiencies or unpreparedness in the use of digital in many parts of the world (Mukuna & Aloka, 2020; Mhlanga & Moloi, 2020). Although institutions have their peculiar challenges in the use of digital technologies, the historically disadvantaged rural ecosystems are the worst affected (Rundel & Salemink, 2021; Mukuna & Aloka, 2020; The Foundation for Blended and Online Learning, 2018). Infrastructural and human resources challenges are greater in rural schools hence affecting e-learning initiatives (Mavhemwa, Jekanyika, & Magomelo, 2017). In the United States, most rural areas are lagging in the use of digital technologies mainly because of a lack of technological gadgets and internet access (The Foundation for Blended and Online Learning, 2018). This has led to widening inequalities between the rural populace and their urban counterparts.

In Australia, research reveals that most rural areas are experiencing some barriers in the utilization of digital platforms. A case study of twenty rural Australian internet users reveals that rural communities suffer from limited access, inconsistent and unreliable services, and rural broadband plans' data restrictions and high prices, which are conceptualized as 'interrupted access' (Freeman & Middleton, 2020). The growing discrepancies of internet access disadvantages rural communities from benefitting from digital learning platforms. Though it is argued that digitalization can be of great benefit in uplifting the livelihoods of the rural populace, this is yet to be fully realized in the

German context. Digital inequalities continue to persist in terms of poor internet connectivity and poor funding of rural schools (Rundel & Salemink, 2021). The continual marginalization of the rural population will continue excluding them from opportunities associated with accessing digital technologies. African rural spaces have been subjects of exclusion in social services dating back from the colonial time hence post-colonial governments have prioritized the reduction of the rural-urban divide, a legacy of colonization (Msila, 2013). This would see rural areas accessing the basic social services enjoyed by their urban counterparts. Although an educational provision in rural areas was set to improve, up to now rural areas are greatly disadvantaged in many African countries (Mavhemwa et al., 2017). This shows itself in persistent academic underachievement by learners.

Rural areas are marginalized to the extent of being excluded from benefiting from online learning platforms. Educational institutions are characterized by poor network connectivity, a lack of digital devices and a lack of qualified teachers in digital technologies (Mukuna & Aloka, 2020; Mhlanga & Moloi, 2020). With the shift to online pedagogies becoming inevitable in the face of the COVID 19 pandemic, many learners in rural spaces now find themselves excluded from schooling and unable to access online resources, due to a lack of infrastructure, the unavailability of electricity and electronic gadgets, and a lack of qualified teachers who can assist with online learning (Dube, 2020). This further widens the gap between the urban and underprivileged rural populace in educational provision. The Zimbabwean scenario is not different from situations experienced in other African rural spaces. From the colonial period up to date, the Zimbabwean rural spaces have been excluded from many forms of development including quality educational provision (Mavhemwa et al., 2017). It is now a norm that national development processes start from urban areas then ends with the rural. The greater percentage of the Zimbabwean population resides in rural areas where most schools are not connected to the electrical power supply (Mavhemwa et al., 2017) hence the bulk of learners are excluded from digital learning.

The digitalization of education in Zimbabwe is quite evident in urban settings and the government is paying lip service to rural ecosystems. Although the government and non-governmental organizations have donated some digital devices mostly in form of computers to some rural schools, their utilization remains a nightmare owing to lack of internet connectivity (Mavuso & Duku, 2014). In places where there is broadband, communities are too poor to afford to buy gadgets and data bundles to access the internet (Freeman & Middleton, 2020). Furthermore, teachers who specialize in information technologies tend to shun rural areas because of the deplorable living standards and lack of resources. As such, the digitalization of the education system is widening the gap of inequalities between the rural inhabitants and their urban counterparts (Daimary, 2020). Poorly resourced unqualified teachers in rural spaces remain technophobic hence the benefits in the use of technological devices are difficult to achieve. A reference to an abrupt shift from face to face to online pedagogies necessitated by COVID-19 lockdown measures is an understatement for Zimbabwean rural communities as teaching and learning stopped in most rural areas leaving educationists in a dilemma whether to have learners proceed to the next levels or not (Mavhemwa et al., 2017). Some non-governmental organizations donated digital devices to Zimbabwean rural schools to enhance teaching and learning during the COVID-19 (Mukute et al., 2020). Though this move was applauded for taking online learning to rural areas, persistent challenges of poor teacher competencies constrained learners from fully benefiting.

Furthermore, parents could not assist learners to do their tasks online. A literature review of parental involvement in children's learning shows that some parents feel that they are not in a good position to take part in education as this is the duty of educators (Matshe, 2014; Mavuso & Duku, 2014; Mukute et al., 2020).This barrier to parental involvement becomes more pronounced in rural areas where parents are illiterate and had a bad experience of school (Matshe, 2014). In these areas, parents cannot assist their children in doing school work and it may sound naïve to think that children will get assistance from their parents on using online platforms. Notwithstanding the challenges encountered, the benefits from this noble project by the non-governmental organization cannot be ruled out, however, it turns to be 'a drop in the ocean' as the majority of rural learners remained locked out of school because they could not access online learning (Mukute et al., 2020). The fact that the majority of the Zimbabwean rural communities cannot do online learning, and did not have the necessary equipment and infrastructure to support online learning means that most learners are left behind (Mukute et al., 2020; Sibanda & Mathwasa, 2021).

Furthermore, cellular network systems are not reliable mainly because cellular operators concentrate in the urban centres where most network usage is (Mavhemwa et al., 2017). It cannot be debated that the COVID-19 pandemic brought a lot of disruptions to human life, however, this period has presented opportunities for many innovations in education (Maatuk et al., 2021). These innovations took the form of online learning from home through radio and television programs, however, despite this effort, the lack of network connectivity in most parts of rural Zimbabwe remains the main hindrance in accessing radio and television programs (Mukute et al., 2020).

The fortunate places with internet connectivity bore the brunt of regular power cuts rendering online learning inconsistent. This argument is supported by the findings from a study by Sibanda and Mathwasa (2021) on the effects of e-learning on the girl child in Matobo district in Zimbabwe. This study concluded that most of the rural secondary school female learners were excluded from education during lockdown due to poverty, unavailability of network or poor network coverage, lack of broadcast transmission services to enable them to access online lessons through the radio, lack of electricity, poor attendance due to lack of smartphones and data bundles, the performance of all household chores including herding of cattle and lack of cooperation from some parents (Sibanda & Mathwasa, 2021). In addition, the online teaching modalities were not suitable for all learners, for instance, radio lessons were not meant to cater for learners' unique needs, and learners with disabilities were not catered for (Mukute et al., 2020). Although learners from rural areas are excluded from digital platforms, they still need to get the necessary support if they are to be productive citizens in the 4IR era.

Teacher and learner support in the use of digital technology for quality education in rural ecosystems

The widening divide between the rural and urban population in educational provision is a known fact (Daimary, 2020; Dube, 2020). This mainly stems from historical legacies in different societies. The shift of teaching and learning pedagogies to digital platforms has further increased the educational divide between the rural and urban. For rural teachers and learners to be adequately supported, there is a need for political will to reduce the educational divide between the rural and urban populace (Freeman & Middleton, 2020). The digital divide is mainly due to poor infrastructure and resources in rural areas. Teachers with little or no competence in the use of digital technologies are normally deployed in rural areas (Mukuna &Aloka, 2020). The basic support teachers and learners can get in the use of digital technology are through increasing access to these platforms. This can be achieved through the effort by the government to provide reliable electric power in rural schools and homes, install internet facilities and avail affordable digital devices and data bundles (Mavhemwa et al., 2017).

The promise for a better life in rural settings has been rhetoric for many years by governments as they only managed to come up with well-articulated plans and policies without significant benefits for the rural population (Msila, 2013). Besides waiting for the central government to directly provide everything, rural communities should create platforms to share ideas on how to confront the problems they are facing (Antony-Newman, 2019). This includes the quest for quality education which can be achieved through accessing and effective use of digital platforms in rural schools. These community initiatives should include all stakeholders notably, parents/guardians, community leaders, non-governmental organizations, ministry of primary and secondary education, schools and the corporate world (Adedoyin & Soykan, 2020). These initiatives can play a crucial role in resource mobilization, facilitation of training of teachers in the use of digital devices and motivating rural communities in achieving the goal of quality education. The barriers faced in the use of digital technologies in teaching and learning can be a result of a negative school climate (Antony-Newman, 2019). The school environments should be welcoming for all stakeholders especially parents whose role in education is well documented (Antony-Newman, 2019; Masabo, Muchopa, & Kuoth, 2017). Teachers should play their professional duties while also appreciating that parents have a role to play. Having workshops with parents and teachers on parental involvement will create a warm relationship between the home and school hence both parties will see the need for purposeful engagement in assisting learners to acquire and use the digital learning platforms. Parental engagement with the school will also help create a positive home environment that is supportive of the school goals (Malone, 2017; Matshe, 2014).

In most cases, teachers deployed in rural areas are not competent in the use of technological devices as such, teachers need to be equipped with the skills through government or community initiative programmes (Blundell, 2021). A case in point is an initiative taken by Higher Life Foundation (a non-governmental organization) to train basic ICT skills to teachers in most rural areas in Zimbabwe (Mavhemwa et al., 2017). The foregoing argument points to the fact that successful online learning in rural ecologies can only be achieved through strong teacher and learner support. This support could be from government or community initiative programs which should see a mobilization of digital resources, teacher capacitation in digital skills and parental motivation for meaningful involvement in online learning activities for their children.

Conclusion

As the world is drifting into the 4IR era given an impetus by the COVID-19 calamity, the pedagogical transformation to match the period is inevitable. The use of digital learning platforms comes with many benefits which were not realized before. Through online teaching and learning, content for many disciplines can be easily shared among learners globally. Online pedagogies offer flexibility and convenience in remote teaching and learning. The unforeseen effects of the COVID-19 pandemic left online learning as one of the most viable modes of education delivery. Notwithstanding the merits that come with online learning platforms, the existing socioeconomic inequalities in many nations are widening due to this new model of education delivery. The historically disadvantaged rural spaces suffer in terms of infrastructure and resources to support online learning. The problems of network connectivity, lack of electricity, digital devices, competence in the use of digital devices by teachers and unaffordability of data bundles are common in most of the rural areas around the globe. Confronted with these challenges, the Zimbabwean rural communities are further marginalized from quality education. In most Zimbabwean rural spaces, the COVID-19 lockdown measures meant a complete shutdown of teaching and learning in its real sense. Unlike their counterparts in urban areas who continued learning online despite some challenges, learners in most rural areas stopped learning abruptly as the face to face traditional mode of teaching was prohibited to contain the spread of the deadly virus. A few rural schools with internet connectivity could not benefit much from online teaching and learning because of other challenges including lack of digital devices and unaffordable data bundles. The right to education was bestowed on all global citizens regardless of their geographical location as such, efforts should be made by all stakeholders to overcome the hindrances in accessing digital platforms as this is now a new reality in education delivery. There is a great need for government commitment to reducing the digital divide between rural and urban spaces. Rural communities should also make their initiatives to confront the problems they are facing. They might involve the formation of committees including all stakeholders in education for the mobilization of resources and motivation of parents so that they support their children in this novel digital pedagogy. Through the concerted effort by the community in supporting teachers and learners in using digital platforms, quality education in rural spaces will be achieved.

References

Adedoyin, O. B., & Soykan, E. (2020). Covid-19 pandemic and online learning: The challenges and opportunities. *Interactive Learning Environments*, 10(1080), 1–13.

Antony-Newman, M. (2019). Parental involvement policies in Ontario: A critical analysis. *School Community Journal*, 29(1), 143–169.

Blundell, C. (2021). Teacher use of digital technologies for school-based assessment: A scoping review. *Assessment in Education: Principles, Policy & Practice*, 28(3), 279–300.

Daimary, P. (2020). E-Learning in schools during Covid-19 pandemic in rural areas. *International Journal of Management*, 11(10), 659–664.

Dube, B. (2020). Rural online learning in the context of COVID-19 in South Africa: Evoking an inclusive education approach. *Multidisciplinary Journal of Educational Research*, 10(2), 135–157.

Erickson, I., & Smallc, R. V. (2013). Digital literacy and informal learning environments: An introduction. *Learning, Media and Technology*, 38, 355–367.

Freeman, J., & Middleton, C. (2020). Technological literacy and interrupted internet access. *Information, Communication and Society*, 23(13), 1947–1964.

Hussain, S., Wang, Z., & Rahim, S. (2013). E-learning services for rural communities. *International Journal of Computer Applications*, 68(5), 15–20.

Khan, S., & Khan, R. A. (2019). Online assessments: Exploring perspectives of university students. *Education and Information Technologies*, 24(1), 661–677.

Lawless, E. (2014). *Facing the Facts: Opportunities and challenges of online learning*. IB Conference of the Americas (pp. 1–12). Washington, DC: Pamoja Education.

Maatuk, A. M., Elberkawi, E. K., Aljawarneh, S., & Rashaideh, H. (2021). The COVID 19 pandemic and E-learning: Challenges and opportunities from the perspective of students and instructors. *Journal of Computing in Higher Education*, 34(1), 1–18.

Malone, D. (2017). Socioeconomic status: A potential challenge for parental involvement in schools. The Delta Kappa Gamma Bulletin. *International Journal for Professional Educators*, 20(4), 58–62.

Masabo, L. P., Muchopa, E. D., & Kuoth, W. B. (2017). Parental involvement in school activities in Kibondo District, Tanzania: Challenges and remedies. *International Journal of Education and Research*, 5(10), 89–96.

Matshe, P. (2014). Challenges of parental involvement in rural public schools in Ngaka Modiri Moleme District of North West Province. *International Journal of Humanities Social Sciences and Education* (IJHSSE), 1(6), 93–103.

Mavhemwa, P., Jekanyika, A., & Magomelo, M. (2017). An investigation into whether access to quality education can be better met with the use of e-learning, analyzing rural and urban schools. A case of Zimbabwe. *International Journal of Engineering Science and Computing*, 7(11), 15341–15351.

Mavuso, M. P., & Duku, N. (2014). Participation of parents in school governance: A case study of two Eastern Cape Schools: A view from below. *Mediterranean Journal of Social Sciences*, 5(3), 454–460.

Mhlanga, D., & Moloi, T. (2020). COVID-19 and the digital transformation of education: What are we learning on 4IR in South Africa? *Education Sciences*, 10(180), 1–11.

Msila, V. (2013). Democratic education through the eyes of the poor: Appraising the post-Apartheid experience. *Universal Journal of Educational Research*, 1(3), 191–199.

Muhtaseb, R. (2015). *Exploring the use of digital technologies in a sample of scientific and educational institutions*. EDULEARN15 Conference (pp. 7598–7606). Barcelona: EDULEARN15.

Mukuna, K. R., & Aloka, P. J. (2020). Exploring educators' challenges of online learning in Covid-19 at a rural School, South Africa. *International Journal of Learning, Teaching and Educational Research*, 19(10), 134–149.

Mukute, M., Francis, B., Burt, J., & Souza, B. d. (2020). Education in times of COVID-19: Looking for silver linings in Southern Africa's educational responses. *Southern African Journal of Environmental Education*, 36, 1–16.

Ndung'u, N., & Signé, L. (2019). *Capturing the Fourth Industrial Revolution.* London: GSM Association.

Obi, J. S., & Obineli, S. U. (2019). *Continuous assessment in counselling.* Enugu: Hugotez Publications.

Okon, U. (2015). ICT for rural community development: Implementing for the development. *Information Technology*, 21(2), 297–321.

Oldfield, A., Broadfoot, P., Sutherland, R., & Timmis, R. (2013). *Assessment in Digital Age: A research review.* Bristol: Graduate School of Education, University of Bristol.

Ramraj, U., &Marimuthu, F. (2019). The impact of technology in expediting learning: A South African experience. *EBEE', 19*, 35–40.

Rapanta, C., Botturi, L., Goodyear, P., Guàrdia, L., & Koole, M. (2020). Online University teaching during and after the Covid-19 Crisis: Refocusing teacher presence and learning activity. *Post-digital Science and Education*, 2, 923–945.

Rundel, C., & Salemink, K. (2021). Bridging digital inequalities in rural schools in Germany: A geographical lottery? *Education Sciences*, 11(4), 1–18.

Sibanda, L., & Mathwasa, J. (2021). Perceptions of teachers and learners on the impact of COVID-19 pandemic lockdown on rural secondary school female learners in Matobo District, Zimbabwe. *European Journal of Social Sciences Studies*, 6(3), 14–33.

The Foundation for Blended and Online Learning. (2018). *Digital learning strategies for Rural America: A scan of policy and practice in K–12 education.* New York: The Foundation for Blended and Online Learning and Evergreen Education Group.

Xu, M., David, J. M., & Kim, S. H. (2018). The Fourth Industrial Revolution: Opportunities and challenges. *International Journal of Financial Research*, 9(2), 90–95.

13. *Influence of Zimbabwean policies on rural female learners progression in advanced level science subjects*

PINIAS CHIKUVADZE & MUNYARADZI CHIDARIKIRE

Introduction

In any given society, the organization of its followers can only be meaningful when there is a definite course of action detailed through enacted policies (Braun, Ball, Maguire, & Hoskins, 2011; Igbo, Okafor, & Eze, 2014). In this regard, the policy is seen as an outcome of power, and control procedures that reflect values, which influence learners' behaviour. In this context enacted policy was seen as a version of structural transcripts, which guide the teaching-learning process (Republic of Zimbabwe, 2008; Shizha & Kariwo, 2011). However, the policy is seldom value-neutral since it represents a particular ideological or ethical standpoint that vests its authority (Coetzee, 2019; Teise, 2013). Therefore, policies, require exploration through paying attention to inconsistencies, omissions, and power relations within a society guided by patriarchal belief systems, in an environment where, traditionally, rural females are accorded a low status (Forde, 2014; Ntim, 2013; Syed & Ozbilgin, 2009). Such an analysis does not only involve policy directives but also negotiation, and tussle between those involved in the policymaking process, and those outside of it (Davies, 2011; Ozga, 2000).

The above-mentioned opinion dismisses the view that policies are simply to be taken up, and, thereafter, transformed into a vibrant course of action (Sava & Orodho, 2014). As a result, education systems reproduce the cultural capital, and opinions of influential groups in societies (Forgasz, Leder, & Tan, 2014). This antagonism was a clear indication that educational policies on their own are never complete in dealing with issues concerning the promotion of rural female learners' progression in education (Shizha & Kariwo, 2011). However, a critical look at these might open up conflicting interpretations by different stakeholders, resulting in, for example, different terms of reference for their application, monitoring, and appraisal (Bell & Stevenson, 2006). Hence, the need for a clear understanding of the social structure and the influence thereof on the setting up of policies that can either promote or discourage rural female learners' progression in Advanced Level science subjects (Dziva, Mpofu, & Kusure, 2011; Jamali, 2009) in rural secondary schools. It is this regard that this chapter critically scrutinizes, gender-related policies with the view to draw insights into their influence on rural female learners' progression in Advanced Level science subjects. This discussion is premised under a conceptual framework derived from feminist theories (liberal, social, and radical), with emphasis on education as a system that supports equal power interactions, equity, social cohesion, participation, and awareness (Ruzvidzo, 2017).

International treaties, and rural female learners' progression in education

In 1980, upon emancipation from the Western colonizers, Zimbabwe faced many challenges that needed attention from the government of the day (Chataika, Mckenzie, Swart, & Lyner-Cleophas, 2012; Mutema, 2012). In addition, the ordinary citizens had their expectations from the government, one of which was education that would equip them with knowledge and skills to empower them, regardless of their gender (Chidhakwa, 2021; Nziramasanga, 1999). Thus, the notion of gender inclusion in various spheres, such as education, was brought to life (Akin-Aina, 2011). According to the liberal feminist standpoint, it was critical for the government, at this point, to apply an open-minded approach in the initial interventions to address gender inequality in education (Mutangadura, 2001; Ndlovu & Mutale, 2013). This mind-set created the potential for Zimbabwe to take note of the existence of inequalities, which then required the nation to embrace scientific socialism as its steering doctrine to transform, among other things, imbalances in the education system (Zhou & Zvoushe, 2012).

This called for proactive interventions, such as the decree of policies with the belief that these would create grounds conducive to equal progression in education (Mwanza, 2015; Rambe & Ndofirepi, 2016). These educational reforms influenced the transformation of how indigenous culture views females (Mareva, 2014). However, it took place at other levels of education, and not the Advanced Level; for example, the transformation reduced the enrolment gap at lower secondary education between rural females, and males, with the gap widening (Sahin, 2011) in Advanced Level science subjects. The implementation of the interventions was a result of the signing of the *Lancaster House Agreement* in London on 21 December 1979, which created a platform for a newly born nation. Zimbabwe participated in several international conferences on citizens' rights, and well-being. The Zimbabwean government endorsed, and consented to, for instance, the following international treaties (Dube, 2013; Ngwenya, 2020):

- The Convention on Rights of the Child (Sections 29 and 30)
- The Universal Declaration of Human Rights (Section 26)
- The Convention on the Elimination of all Forms of Discrimination Against Women (1991)
- The Beijing Declaration on the Platform for Action (1995)
- The 2004 Solemn Declaration on Gender and Equality in Africa
- The Dakar Platform for Action
- The Beijing Declaration
- The SADC Declaration on Gender and Development
- The Millennium Declaration

This led to better designing of strategies to fight against, for example, gender inequality in education as the basis for policy formulation (Kurasha & Chabaya, 2013). Therefore, it can be argued that these conferences and conventions supposedly brightened the expectations of disadvantaged groups, wishing to have a gender-neutral, and gender-sensitive approach to education, among other things. At face value, Zimbabwe consented, and agreed to these declarations, resolutions, and procedures, to initiate a permitting atmosphere for the realization of gender equality (Dube & Dziva, 2014; Maphosa, Tshuma, & Maviza, 2015). The intention was to improve the operating base for policies to inhibit the bias that is grounded on gender (Mavhunga & Bondai, 2015).

However, a closer look at the reality on the ground shows that this did not in any way guarantee an automatic inclusion of themes derived from international treaties into indigenous policies, since the process needed approval through an act of parliament to be incorporated into policy (Machacha & Alexander, 2010). This created a gap between the demand for gender equality as enshrined in the conventions, and what was obtained on the ground, with rural females encountering challenges in their progression in education

(Booysen & Nkomo, 2010; Nani & Sibanda, 2019); these intentions did not always come to the realization. Against this background, female pressure groups have been challenging society's stance towards defending the code of equal opportunities as delineated in various treaties (Zimbabwe Women Lawyers Association, 2012).

On paper, these *acts* (e.g. *Matrimonial Causes Act* [1987]; *Maintenance Act* [1999]; *Education Act* [1987]; *Domestic Violence Act* [2007]; *National Gender Policy* [2004; 2013–17] right sound practical in providing answers to rural females' concerns, but the implementation thereof leaves more questions than answers. Thus, *Chapter 25/04, Part II, Section 4* of the *Education Act* (1987) brought with it obstructive gaps in its framework, which made it strenuous to realize the full capacity of the policies (Chinomona & Maziriri, 2015). In this regard, policies are indeed written in a complex socio-political environment, with key issues, at times, being raised by ordinary citizens who are set aside in preference of apparently so-called *'doable'* approaches, together with *'feasible'* goals for various sectors, such as education (Mutanana & Bukaliya, 2015). Consequently, in most cases, policies are portrayed as a symbol of political achievement from the colonial to the current society – mere symbolism (Jansen, 2000).

Taking into account the patriarchal nature of both the state, and the social order, and given the preconceived notion in the dispensation of impartiality concerning gender parity, it is not rational to imagine that policies can ever be a vigorous force for transforming prevailing social configurations in this post-colonial era (Ntlama, 2010). In this context, through a lens that incorporates the feminist, and symbolic interactionist theories, the authors discussed how some pieces of policies influence rural female learners' progression in Advanced Level science subjects. For the empowerment of rural females, and males, several gender-sensitive policies were enacted, and existing ones were mostly brought in line with tenets of equality. However, wide-ranging inequalities against rural females continue in the socio-economic, socio-political, environmental, and socio-cultural spheres (Mazonde & Carmichael, 2016; Moreira & Rabenevanana, & Picard, 2017). It is against this background that rural female learners' progression in education has been observed to be marginal, mostly owing to colonial remnants of interactions between femininity, and masculinity, and procedures in policy changes (Chikuvadze, 2020; Masinire, 2015). This chapter gives insights into the influence of the *Constitution of Zimbabwe*, the *National Gender Policy, Affirmative Action Policy, and education policies* on rural female learners' progression in education in Advanced Level science subjects.

Constitution of Zimbabwe, and its influence on rural female learners' education

The *Lancaster House Constitution* (Republic of Zimbabwe, 1980) was enacted as a guide in the operation of various spheres of life in independent Zimbabwe. The citizens had definite expectations to bring about equality and congruent nation-building (Mlambo, 2013), also in the context of education. Those in authority were expected to create conditions that empower rural females through education (Heymann, Raub, & Cassolap, 2014). With this in mind, this section looks at how the Constitution influenced the setting up of a female-friendly environment in different spheres, such as education (Selebogo & Ojakorotu, 2013). A closer look at the *Lancaster House Constitution* (Republic of Zimbabwe, 1980) reveals that in a bid to please the indigenous population, the customary law, and the application thereof to issues relating to people's rights and lives were preserved (Makonese, 2016). For instance, *Sections 23(a)* and *(b)* state as follows:

> Nothing contained in any law shall be held in contravention of subsection (1) (a) [the non-discrimination provision] to the extent that the law in question relates to any of the following matters – (a) matters of personal law; and (b) the application of African customary law in any case involving Africans (Republic of Zimbabwe, 1980)

This lay the foundation for the application of the requirements of *Section 20(5)* (Republic of Zimbabwe, 1980) in discouraging the implementation of the practice of expelling pregnant learners from schools (Hapanyengwi-Chemhuru, 2015). The authors observed that the principle of equality is also catered for in *Section 14(23)(i)(a)* (Republic of Zimbabwe, 1980), as it directed that no law shall make discriminatory conditions. In the context of education, secondary schools could no longer prevent pregnant rural learners or those who have given birth from progressing in their studies (Heymann et al., 2014). Still, despite some positive aspects from the perspective of equality, one has to understand that first and foremost, the concern at this point in history was to establish a sovereign state. Secondly, the *Lancaster House Constitution* (Republic of Zimbabwe, 1980) was ushered in without a referendum being done (Madebwe, 2014). Therefore, there was a need for the constitution to be amended in line with concerns raised by different stakeholders in society.

Now, the discussion shifts its focus to probing the extent to which the *2005 Constitutional Amendment* (No. 17) (Republic of Zimbabwe, 2005) and *2013 Constitution Amendment* (No. 20) (Republic of Zimbabwe, 2013) protect females' rights with specific reference to progression in education. These amendments were a result of endeavours by different interested parties such as females' groups (e.g. the Campaign for Female Education, the Girl Child Network, the Musasa Project, the Women Action Group, Women of Zimbabwe Arise, and the Zimbabwe Women Lawyers' Association), to strengthen the demand for a legal framework that intensifies the issue of gender parity in education (Africa Union, 2009; UN, 2014).

Therefore, looking at the diversity in terms of females' concerns, those consulted in the formulation of the *2005 Constitutional Amendment (No. 17)* and the *2013 Constitution Amendment (No. 20)* enabled them to be widely recognized for their well-founded pledge to gender equality and the right to education (Kapinga, 2010). Thus, the provisions of the Amended Section 23 of the *2005 Constitution on Protection from Discrimination* (Republic of Zimbabwe, 2005) clarify confusion and provide more detail by replacing specific terms, and supporting equity:

> (a) in subsection (2) by the deletion of "or gender" wherever it occurs and the substitution of "sex, gender, marital status or physical disability"; (b) in subsection (3) – (i) by the repeal of paragraph (a) and the substitution of – (a) matters of personal law; (ii) in paragraph (d) by the deletion of "or gender" and the substitution of, "sex, gender, marital status or physical disability" or (g) the implementation of affirmative action programmes for the protection or advancement of persons or classes of persons who have been previously disadvantaged by unfair discrimination.

This was intended to speed up the socio-cultural, political, and economic transformation through the application of standards that allow for an improved number of individuals, regardless of their gender, to access, and be treated in the same manner in different activities, such as education in general and Advanced Level science subjects in particular (Mkude, 2011). In addition, the *2005 Constitution Amendment* (No. 17) shows transformative foresight on the *Declaration of Rights,* since it organizes epic intentions that extend from the indivisibility and inter-connectedness of human rights and functional parity to addressing the imbalances (Gaidzanwa, 2016; Moyo, 2019) in education in general, and Advanced Level science subjects in particular. Thus, the *2013 Constitution* (Amendment No. 20), in *Chapter IV, Part II* – Declaration of Rights on *Section 56* (equality, and non-discrimination), provides that –

> (2) Women and men have the right to equal treatment, including the right to equal opportunities in political, economic, cultural, and social spheres (3) Every person has the right not to be treated in an unfairly discriminatory manner on such grounds as their nationality, race, color, tribe, place of birth, ethnic or social origin, language, class, religious belief, political affiliation,

opinion, custom, culture, sex, gender, marital status, age, pregnancy, disability or economic or social status, or whether they were born in or out of wedlock (Republic of Zimbabwe, 2013).

An essential point to note is that the *Declaration of Rights* singles out explicit categories (e.g. ethnic or social origin, religious belief, custom, culture, sex, gender, and pregnancy). In this regard, the *2013 Constitution* concedes the presence of hindrances to the realisation of rural females' rights, hence the need to lay a legal foundation upholding the eradication of such impediments. In addition, preamble of the *2013 Constitution Amendment* (No. 20) (Republic of Zimbabwe, 2013) depicts people of Zimbabwe's commitment towards safeguarding the essential human rights, and sovereignty. Thus, the *constitution* goes further than just recognising these rights, as it guarantees that they are realized. For example, Section 17(1) provides that the state must promote full gender balance in Zimbabwean society, and, in particular, *'(a) [t]he State must promote the full participation of women in all spheres of Zimbabwean society based on equality with men'* (Republic of Zimbabwe, 2013). With specific reference to education, Section 27(2) provides that *'[t]he State must take measures to ensure that girls are afforded the same opportunities as boys to obtain an education at all levels'* (Republic of Zimbabwe, 2013).

The citations from the *2013 Constitution Amendment* (No. 20) (Republic of Zimbabwe, 2013) advocate for full participation based on equality in spheres, such as education, at all levels; one could infer that it implies Advanced Level science subjects as well. Hence, in this *Constitution*, education is seen as a tool for promoting other rights, for example, equality and non-discrimination. It took cognizance of this by regarding females' rights in light of the disadvantaged status under the previous dispensation and the first Constitution. Concerning the right to education, the *2013 Constitution* (Amendment No. 20) through Section 75(1) states that *'[e]very citizen of Zimbabwe has a right to (b) further education, which the State through reasonable legislative measures must make progressively and available and accessible'* (Republic of Zimbabwe, 2013). Of significance in this clause is the word 'every', as it is taken to include rural females. This can be regarded as a positive development in light of past injustices. However, the document does not explicitly state how legislative measures ought to be interpreted within the ideals set, and as such, this can be noted as silence (Zanhi, 2014).

Furthermore, despite statements to advance equality, it must be noted that the *2005 Constitutional Amendment* (No. 17) (Republic of Zimbabwe, 2005) and the *2013 Constitution Amendment* (No. 20) (Republic of Zimbabwe, 2013) had limitations on the *Declaration of Rights* in Chapter

IV since they fell short about conceptual simplicity in rural females' rights (Dziva, 2018). It silences females through, for instance, the language used, as citizens are referred to by other words such as 'he' and 'him', with the words 'she' and 'her' appearing nowhere (Zungura & Nyemba, 2013). Females are thus subconsciously excluded and forced by the belief systems to accept discrimination among the sexes as 'normal' in society (Gutsa, Tom, Chihambakwe, & Chideya, 2011). This oppresses rural females in areas such as education since laws and policies have been turned into the very apparatus of gender discernment (Ifemeje & Ikpeze, 2012).

Furthermore, the *2013 Constitution Amendment* (No. 20) (Republic of Zimbabwe, 2013) does not outline the implementation procedure. Thus it falls short of a clear objective on how rural females' right to education should be developed and treated. This portrays the use of a catch-all formula in terms of the right to education, which renders the clause unclear and makes it subject to different interpretations by stakeholders in rural secondary schools. Against this background, any policy that guarantees the right to education but does not guarantee gender equality in education fails to enact equality, and, by implication, equal access to the so-called *'masculine'* Advanced Level science subjects.

Of note too is that some of these clauses are enacted without a stipulated monitoring procedure. Thus, in instances where monitoring and evaluating, is done, it monitors the progress of how rural males have progressed or assisted, and not rural females. Hence, rural females are again continuously ignored from the actual planning that the monitoring is based on. Of note too is that some of these clauses are enacted without a stipulated monitoring procedure. Although there are bodies, such as the Ministry of Women Affairs, Small and Medium Enterprise and Community Development, and the Zimbabwe Gender Commission, that direct the drafting of gender-related policies, no mechanism is in place to monitor compliance by other ministries (e.g. the Ministry of Primary and Secondary Education) or grassroots stakeholders (Akotia & Anum, 2015; Chikuvadze, 2020). Hence, policy formulation without a clear statement of whose responsibility, it is to enforce the implementation and monitoring amounts to carrying on with an existing policy in education (Bamgbose, 1991). Of concern now is that not much has been done in terms of research to look into the influence of the gender-related aspects in the *2013 Constitution Amendment* (No. 20) on rural female learners' progression in education in general and Advanced Level science subjects in particular (Unterhalter, 2008).

Several authors (Carinci & Wong, 2009; Mapfumo, Chireshe, & Peresuh, 2002; Manion, 2011; Wudie & Philipos, 2014) argue that, in a structured society where females' mind-sets are influenced by cultural beliefs on their inferior status, they take a back seat in, among other environments, the *'masculine'* Advanced Level science environment. It is in this context that feminists have advocated for the appreciation and involvement of rural females in education (Mapuva, 2013). This was driven by the need to transform from an elitist, settler, racially-biased, and dual education structure to an inclusive one (Mugweni & Dakwa, 2013). This can, however, only happen if legislation and policies resonate with the stipulation in the *constitution* and action is taken to implement these. It is, therefore, imperative to look at other forms of official text that relate to these versions of the *constitution*.

The post-colonial government in Zimbabwe tried to create a doctrine of a non-discriminatory society to enable females to develop themselves to their full potential (Atta, 2015). In this regard, the *constitution* departs from its rather artificial categorization of rights to a position that makes rights read holistically and be 'given full effect' through implementation (Moyo, 2019). But the existence of provinces demarcated along tribal or ethnic lines, such as the structures and systems of the institution of management in the Ndebele, Karanga, Zezuru, Kalanga, Tonga, and Venda societies, have some notable variances and, together with the introduction of plural legal systems (customary law and labour courts) (Helium, 2000; Kameri-Mbote, 2018), proved detrimental to rural females' progression in different spheres, such as education in general, and Advanced Level science subjects.

Within these community settings based on ethnicity, traditional laws continued to provide a basis for discriminatory tendencies against rural females (Jayachandran, 2015). In addition, the superstructure in Zimbabwe was still firmly established in socio-cultural, socio-economic, and socio-political inequality, with education inclined towards the enforcement of cultural essentialism (Shizha, 2006). In this regard, the customary policies portrays a false picture of the existence of a uniform set of customs, notwithstanding the diversified society with multi-cultural belief systems (Ndulo, 2011). Hence the existence of an immense fissure on the application of customary law vis-à-vis common policies codes, thereby creating parallel structures to resolve issues related to inequalities. Hence, there is no coordination between the two lines of thought (e.g. Western legislature and the indigenous customary belief system) on equality between rural females and males. In this context, it can be noted there exists a contradiction between the requirements of the *Lancaster House Constitution* (Republic of Zimbabwe, 1980) in *Section 23(3(b))* and the expectations of indigenous customs (Mboreke, 1988). For instance, *Customary Law* (Act 2 of 1990) had no clause on how to promote gender equality; instead, it was a source of policies that was used to subjugate females and continue to regulate the lives of citizens (Heidi & Jen, 2009).

With most African females, such as those in the rural areas in Zimbabwe, married under customary law, their consent to its broader application of gender equality-related policies would therefore be regarded as *de facto* (FAO, 2017). This explains relations of power, gender, and domination in social establishments and the revelation of issues of disparity and subjugation within the social structures of human existence (Mutekwe & Mutekwe, 2012). The aforementioned idea is an antithesis of the human capital perspective, which advocates for an educational policy that correlates with gender relations through the identification of cost-effective strategies to allow for the progression of rural female learners (Manion, 2011) in Advanced Level science subjects. Therefore the integration of indigenous customs into the Western legal courts to give rise to females' rights being ensnared between formal policies and customary policies.

A plural legal system was created, with customary policies mostly guided by the belief systems that are influenced society's desire for its inhabitants to adhere to particular traditional practices (Diala, 2017; Tamale, 2014). However, these traditional beliefs that were grounded in the customary policies (Rwafa, 2016; Vambe & Mupfariseni, 2011), tended to contradict with that is legislated in the constitution. For instance, the issue by the state to promote the element of inclusivity tends to hit a brick wall, since there are still individuals or groups that conceal their own sub-cultural beliefs (Mutekwe & Mutekwe, 2012). This has led gender activists to suggest that although on paper the policy seems excellent; it needs time to prove that the provisions are not merely a facade for politicians (Muzulu, 2014). For example, in the constitution, it is not stated to which extent the state should fund basic education, leaving it open to interpretation that the state is partially responsible for funding (UN, 2014).

In response to the outcry from female pressure groups, numerous policies were enacted through the *Lancaster House Constitution* (Republic of Zimbabwe, 1980) and the *Constitution Amendment* (No. 17) (Republic of Zimbabwe, 2005), the *Domestic Violence Act* (2007), the *Legal Age of Majority Act* (1982), the *Matrimonial Causes Act* (1985), the *Sexual Discrimination Removal Act* (1986) and the *Sexual Offences Act* (2001) (Hlatshywayo et al., 2014). In support of the emancipation of females, the Constitutional Court ruled that *Chapter 5:07* of the *Marriage Act* (Republic of Zimbabwe, 1980), which allowed females as young as 16 to be married with parental consent, was unconstitutional (Sachiti, 2016). However, the issue of child marriage remains a menace to the rights of young rural females (UNFPA, 2012). This concurs with the liberal feminist perspective, which sees it as a product of diminished access to civil liberties (Giddens, 2001). Thus, customary law creates biased patriarchal supremacy that gives males more power and control over decision-making processes (Losindilo, Mussa, & Akarra, 2010).

The prevailing situation about females' rights, as enshrined in the *Lancaster House Constitution* (Republic of Zimbabwe, 1980), the *2005 Constitution Amendment* (No. 17) (Republic of Zimbabwe, 2005), the *2013 Constitution Amendment* (No. 20) (Republic of Zimbabwe, 2013), and the traditional belief system, seems to create a gap in the legislative framework. Against this background, the next section centres on the need for the post-modern era to discuss strategies to be used to dismantle the inequalities between rural females and males in different spheres of life, education in general, and Advanced Level science subjects included.

Rural female learners' progression in advanced level science subjects, and the National Gender Policy

This section focuses on the influence of policies and their content on the mutually exclusive categories of *'femaleness'* or *'maleness'* on progression in education (Republic of Zimbabwe, Ministry of Women Affairs, Gender and Community Development, 2013). These policies recognize the existence of disparities among rural females and males that are socially constructed and are learned through socialization (Zinn, Eitzen, & Wells, 2008). In this discussion on female empowerment, *Goal Number Five: Achieve gender equality and empower all women and girls* of the *Sustainable Development Agenda 2030* and *Goal Seventeen: Full gender equality in all spheres of life* of the *African Union Agenda 2063* (UN, 2016) are investigated. These led to the setting up of 'gender machinery' directed towards upholding and supporting gender equality and equity, which filter into society through laws and policies (Van der Westhuizen, 2013). In this context, gender disparity in progression in education forms the nucleus of the discussion, looking at how these policies, directly or indirectly, foster equality and equity (Kaimenyi & Ngeretha, 2014) in rural female learners' progression in Advanced Level science subjects.

In recognition that there are gender imbalances in the operation of the institution, the government, guided by the *constitution*, has developed and introduced policies, among them *Affirmative Action*, the *National Gender Policy*, and the abolition of child marriages (Chauraya, 2012). These policies are rooted in the *African Charter on Human and Peoples Rights*, the *Protocol to the African Charter on Human and People's Rights on the Rights of Women in Africa*, and the *Solemn Declaration on Gender Equality in Africa* (Omotosho, 2015). However, these policies and intervention programmes focused on expanding rural female learners' progression in education with little reflection (Masinire, 2015) on rural female learners' experiences in progression in Advanced Level science subjects. In this context, Gaidzanwa (1989) articulates concern over the significantly low figures of rural female learners progressing to Advanced Level science subjects, and beyond.

Zungura and Nyemba (2013) portrayed that this discourse interrogates how policies such as the *Affirmative Action Policy* (1993) and the *National Gender Policy* (2004; amended in 2013), designed under the direction of exterior powers, influence female learners' progression in education in learning ecologies. Accordingly, these national policies are aimed at affording a viable conduit through which the government interconnects and acts in response to petitions by the natives (Machiridza, Kihonge, & Ochieng, 2016; Zhou & Zvoushe, 2012). This was because of the realization that the contribution of rural females should be brought to the limelight through policy guidelines (Mabhanda, 2016). For example, the gender equality strategies of Zimbabwe (2013–2017) and the strategic implementation plan (2013–2017) seek to achieve a gender-just society, where females, and males enjoy equality, and equity, and participate as equal partners in the development process of the country (Republic of Zimbabwe, Ministry of Women Affairs, Gender and Community Development, 2013). This meticulously worded local undertaking ensures the inculcation of the tenets of equality, as enshrined in the Beijing resolutions (Agu & Omenyi, 2013).

In addition, the *Affirmative Action Policy* (1993) was introduced to correct historical inequalities encountered by mostly females in their progression in Advanced Level science subjects (Stewart et al., 2000). This policy placed much emphasis on equal access to learning opportunities for all (both females and males) at higher institutions of education (Munemo, 2017; Zimbabwe Women Lawyers Association, 2012). Feminists viewed this as a legislative attempt to reduce disparities in the social structure by uplifting disadvantaged rural female learners (Manion, 2011).

This advocates for a substantive approach in the realization of gender equality that focuses not only on the difference between rural female, and male learners but rather on how these policies weigh into the historic systemic drawback (Selebogo & Ojakorotu, 2013). Authors such as Mubika and Bukaliya (2011); Zivengwa, Hazvina, Ndedzu, and Mavesere (2013) argue that, although in affirmative action there are instances where all citizens cannot be treated the same, there are instances where there is a need to level the playing field, such as allowing rural female learners who have been marginalized in spheres such as education to progress to other levels. Mwamwenda (2013) insists that policy planning fails mostly due to decision-makers who are unaware of the prevailing situations in institutions such as rural secondary schools. Therefore, ideas, and initiatives of policy generation and implementation must come from, and are supported by ordinary citizens in the remotest parts of the country.

Although this was considered to be a positive move in confronting gender inequality, no mechanism was put in place to spearhead the implementation thereof (Pedzisai, Tsvere, & Nkhondo, 2014). This raises questions about the practicability of gender-related policies in a set-up where a *'son syndrome'* prevails, which entails giving preference to males and seeing females as the fragile sex, which needs to be aided (Sinnes & Locken, 2014). From this discussion, the authors allude to the fact that the *Affirmative Action Policy* is taken to adversely put forward rural female learners' reputation, which suggests that they are incompetent to do the things males can (Musingafi & Mufumbate, 2014). This can be seen as contradicting the basis of equal conduct under the *constitution,* thus giving rise to activist bias, for example where female learners with lesser quality Ordinary Level passes (Grade B or C) in science subjects are enrolled, with their male counterparts with quality symbols (Grade A) at the Ordinary Level being omitted from the classes to proceed in Advanced Level science subjects.

Hence it can be contended that the policy is simply concerned with making secondary schools more expressive of gender composition in Advanced Level science subjects; however, it does not confront the existing patriarchal beliefs in society. Against this background, the decision to legislate a *National Gender Policy* to direct, and guide gender equality in all sectors under the auspices of the Republic of Zimbabwe's Ministry of Women Affairs, Gender and Community Development (Maposa & Maposa, 2013). Thus, the *National Gender Policy* (2013–2017) sought to eradicate discrimination to create a gender-impartial society where females and males experience equality and participate as equal partners in all spheres of life (Republic of Zimbabwe, Ministry of Women Affairs, Gender and Community Development, 2013). From the previous discussion, it can be recognized that on education and training, the *National Gender Policy* (2013–2017) has the following objectives:

> To promote (i) equal access to education for boys and girls and their retention at all levels of education; and (ii) access to training opportunities for men and women, to make possible their equal participation in the workplace and governance structures (Republic of Zimbabwe, Ministry of Women Affairs, Gender and Community Development, 2013)

In this regard, the policy advocates for the amendment of all pertinent legal mechanisms, with support from various international treaties and conventions to stimulate gender equality by supporting and inspiring rural females to take up science subjects at all levels (Republic of Zimbabwe, Ministry of Women Affairs, Gender and Community Development, 2004). This is against the backdrop of society often being unaware of the low levels of rural female learners' progression in Advanced Level science subjects, and, thus, not realizing the need to confront such concerns (Masinire, 2015).

In this context, the state enacted strategies such as amending all relevant legal channels to deal with females' progression in education in general and Advanced Level science subjects in particular, but with accountability procedures to monitor the effectiveness and efficiency thereof (Chingarande, 2007). In support of this argument Win (2004) and Beuchler (2011), put forward that the lack of legal back-up or any sanctioned announcement on how this instruction was to be applied creates fragile and inconsistent powers of gender policy determination. Accordingly, while education guidelines are deliberated at the higher level of influence, the application thereof hinges on the subordinate echelons, such as schools, where social proxies could construe policy goals, and use their substantial discretion on implementation (Maposa & Mugabe, 2013). This is probable to ensue in a patriarchal society where, to some extent, policy implementers continue to socialize females, and males on their roles instead of being urged to promote gender equality in *'masculine'* science subjects (Shabaya & Konadu-Agyemang, 2004). This calls for the use of feminist theories in critiquing the extent to which conventional policy priorities are put in place without the involvement of policy implementers and the intended right beneficiaries (Runhare & Vandeyar, 2011). In this context, the next section explores how the existence of education acts influences rural female learners' progression in Advanced Level science subjects.

Education acts, and rural female learners' progression in advanced level science subjects

In the pre-colonial era, indigenous society had its form of education, where grandfathers, and grandmothers played a critical role in inculcating social values and expected roles for rural females, and males in their day-to-day lives. In a nutshell, this informal education created a scenario whereby rural females, and males are socialized according to their gender, which influenced their identity. On the other hand, the arrival of colonization brought with it a Western education system guided by policies, which were later amended in the post-colonial era. In this regard, policies and their influence on rural female learners' progression in education should not be seen in this section as a fixed structure but as a continuing social creation of human interpretation.

To begin with, the pre-independence era was characterized by biased policies, as they banished, and deprived the natives (Republic of Zimbabwe, Ministry of Education, Sport, and Culture, 2005). Thus, upon realizing that most of the general public were excluded from formal education during the colonial era, post-independent Zimbabwe embarked on a massive education transformation crusade to make available much sought-after education (Mubika & Bukaliya, 2011). It is broadly acknowledged that education has a momentous function in making learners ready to take up the fortunes, and potentialities (Chikuvadze & Matswetu, 2013) in education in general and Advanced Level science subjects in particular.

However, even with the declared success story of legislated policies aimed at improving females' progression in education, a sizeable number of rural females still find themselves excluded from Advanced Level science subjects in particular (Chinyoka, 2014). In this case, education policies are portrayed as an effort towards the attainment of comprehensive constitutional imagery of moving from the colonial era to the sovereign society (Jansen, 2000). This calls for the need to own up that gender equality is more extensive than just the completion of primary, and secondary education (Olowu, 2012). This was done through enacting gender-related policies aimed at eradicating and exposing stumbling blocks in rural female learners' progression in Advanced Level science subjects (Zezekwa, Madau, & Nkpodi, 2013).

This was in line with feminist ideals, which hope that education would help to reduce disparity by developing the possibility that subsists within all human beings. Within the context of bringing about reform, the post-colonial government promulgated the *Education Acts of 1987 and 1991* (amended in 1992), revised in *1996, 2004*, and *2006,* with emphasis on education as a basic human right available to all pupils, irrespective of religion, culture or sexual inclination (Runhare & Gordon, 2004; Samkange, 2015). These education acts, through amendments, recognized the liberating role played by education by acknowledging it as a right, with no child being refused admission based on sex, among other concerns. In this way, educational institutions are assumed to be places of learning, growth, and empowerment, in particular for rural female learners who are regarded as a marginalized group (Chikuvadze & Matswetu, 2013) in Advanced Level science subjects. This is a clear indication that concerns about equality and inclusion prop up the actual underpinnings of the society in which rural female learners live, and how they associate with others at the community and national levels.

In some cases, although education acts specify that every child has a right to education, it does not immediately translate into equal opportunities for both rural females, and males, as chauvinist views on rural female learners' progression in Advanced Level science subjects still exist (Republic of Zimbabwe, Ministry of Education, Sport, and Culture, 2005). Consequently, it is not that gender equality is not seen as a priority, but there is a wide implementation gap between declared policy intents and proceedings for legislative, and social transformations (Mukoro, 2013). In such a scenario, underprivileged rural female learners run the risk of being uncared for and, ultimately, dwindling if the system falls short in addressing their concerns (Chikuvadze, 2020; Slavin, 2005).

As a result education acts and policies tend to concentrate more on the symptoms rather than attend to the relentless triggering bases of gender disparity in Advanced Level science subjects (Economic Commission for Africa, 2008). In addition policies put in place, are not an end in themselves, since achieving gender equality does not only comprise the taking on of detailed regulations, instead their enactment (Matonhodze & Guzura, 2014). It is in this context that it can be noted that, policies and circulars have no definitive schedules to provide for exact requirements for female, and male learners; as a result, differential prospects in education between the two sexes seem to persist (Chauraya, 2012). This is contrary to human capital theorists' perspective that the provision of quality education to rural female learners is an investment crucial for the development of society (Iyoboyi & Muftau, 2014). In line with this, Stromquist (2007) appeals for cross-examination of the hurdles to open-minded execution of educational policies, in a bid to transform the social gender interactions in Advanced Level science subjects.

In upholding global values of non-discrimination in learning institutions, *Part II, Subsection 4(1)* of the *Education Act* emphasizes that every child shall have the right to education (Republic of Zimbabwe, 1996). The widespread contention concerning this nationalist education policy proclamation was to bring Zimbabweans into the realm of social conscience within the structures of the post-colonial circumstances. Thus, the education sector set-up was assumed the principal place for the creation of a well-versed and analytical public sharing of knowledge among the diverse population. Nevertheless, *Section 4(2)* of the *Education Act* (Republic of Zimbabwe, 1996) does not include gender as a basis on which inequity on enrolment is outlawed (Zimbabwe Human Rights Non-Governmental Organisation Forum, 2001). This controverts the feminism codes of beliefs, which are in favour of evenly balanced privileges, and access to all aspects of existence, such as education. In response, the *Education Act* (as amended) (Republic of

Zimbabwe, 2006) emphasizes the authoritarian, top-down approach, which empowered the responsible minister to unilaterally declare what should be taught in an area without consulting the concerned grassroots stakeholders (Dube & Ncube, 2013).

Judging from the amount of literature available on education policies, authors argue that, of all aspects of the protection of children's rights in education, policies, to a larger extent, have received attention (Nkomo, 2008). For Zimbabwe, this is true, as children's rights to education are enshrined in the *Education Act* (1987), of which the relevant section of the policy has been amended twice – in 1990 and 2006. On the amendment in *Chapter 25:04, Section IV* on children's fundamental right to education and entitlement to enrolment in government primary and secondary schools reads: '*(1) Notwithstanding anything to the contrary contained in any other enactment, but subject to this Act, every child in Zimbabwe shall have the right to school education*' (Republic of Zimbabwe, Education [Amendment] Act, 2006). This seems to resonate with the demands in the *constitution* on their right to education, as, in its articulation, it refers to 'every child', which authors presumed to be inclusive of both rural female, and male children. However, in *Chapter 25:04, Part III, Section 10* the following is stated:

> Every child of school-going age shall be entitled to be enrolled at the Government primary or secondary school, as the case may be, nearest to the place where he is ordinarily resident unless such primary or secondary school is fully enrolled (Republic of Zimbabwe, Education Act (Amendment, 2006).

It can be observed that there is a contradiction in the citation, as at first, it referred to '*every child*', but inspecting it more closely, it can be noted that this section referred to 'he' instead of constantly being gender-sensitive by using the term '*every child*', which accommodates both rural female and male learners. In the absence of gender-sensitive language in the policy document, this brings more questions than answers in the extent to which it can be implemented to the satisfaction of the disadvantaged rural female learners. From the above discussion, it can be noted that the consultations leading to the crafting of *the Education Act* (*1990; 2006*) with limited participation from rural parents and learners (Kadodo & Zanga, 2015).

As a result, without the translation of policy intentions into reality, the recent amendment stipulations are not likely not to benefit children in the selection of either primary or secondary schools of their choice. Thus, the new demands for gender equality require female learners to be re-admitted into the education system upon giving birth so that they can continue with their studies. This stance is backed by *Policy Circular 35* of the Republic of Zimbabwe, Ministry of Primary and Secondary Education, which grants pregnant learners the right to continue with their education upon giving birth (Mawere, 2013). However, it is a matter of concern that this change comes up with a scenario that seems as if the policy circular was specifically meant for disciplinary issues, making the whole process gender-blind (Mawere, 2013). So, while they have thought of withdrawing rural female learners from inconvenient situations, it remains to be seen how this has weighed in to address gender discrepancies, as some schools still do not allow pregnant learners to attend classes in secondary schools (Samkange, 2015).

Furthermore, there is no guarantee that nursing mothers can return to school, as their return depends on the availability of a place in the relevant class (Molosiwa & Moswela, 2012). This enacted policy was expected to operate in a society where specific groups, such as church and traditional leaders, regarded it as taboo and unmentionable in African culture to allow females of school-going age to get pregnant (Sithole, Manwa, & Manwa, 2013). Accordingly, this gives the impression that the legal framework is favourable, but it is not matched by action on the ground where, at times, policies are viewed as propping up promiscuity and are believed to bring about a lenient atmosphere at a time when children are experimenting with sex. Although much has been said about moving towards equality in science subjects in secondary schools in terms of enrolment, how these rural female learners are socialized into subjugated positions has not been taken into cognizance (Khan & Ara, 2006).

For instance, Zimbabwe's *2004 Education Act* does not look precisely into gender-related issues in learning institutions, as it only gives reference to the matter of no nepotism on admission in schools, without taking note of learners' different socialization circumstances (Gudyanga, 2016). Against this background, educational policies that are centred on enrolment only are scratching on the outer borders of gender inequality, without getting deeper into the nucleus of the causative factors (Marshall & Arnot, 2008). This is a case of the act, in theory, providing equal rights of entry into education, but, on the ground, the reality is different, as rural female learners still come across challenges in their progression in Advanced Level science subjects (Chikuvadze & Matswetu, 2013). Consequently, the *Act* consciously prefers to presume that all learners are equal and need access to education, without balancing the incongruity already impressed upon rural learners during the socialization process.

It is contended that policy intents are rarely if ever, transformed into reality, the way they have been envisioned (Ntshoe, 2009). Furthermore, policies are socially put together, and are frequently exposed to varied understandings

(Schauer in Ntshoe, 2009). For example, in Zimbabwe, policy, such as the *Education Act*, positions all learners into a single group, signifying that an education system is a gender-neutral place where rural female learners can transverse without restrictions (Primrose & Alexander, 2013). However, in this patriarchal society, rural female learners form a group of their own, with their own needs, which should be accommodated. If this is not recognized at the policy design level, it might not be addressed at the policy application level. This is against the feminist perspective, which advocates for equality, and equity in all spheres of society, such as education. For example, in the *Basic Education Assistance Module*, the position of the government is that monies are supposed to be allocated on a *50/50* basis between rural female, and male disadvantaged learners (Dlakama, 2015).

This perpetuates inequalities, as in Zimbabwe, females comprise 52 % of the population (Republic of Zimbabwe, Ministry of Women Affairs, Gender, and Community Development, 2004). This is a clear indication of gender-blind and unresponsive interventions that are not equitably distributed as more rural male learners will benefit, creating a weak basis for rural female progression in education in general and Advanced Level science subjects in particular. This is restrictive, as it caters to only those still in school and is silent on those out of school, who are mostly rural female learners. It can be noted that policies, and policy circulars place children in a single category, thereby suggesting that the education system is a gender-neutral space (Chirimuuta, 2006). According to Makura (2012), social responsibilities, and potential within the Zimbabwean setting stress that females, and males carry out functions consistent with their sex, which generates a gender disparity in rural learners' progression in Advanced Level science subjects.

Conclusion

From this chapter, it can be noted that policy proclamation is one thing, but instigating that policy is another since socio-spatial *'othering'* of rural female learners emerges from broadly conceived imaginings of femininity. It is against this background this chapter concludes that though policies in black, and white guarantee rural female learners unrestricted and equal rights to progress in education in general, and Advanced Level science subjects in particular, but the existing situation exposes them to patriarchal inclinations grounded in gender stereotypes. Hence, our belief that researches on gender inequalities in education and training should continue to embrace inputs from rural female learners without compromising their integrity.

References

African Union. (2009). *African Union gender policy.* http://www.wgd.au.int/en/content/african-union-gender-policy (Accessed on 29 May 2021).

Agu, N., & Omenyi, A. S. (2013). Gender enrolment status in higher education courses: A situation assessment and analysis of a South Eastern Federal University. *Journal of Emerging Trends in Educational Research and Policy Studies, 4*(3), 517–524.

Akin-Aina, S. (2011). *Beyond an epistemology of bread, butter, culture and power: Mapping the African Feminist Movement.* Ottawa: Nokoko Institute of African Studies Carleton University.

Akotia, C. S., & Anum, A. (2015). Gender, culture, and inequality in Ghana: An examination of sociocultural determinants of gender disparity. In *Psychology of gender through the lens of culture* (pp. 375–394). Cham: Springer.

Atta, G. P. (2015). Education inequality: How patriarchy and policy collide in Ghana. *International Journal of Humanities and Social Sciences, 57*(1), 11–19.

Bamgbose, A. (1991). *Language and the nation: The language question in sub-Saharan Africa.* London: Transaction Publishers.

Bechhofer, F., & Paterson, L. (2012). *Principles of research design methods.* Oxford: Oxford University Press.

Bell, L., & Stevenson, H. (2006). *Education policy: Process, themes and impact.* New York, NY: Routledge.

Beuchler, S. M. (2011). *Women's movements in the United States: Woman suffrage, equal rights and beyond.* New Brunswick, NJ: Rutgers University Press.

Booysen, L. A., & Nkomo, S. M. (2010). Gender role stereotypes and requisite management characteristics: The case of South Africa. *Gender in Management: An International Journal, 25*(4), 285–300.

Braun, V., & Clarke, V. (2006). Qualitative research in psychology. *Journal of Psychology, 3*, 77–101.

Carinci, S., & Wong, P. L. (2009). Does gender matter? An exploratory study of perspectives across genders, age and education. *International Review of Education, 55*(5), 523–540.

Chauraya, E. (2012). The African view on gender and its impact on implemented gender policies and programmes in Africa. *Journal of Sustainable Development in Africa, 14*(3), 252–261.

Chauraya, E. (2013). Gender discrimination in transnational academic mobility of lecturers: A Zimbabwean case. *The Dyke, 7*(3), 90–106.

Chidhakwa, N. (2021). Mitigating multiple vulnerabilities in Zimbabwean rural schools: An asset-based approach. *International Journal of Research & Innovation in Social Science, V*(IV), 71–78.

Chikuvadze, P. (2020). *Female pupils' perspective on societal factors influencing their progression in Advanced Level science subjects in Zimbabwe.* (Unpublished PhD thesis) University of the Free State, Bloemfontein.

Chikuvadze, P., & Matswetu, V. S. (2013). Gender stereotyping and female pupils' perception of studying advanced level sciences: A survey of one province in Zimbabwe. *Gender & Behaviour, 11*(1), 5285–5296.
Chingarande, S. D. (2007). An analysis of gender-related developments and challenges in Zimbabwe since independence. In F. Maphosa, K. Kujinga, & S. D. Chingarande (Eds.), *Zimbabwe development experiences since 1980: Challenges and prospects for the future.* Harare: Organisation for Social Sciences Research in Eastern and Southern Africa, Zimbabwe Chapter.
Chinomona, E., & Maziriri, E. T. (2015). Women in action: Challenges facing women entrepreneurs in the Gauteng Province of South Africa. *International Business & Economics Research Journal, 14*(6), 835–850.
Chinyoka, K. (2014). Causes of school drop-out among ordinary level learners in a resettlement area in Masvingo, Zimbabwe. *Journal of Emerging Trends in Educational Research & Policy Studies, 5*(3), 294–300.
Chirimuuta, C. (2006). Gender and the Zimbabwe Education Policy: Empowerment or perpetuation of gender imbalances. *Quiet Mountain Essays, Open Issue*, 1–5.
Coetzee, D. (2019). The effect of the ideology of new managerial professionalism on the South African education system. *South African Journal of Education, 39*(4), 1–9. https://doi.org/10.15700/saje.v39n4a1871 (Accessed on 10 January 2021).
Davies, J. S. (2011). *Challenging governance theory: From network to hegemony.* Bristol: The Policy Press.
Diala, A. C. (2017). The concept of living customary law: A critique. *The Journal of Legal Pluralism & Unofficial Law, 49*(2), 143–165.
Dlakama, B. (2015). *An examination of Zimbabwe's attainment of MDG 2 – Achieve Universal Primary Education: The case of Insiza Constituency Ward 10.* Midlands State University: Department of Development Studies.
Dube, B., & Dziva, C. (2014). The appointment of 2013 cabinet ministers in Zimbabwe: A lost opportunity for gender parity in decision making positions. *International Journal of Politics and Good Governance, 5*(5.1), 1–23.
Dube, L., & Ncube, B. (2013). Language policy and linguistic rights in post-colonial Zimbabwe: The case of IsiNdebele. *Greener Journal of Social Sciences, 3*(5), 249–255.
Dube, T. (2013). Engendering politics and parliamentary representation in Zimbabwe. *Journal of African Studies and Development, 5*(8):200–207.
Dziva, C. (2018). The 2013 Constitutional reform and the protection of women's rights in Zimbabwe. *Eastern Africa Social Science Research Review, 34*(2), 21–35.
Dziva, D., Mpofu, V., & Kusure, L. P. (2011). Teachers' conception of indigenous knowledge in science curriculum in the context of Mberengwa District, Zimbabwe. *African Journal of Education and Technology, 1*(3), 88–102.
European Commission. (2010). *Gender differences in educational outcomes: Study of the measures taken and the current situation in Europe.* Brussels: Education, Audiovisual and Culture Executive Agency.

FAO. (2017). *Legal pluralism, women's land rights and gender equality in Mozambique: Harmonizing statutory and customary law.* Rome: FAO.

Forde, C. (2014). Is gender-sensitive education a useful concept for educational policy? *Cultural Studies of Science Education, 9*, 369–376.

Forgasz, H., Leder, G., & Tan, H. (2014). Public views on the gendering of mathematics and related careers. International comparisons. *Educational Studies in Mathematics,* 87, 369–388.

Gaidzanwa, R. B. (2016). Women and land in Zimbabwe: State, democracy and gender issues in evolving livelihoods and land regimes. In A. Pallotti & C. Tornimbeni (Eds.), *State, land and democracy in Southern Africa* (pp. 149–166). New York, NY: Routledge.

Gaidzanwa, R. B. (1989). *The experiences of women in post-revolutionary reconstruction: Women in higher education administration.* (Working Paper No. 2:1–20). Human Resources Research Centre.

Giddens, A. (2001). *The global third way debate.* Cambridge: Polity Press.

Gudyanga, A. (2016). Zimbabwean female participation in Physics: Factors of identity formation considered as contributing to developing: An orientation to Physics by female students. *Journal of Education & Practice, 7*(26), 159–171.

Gutsa, I., Tom, T., Chihambakwe, W., & Chideya, T. N. (2011). *Gender and development.* Harare: Zimbabwe Open University.

Hapanyengwi-Chemhuru, O. (2015). Education for all in Zimbabwe: A critical appraisal. *Journal of the African Educational Research Network, 15*(1), 12–19.

Helium, A. (2000). Human rights and gender relations in postcolonial Africa: Options and limits for the subjects of legal pluralism. *Law & Social Inquiry, 25*(2), 635–655.

Heymann, J., Raub, A., & Cassolap, A. (2014). Constitutional rights to education and their relationship to national policy and school enrolment. *International Journal of Educational Development, 39*, 131–141.

Hlatshywayo, L., Hlatshywayo, S., & Muranda, Z. A. (2014). The extent to which females occupy leadership positions in Zimbabwean teachers colleges. *Journal of Humanities & Social Science, 19*(9), 28–36.

Ifemeje, S., & Ikpeze, O. (2012). Global trend towards gender equality: Nigeria's experience in focus. *Kuwait Chapter of Arabian Journal of Business and Management Review, 2*(3), 51–63.

Igbo, J. N., Okafor, R. A., & Eze, J. U. (2014). The role of socio-economic background on self-concept and academic achievement of in-school adolescents in Nigeria. *International Journal of Research in Humanities, Arts and Literature, 2*(2), 1–10.

Iyoboyi, M., & Muftau, O. (2014). An assessment of human capital development in Nigeria through the lens of education. *International Letters of Social and Humanistic Sciences, 35*, 1–14.

Jamali, D. (2009). Constraints and opportunities facing women entrepreneurs in developing countries: A relational perspective. *Gender in Management: An International Journal, 24*(4), 232–251.

Jansen, J. (2000). Rethinking education policy-making in South Africa: Symbols of change, signals of conflict. In A. Kraak & M. Young (Eds.), *Education in retrospect.* Pretoria: HSRC.

Jayachandran, S. (2015). The roots of gender inequality in developing countries. *Annual Review of Economics, 7,* 63–88.

Kadodo, W., & Zanga, S. (2015). Implementation of the 2006 Education Amendment Act on indigenous languages in Zimbabwe: A Case of the Shangaan Medium in Cluster 2 primary schools in the Chiredzi District. *International Journal of Learning, Teaching and Educational Research, 11*(1), 117–127.

Kaimenyi, C. K., & Ngeretha, A. (2014). Gender instruments, laws, policies and guidelines: A tool for human resource managers in Kenya. *International Journal of Academic Research in Business and Social Sciences, 4*(7), 220–228.

Kameri-Mbote, P. (2018). Constitutions as pathways to gender equality in plural legal contexts. *Oslo Law Review, 5*(1), 21–41.

Kapinga, B. B. (2010). Women access to science at the University of Dar es Salaam, Tanzania. *European Journal of Educational Studies, 2*(3), 273–281.

Khan, M. R., & Ara, F. (2006). Women, participation and empowerment in local government: Bangladesh Union Parishad perspective. *Asian Affairs, 29*(1), 73–92.

Kurasha, P., & Chabaya, R. A. (2013). Curriculum development and implementation: Factors contributing towards curriculum development in Zimbabwe higher education system. *European Social Sciences Research Journal, 1*(1), 1–12.

Losindilo, E., Mussa, A. S., & Akarro, R. R. J. (2010). Some factors that hinder women participation in social, political and economic activities in Tanzania. *Arts and Social Sciences Journal, 4,* 1–10.

Mabhanda, W. (2016). The call for gender balance, levelling the engineering gradient for more female students: The case of Gweru Polytechnic College. *International Journal of Business Marketing and Management, 1*(3), 23–30.

Maboreke, M. (1988). Women under Zimbabwean law. *Zimbabwe Law Review, 6,* 64–78.

Machacha, L., & Alexander, E. (2010). Gender experiences and mainstreaming in Botswana. In T. Matebu & D. Abiye (Eds.), *Gender mainstreaming experiences from Eastern and Southern Africa.* Addis Ababa: Organization for Social Science Research in Eastern and Southern Africa.

Machiridza, A. T., Kihonge, E., & Ochieng, P. A. (2016). Factors influencing women's career progression to leadership positions in Harare City Council, Zimbabwe. *International Journal of Scientific & Technology Research, 5*(5), 95–102.

Madebwe, T. (2014). Constitutionalism and the new Zimbabwean Constitution. *Midlands State University Law Review, 1,* 6–19.

Makonese, M. (2016). Women's rights and gender equality in the new Zimbabwean the role of constitution: Civil society in implementation and compliance. In C. M. Fombad (Ed.), *The implementation of modern African constitutions: Challenges and prospects.* Pretoria: University of Pretoria Press.

Makura, A. H. (2012). Leadership styles of female educational leaders: In search of a gender inclusive leadership theory. *Journal of Social Sciences, 31*(3), 279–287.

Manion, C. (2011). Girls' education as means or end of development? A case study of gender and education policy knowledge and action in the Gambia. (Unpublished DPhil thesis.) University of Toronto, Toronto.

Mapfumo, J., Chireshe, R., & Peresuh, M. (2002). Career perceptions and visions of boys and girls in secondary schools in Zimbabwe: Some implications for teachers and parent. *Zambezia, XXIX* (ii), 156–173.

Maphosa, M., Tshuma, N., & Maviza, G. (2015). Participation of women in Zimbabwean politics and the mirage of gender equity. *Ubuntu: Journal of Conflict and Social Transformation, 4*(2), 127–159.

Maposa, A. D., & Mugabe, M. J. (2013). "To be or not to be": The plight of female educational leaders in Masvingo Province Zimbabwe. *Afro-Asia Journal of Social Sciences, 4*(4.4), 1–15.

Mapuva, J. (2013). The feminist discourse and the development of a civic virtue in Zimbabwe: Case of Women of Zimbabwe Arise. *Journal of African Studies and Development, 5*(8), 261–270.

Mareva, R. (2014). Affirmative action by lowering university entry points for females: Great Zimbabwe university students' views. *Global Journal of Interdisciplinary Social Sciences, 3*(4), 173–178.

Marshall, H., & Arnot, M. (2008). Globalising the school curriculum: Gender, Education for All and global citizenship education. In S. Fennell & M. Arnot (Eds.), *Gender education and equality in a global context: Conceptual frameworks and policy perspectives.* London: Routledge.

Masinire, A. (2015). Teachers' perceptions and students' lived experiences in vocational-technical subjects in a rural high school in Zimbabwe. *Gender & Education, 27*(6), 618–634.

Matonhodze, L., & Guzura, T. (2014). Are we there yet? An evaluation of the impact of the Zimbabwe national gender policy on gender mainstreaming in Zimbabwe. *Global South SEPHIS E-Magazine,* 39–51.

Mavhunga, P. J., & Bondai, B. (2015). Gender mainstreaming in education in Zimbabwe: Mirth? *Educational Research International, 4*(4), 9–12.

Mawere, D. (2013). Evaluation of the Nziramasanga commission report of inquiry into education in Zimbabwe, 1999: The case of gender equity in education. *International Journal of Asian Social Sciences, 3*(5), 1077–1088.

Mazonde, N. B., & Carmichael, T. (2016). The influence of culture on female entrepreneurs in Zimbabwe. *Southern African Journal of Entrepreneurship and Small Business Management, 8*(1), 1–10.

Mkude, D. (2011). Higher education as an instrument of social integration in Tanzania: Challenges and prospects. *Research in Comparative and International Education, 6*(4), 366–373.

Mlambo, A. S. (2013). Becoming Zimbabwe or becoming Zimbabwean: Identity, nationalism and state building. *Africa Spectrum, 48*(1), 49–70.

Molosiwa, M., & Moswela, B. (2012). Girl-pupil in secondary schools in Botswana: Influencing factors, prevalence and consequences. *International of Business and Social Sciences, 3*(7), 265–271.

Moreira, C. S., Rabenevanana, M. N., & Picard, D. (2017). Boys go fishing, girls work at home: Gender roles, poverty and unequal school access among semi-nomadic fishing communities in Southern Western Madagascar. *Compare: A Journal of Comparative and International Education, 47*(4), 499–511.

Moyo, A. (2019). *Selected Aspects of the 2013 Zimbabwean Constitution and the Declaration of Rights.* Lund: Raoul Wallenberg Institute of Human Rights and Humanitarian Law.

Mubika, A. K., & Bukaliya, R. (2011). Education for all: Issues and challenges: The case for Zimbabwe. *International Journal of Social Sciences and Education, 1*(4), 315–325.

Mugweni, R. M., & Dakwa, F. E. (2013). Exploring the implementation of 'Education for All' in Early Childhood Development in Zimbabwe: Success and challenges. *Case Studies Journal,* 1–9.

Mukoro, A. S. (2013). The phenomenon of gender inequality in access to and equity in university education in Nigeria. *Mediterranean Journal of Social Sciences, 4*(7), 129–136.

Munemo, P. (2017). Women's participation in decision making in public and political spheres in Ghana: Constrains and strategies. *Journal of Culture, Society and Development, 37,* 47–52.

Musingafi, M. C. C., & Mafumbate, R. (2014). Students' perception of girl child affirmative action in high schools in Masvingo urban, Zimbabwe. *International Journal of Education and Practice, 2*(9), 192–212.

Mutanana, N., & Bukaliya, R. (2015). Women empowerment and gender related programmes implementation in Hurungwe District, Zimbabwe. *International Journal of Research in Humanities and Social Sciences, 2*(2), 1–12.

Mutangandura, P. (2001). Handicaps to women's rights in Zimbabwe. *Gender gaps in our constitutions: Women's concerns in selected African countries.* Conference Documentation, 1–3 October. Nairobi: Heinrich Boell Foundation.

Mutekwe, E., & Mutekwe, C. (2012). Manifestations of the gender ideology in the Zimbabwean school curriculum *Journal of Educational and Instructional Studies in the World, 2*(3), 193–209.

Mutema, E. P. (2012). The fast track land reform programme: Reflecting on the challenges and opportunities for resettled former farm workers at Fairfield Farm in Gweru District, Zimbabwe. *Journal of Sustainable Development in Africa, 14*(5), 96–106.

Muzulu, P. (2014). *Gender activists slam Zimbabwe's Judicial Service Commission. News Day*, 7 February.

Mwamwenda, T. S. (2013). Reception and treatment of HIV-AIDS children in schools. *Journal of AIDS and HIV Research, 15*(12), 472–478.

Mwanza, P. (2015). The state of girl-child's education in Zambia: The case of Chongwe District. *Journal of International Cooperation in Education, 17*(2), 95–110.

Nani, G. V., & Sibanda, L. (2019). Choice of practical subjects: Is it still a gendered phenomenon? A case of selected co-educational secondary schools in Bulawayo Metropolitan Province, Zimbabwe. *Journal of Educational and Social Research, 9*(3):1–10.

Ndlovu, S., & Mutale, S. B. (2013). Emerging trends in women's participation in politics in Africa. *American International Journal of Contemporary Research, 3*(11), 72–79.

Ndulo, M. (2011). *African customary law, customs and women's rights.* (Cornell Law Faculty Publications, Paper, 187.) http://www.scholaship.law.cornell.edu/facpub/187 (Accessed on 10 February 2019).

Ngwenya, V. C. (2020). Curriculum implementation challenges encountered by primary school teachers in Bulawayo Metropolitan Province, Zimbabwe. *Africa Education Review, 17*(2), 158–176.

Nkomo, D. (2008). Language in education and language development in Zimbabwe. *Southern African Linguistics and Applied Language Studies, 26*(3), 351–362.

Ntim, S. (2013). The academic progression paradox: Socioeconomic determinants of the mismatch between boys and the girl-child education in rural Ghana. *International Journal of Humanities and Social Science, 3*(14), 177–191.

Ntlama, N. P. (2010). Impediments in the promotion of the right to gender equality in post-apartheid South Africa. (Unpublished LLD thesis.) University of South Africa, Pretoria.

Ntshoe, I. M. (2009). Hidden and subtle effects of racism in law and school policy in post-apartheid South Africa. *Southern African Review of Education, 15*(2), 85–104.

Nziramasanga Commission. (1999). *Report on Presidential commission of inquiry into education and training.* Harare: Government Printers.

Olowu, D. (2012). Gender equality under Millennium Development Goals: What options are for sub-Saharan Africa? *Agenda: Empowering women for Gender Equality, 26*(1), 104–111.

Omotosho, B. J. (2015). African Union and gender equality in the last ten years: Some issues and prospects for consideration. *Journal of Integrated Social Sciences, 5*(1), 92–104.

Ozga, J. (2000). *Policy research in educational settings: Contested terrain.* Buckingham: Open University Press.

Pedzisai, C., Tsvere, M., & Nkhondo, M. (2014). The Zimbabwe two pathway education curriculum: Insights into policy implementation challenges and opportunities. *International Journal of Advanced Research in Management and Social Sciences, 3*(4), 158–169.

Primrose, K., & Alexander, C. R. (2013). Curriculum development and implementation: Factors contributing towards curriculum development in Zimbabwe higher education system. *European Social Sciences Research Journal, 1*(1), 55–65.

Rambe, P., & Ndofirepi, T. M. (2016). Gender differences in the perceptions of entrepreneurship hindrances: A case of vocational education students in Zimbabwe. *Journal of Economics and Behavioral Studies, 8*(6), 94–113.

Republic of Zimbabwe, Ministry of Women Affairs, Gender and Community Development. (2004). *National Gender Policy.* Harare: Government Printers.

Republic of Zimbabwe, Ministry of Women Affairs, Gender and Community Development. (2009). *Progress report of the Republic of Zimbabwe on the implementation of the Beijing Declaration and Platform for Action (1995) and the Outcome of the Twenty-third Special Session of the General Assembly (2000).* Harare: Ministry of Women's Affairs, Gender and Community Development. http://www.uneca.org/eca_programmes/acgd/ (Accessed on 27 October 2020).

Republic of Zimbabwe. (1980). Lancaster House Constitution/*Constitution of Zimbabwe incorporating all amendments made by the Constitution of Zimbabwe Amendment (No. 17) Act, 2005 (Act No. 5 of 2005).* Harare: Government Printers.

Republic of Zimbabwe. (1996). *Education Act Revised Edition.* Harare: Government Printers.

Republic of Zimbabwe. (2005). *The Constitution of Zimbabwe Amendment Act (No. 17).* Harare: Government Printers.

Republic of Zimbabwe. (2006). *Education Act (Amendment).* Harare: Government Printers.

Republic of Zimbabwe. (2008). *National report on the status of education by Zimbabwe.* Geneva: UNESCO.

Republic of Zimbabwe. (2013). *The Constitution of Zimbabwe Amendment Act (No. 20).* Harare: Government Printers.

Republic of Zimbabwe, Ministry of Women Affairs, Gender and Community Development. (2013). *National Gender Policy (2013–2017).* Harare: Government Printers.

Republic of Zimbabwe, Ministry of Education, Sport and Culture. (2005). *National gender action plan of Zimbabwe: Education for All towards 2015.* Harare: Government Printers.

Runhare, T., & Gordon, R. (2004). *The comprehensive review of gender issues in the education sector.* Harare: UNICEF/Ministry of Education Sports & Culture.

Runhare, T., & Vandeyar, S. (2011). Loss of learning space within a legally inclusive education system: Institutional responsiveness to mainstreaming of pregnant learners in formal education. *Gender & Behaviour, 9*(2), 4100–4124.

Ruzvidzo, C. (2017). *Spare a thought for the rural learner in the new curriculum.* https://www.chronicle.co.zw/spare-a-thought-for-the-rural-learner-in-the-new-curriculum/ (Accessed on 24 June 2020).

Rwafa, U. (2016). Culture and religion as sources of gender inequality: Rethinking challenges women face in contemporary Africa. *Journal of Literary Studies, 32*(1), 43–52.

Sachiti, R. (2016). Education for girls, women lead to development. *The Herald Newspaper,* 11 May.

Sahin, E. (2011). Gender equity in education. (Paper presented at the International Conference on New Trends in Education and Their Implications held at Antalya, Turkey on 11–13 November: 216–220).

Samkange, W. (2015). Gender disparities in education: Examining the role of gender mainstreaming and gender policies in achieving gender parity. *International Journal for Research in Social Science & Humanities, 1*(2), 1–12.

Sava L. A., & Orodho, J. A. (2014). Socio-economic factors influencing pupils' access to education in informal settlements: A case of Kibera, Nairobi County, Kenya. *International Journal of Education and Research, 2*(3), 1–16.

Selobogo, M. Y. P., & Ojakorotu, V. (2013). SADC gender and development protocol: An evaluation of equality, empowerment and gender based violence in South Africa (2008–2012). *Gender and Behaviour, 11*(1), 5175–5196.

Shabaya, J., & Konadu-Agyemang, K. (2004). Unequal access, unequal participation: Some spatial and socio-economic dimensions of the gender gap in education in Africa with specific reference to Ghana, Zimbabwe and Kenya. *Compare, 34*(4), 395–424.

Shizha, E., & Kariwo, M. T. (2011). *Education and development in Zimbabwe: A social, political and economic analysis.* AW Rotterdam: Sense Publishers.

Shizha, E. (2006). Legitimizing indigenous knowledge in Zimbabwe: A theoretical analysis of post-colonial school knowledge and its legacy. Youth and Children's Studies. Paper 2. *Journal of Contemporary Issues in Education, 1*(1), 20–35.

Sinnes, A. T., & Loken, M. (2014). Gendered education in a gendered world: Looking beyond cosmetic solutions to the gender gap in science. *Cultural Studies of Science Education, 9,* 343–364.

Sithole, J. C., Manwa, L., & Manwa, L. (2013). Gender equity in education: An analysis of perceptions of Masvingo urban female students, parents and teachers towards the maternity leave policy for high school girls in Zimbabwe. *Journal of African Studies and Development, 5*(4), 64–69.

Slavin, R. E. (2005). *Educational psychology: Theory and practice.* New York, NY: Allyn and Bacon.

Stewart, J., Sithole, E., Ncube, W., Moyo, T., Gwaunza, E., Nzira, T., Dengu-Zvobgo, K., Mashiangaidze, D., Donzwa, B., & Kazembe, N. (2000). *In the shadow of the law-women and justice delivery in Zimbabwe.* Harare: Bardwell Press.

Stromquist, N. P. (2007). The gender socialisation process in schools: A cross-national comparison. (Background paper prepared for the *Education for All Global Monitoring Report 2008 Education for All by 2015: Will we make it?*) http://www.unesdoc.unesco.org/images/0015/001555/155587e.pdf (Accessed on 12 May 2021).

Syed, J., & Ozbilgin, M. (2009). A relational framework for international transfer of diversity management practices. *International Journal of Human Resource Management, 20*(12), 2435–2453.

Tamale, S. (2014). Exploring the contours of African sexualities: Religion, law and power. *African Human Rights Law Journal, 14*(1), 150–177.

Teise, K. L. G. (2013). *Education for sustainable development exposing social sustainable policy imperatives for South African education.* (Unpublished PhD thesis.) University of the Free State, Bloemfontein.

UN. (2014). *Gender equality: Zimbabwe United Nations Development assistance framework.* Harare: UN.

UN. (2016). *Concept note: 'The Africa we want in 2030, 2063 and beyond.'* High level forum: 'Early action and results on the 2030 Agenda for Sustainable Development, in the context of the first ten-year implementation plan of Africa's Transformative Agenda 2063: Opportunities and challenges.' New York, NY: UN.

UNFPA. (2012). *Marrying too young: End child marriage.* New York, NY: UNFPA.

Unterhalter, E. (2007). *Gender, schooling and global social justice.* London: Routledge.

Unterhalter, E. (2008). Cosmopolitanism global social justice and gender equality in education. *Compare,* 38(55):539–554.

Vambe, B., & Mupfariseni, B. (2011). Negotiating property rights in Southern Africa through the Novel magora panyama: A legal perspective. *Journal of Literary Studies, 27*(3), 93–110.

Van der Westhuizen, G. J. (2013). Post-colonial perspectives on education policy research. *Africa Education Review, 10*(4), 689–708.

Vavrus, F. (2002). Making distinctions: privatisation and the (un)educated girl on Mount Kilimanjaro, Tanzania. *International Journal of Educational Development, 22,* 527–547.

Win, E. J. (2004). When sharing female identity is not enough: Coalition building in the midst of political polarisation in Zimbabwe. *Gender and Development, 12*(1), 19.

Wudie, A. T., & Philipos, P. (2014). Factors affecting female students' academic performance at higher education: The case of Bahir Dar University, Ethiopia. *African Educational Research Journal, 2*(4), 161–166.

Zanhi, L. M. (2014). *Gender equality in Zimbabwe.* Harare: Legal Resources Foundation.

Zezekwa, N., Madau, A. V., & Nkopodi, N. (2013). A comparative study of South African and Zimbabwean science teacher education programme: Some theoretical reflections. *Mediterranean Journal of Social Sciences, 4*(13), 317–324.

Zhou, G., & Zvoushe, H. (2012). Public policy making in Zimbabwe: A three decade perspective. *International Journal of Humanities and Social Science, 2*(8), 212–222.

Zimbabwe Women Lawyers Association. (2012). *Zimbabwe Civil Society's shadow report to the CEDAW committee.* Harare: Zimbabwe Women Lawyers Association.

Zinn, M. B., Eitzen, D. S., & Wells, B. (2008). *Diversity in families* (8th ed.). Boston, MA: Pearson.

Zivengwa, T., Hazvina, F., Ndedzu, D., & Mavesere, I. M. (2013). Investigating the casual relationship between education and economic growth in Zimbabwe. *Asian Journal of Humanities and Social Sciences, 1*(5), 399–410.

Zungura, M., & Nyemba, E. Z. (2013). The Implications of the quota system in promoting gender equality in Zimbabwean politics. *International Journal of Humanities and Social Science, 3*(2), 204–211.

Contributors' Biographies

Ndondo Semkeliso is a holder of a Masters of Education Degree in early Childhood Development. Currently, she is a Teacher In charge of the ECD department at a primary school. Her research interest is in the teaching and learning of ECD learners in rural settings.

Nhlanhla Mkwelie has a Master's in Mathematics from the Bindura University of Science Education in Zimbabwe, and he is a Lecturer of Mathematics in the Department of Science, Mathematics and Technology Education at the National University of Science and Technology Education in Zimbabwe. He taught mathematics at high school for over 15 years. Currently, he teaches mathematics and statistics courses at university level and is doing a doctoral study with the University of South Africa. He has presented over 10 research papers at local conferences and one paper at an international conference. He has 3 research papers under review. His research interest is cultural mathematics.

Mlungisi Moyo has a Master's in Education in Curriculum Studies. He taught at the primary school level in Zimbabwe for 9 years before joining the tertiary education system where he has been a lecturer for 13 years. He has a lot of interest on issues to do with quality education at all levels, that is, from early childhood development (ECD) to teacher education. Mlungisi has presented 18 researched articles at both national and international conferences in addition to the 8 articles published in renowned journals.

Christopher Ndlovu has a Ph.D. in Sociology of Education from the University of KwaZulu-Natal in South Africa, and a Senior Lecturer in the Department of Educational Foundations at Lupane State University in Zimbabwe. His research interest is in indigenous knowledge systems and their integration into the formal school curriculum, and in the advancement of rural education. He is a product of National Institute of Humanities and Social Sciencs (NIHSS).

Siphiwo Ncube is an M.Phil. student with Lupane State University in the field of Educational Agriculture. Her research interest are in using agriculture for the betterment of livelihoods in rural communities. She has presenting papers on local and international conferences on the role of agriculture in empowering communities at grassroots levels.

Mandlenkosi Ndlovu holds a Ph.D. in Political Studies from the University of Johannesburg in South Africa. His research interests are on post-conflict peace building based on indigenous knowledge systems. He advocates for inclusive, participatory, bottom-up peace building processes that are informed by contextual specificity as opposed to universal liberal approaches predicated on one--size-fits-all models.

Ndondo Shepherd has a Ph.D. in Education from the University Of Fort Hare in South Africa. He is a Senior Lecturer in Educational Foundations at Lupane State University in Zimbabwe. His research interest is in African philosophy, moral philosophy and finding out how problems confronting humanity today can be alleviated through blending of contemporary methods with indigenous knowledge systems.

Tinashe Pikirai is a Lecturer at Hillside Teachers College in Zimbabwe. He is a holder of a first degree and a Master of Science degree from Bindura University of Science Education in Zimbabwe. Currently, he is the Head of Department of Research at Hillside and has written two geography textbooks. He has also written and presented several research papers at local and international research conferences. His research area of interest in is environmental sustainability.

Ntandoyenkosi Satamwe is a Lecturer of Mathematics at the Hillside Teachers' College in Zimbabwe. She has taught mathematics at high school for over 12 years. She has also taught mathematics and statistics courses at college and university levels. She received her Master of Science Education in Mathematics at the Bindura University of Science Education in Zimbabwe. Currently she is working towards starting her doctoral studies. She has presented 4 research papers at local conferences and one paper at an international conference. Her research interest is in using ICTs in the teaching and learning of mathematics.

Mudimba Collen is a lecturer at Great Zimbabwe University in the Early Childhood Development department. Mudimba, holds a Masters and Bachelors Degree in Early Childhood Development from Great Zimbabwe University. He is currently pursuing a D/Phil in the same area of specialisation. His research interests are in integrating indigenous knowledge systems in ECD programmes to promote a Heritage based philosophy. Currently, he has three publications, with six being at different stages towards publication.

Samkeliso Mathe has accomplished Bachelor of Education in Early childhood Development with Zimbabwe Open University (ZOU) and did Masters of Education in Early childhood Development with Women University of Africa. Her research areas are on the effectiveness of learner centered approach in remote schools, and online teaching and learning of ECD children in rural areas.

Pinias Chikuvadze holds a PhD in Philosophy and Policy Studies in Education from the University of Free State. He is currently working as a lecturer in Bindura University of Science Education, in the educational management section.

Munyaradzi Chidarikire is a PhD holder in the in Educational Psychology, obtained from the University of Free State. Currently he is working as a lecturer at the University of KwaZulu-Natal, in the department of Educational Psychology.

Mkwananzi Dumisani is an Information and Communication Technology (ICT) and Computer Science specialist who has two journal publications and a number of Teacher Education Module chapters published by the University of Zimbabwe. Has a keen interest in system design, assistive technology, innovation and industry. A holder of a Master's of Science Education (Computer Science) Degree with National University of Science and Technology (NUST) and a Bachelor of Science Education (Honors) in Computer Science with NUST.

Cynthia Ncube is an Early Childhood Development Specialist, currently stationed at United College of College of Education as an ECD lecturer with

14 years of experience. Presenter of various papers on early childhood issues with a focus on curriculum development. A holder of a Master's of Education (Early Childhood Development) Degree with Great Zimbabwe University.

Nkosilathi Sibanda holds an M.A. in African languages from Great Zimbabwe University, B.A. Honours in IsiNdebele from Lupane State University, Post graduate diploma in Education from Lupane State University and Diploma in Applied language studies from Lupane State University. His research interests are in the betterment of rural teaching and learning.

Mpumelelo Ncube is a holder of an M.A.in African languages from Great Zimbabwe University and an Honours degree in Linguistics from the University of Zimbabwe. He also has a diploma in Personal Management from IPMZ. He enjoys researching in Oral Literature, African Literature and Indigenous Knowledge Systems as they affect education.

Pikirai Teckla is a primary school trained teacher. She has a vast experience in teaching at primary level from Kindergarten to grade seven. She has a Diploma in Education (Primary). She has written a lot of short stories for the primary sector and she has also written seven research papers of which she presented some of the research papers at different research conferences. Her area of research is in education particularly education of the disadvantaged. She is also interested in heritage education.

Judith Musengi holds a Master of Education Degree in History. She is a lecturer at Hwange Teachers College. She is interested in undertaking research in History, Education and Culture. The author has co-authored a Journal article with Chikuvadze, Magutsa and Gonzo, "Exploring Challenges faced by Rural Zimbabwean School-Going Single Mothers in Nurturing Children: A Literature Perspective." https://www.richman.org/journal.

www.ingramcontent.com/pod-product-compliance
Ingram Content Group UK Ltd.
Pitfield, Milton Keynes, MK11 3LW, UK
UKHW021008120926
8556IPUK00028B/206

9 781433 198267